DISCOVERING

DIXIE

"A valuable companion for the first-time visitor or for the veteran who wants to rekindle an old romance with the Deep South."
— *Dick Alexander, San Francisco Examiner*

"Polese wends the reader on a 2700-mile drive through the most scenic highways of the South, from Bourbon Street in New Orleans to the Blue Ridge Parkway in North Carolina. This will be very welcome addition to travel collections."
— *Library Journal*

"Very much an Old South guide . . . handily organized!"
— *Atlanta Constitution*

"Definitely *the* guide to one of America's most alluring regions!"
— *Bookpaper*

"Good reading!"   — *New Orleans Times-Picayune*

"This is a TOURING AMERICA kind of travel guide: a personal blueprint for a three-week trip. Polese gives first-time visitors a wide-ranging experience of the best Dixie has to offer. *Discovering Dixie* is the kind of guidebook every touring motorist would like to have, both for planning the trip and to refer to enroute."   — *Touring America*

DISCOVERING
DIXIE

Along the Magnolia Trail

*The Day by Day Travel Guide
to the Best of the Deep South*

Richard Louis Polese

OCEAN TREE BOOKS
ADVENTURE ROADS TRAVEL

Special Thanks: Many Dixie denizens and Confederate sympathizers helped this book come to be, especially Beth and Corky McFarland, Shelley Welman, Barbara Lee Harding, Patricia Yohn, Ann Reilly Jones, Cynthia Tomlin, Cynthia Riggs, Linda Olson, Beverly Gianna, Bill and Martha Lum, Mattie Jo Ratcliff, Jeff Penny, Elizabeth McGuffey, Marcy Cobun, Elaine Gilmartin Beaumet, Natasha Williamson, Jimmy Spikes, Vicki Stamler, B.J. Smith, Cindy Ellsworth, Jean Schaum, Laura Holt, John Vavruska, Jim and Esther Polese, Joanna Hill, Carol Niemeyer, Jim Childers, Vera Daimwood, Jo Wright, Ann Vaughan, Mary Gaubert, Janet Foley, Jackie Burch, Paula Pate, Carol Kirby, and Jack and Mary Hartsfield.

Extra appreciation to my friend Bettina Rohrbach for her clarity; to a very talented travel editor, Richard Harris; and to Jack D. Rittenhouse, Carl Franz and Rick Steves — the trailblazers of user-friendly travel writing.

Published by:
OCEAN TREE BOOKS
Post Office Box 1295
Santa Fe, New Mexico 87504
(505) 983-1412

Cover: Holly Wood
Maps: Michael Taylor
Typography: Buffalo Publications
Printing: Rose Printing Co., Tallahassee, Florida

ISBN: 0-943734-18-5

Library of Congress Cataloging in Publication data:

Polese, Richard.
    Discovering Dixie: along the Magnolia Trail: the day by day travel guide to the best of the Deep South / by Richard Louis Polese.
    (Adventure Roads Travel)
    Includes bibliographical references and index.
    ISBN 0-943734-18-5
    1. Southern States — description and travel — 1991 — Tours.
2. Family recreation — Southern States — Guidebooks. 3. Children — Travel — Southern States — Guidebooks. I. Title. II. Series.
F207.3.P5 1991
917.504′43 — dc20   91-15728   CIP

"Life is either a great adventure, or it is nothing."

— Alabama's Helen Keller

This book is for

Tamsin, Vanessa, and **Martin**

who make my life a great adventure.

The Magnolia Trail through Dixie

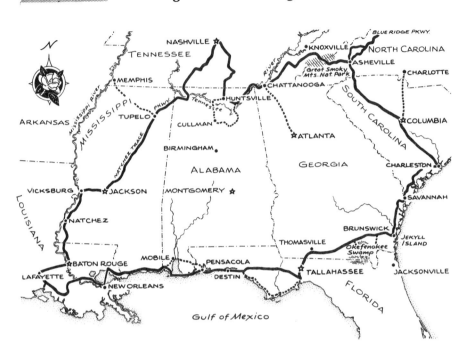

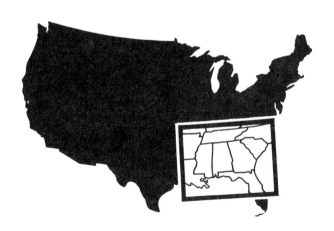

Contents

MAGNOLIA TRAIL MAPS

 *Preface*

YOU HOLD IN YOUR HANDS the first guidebook with a daily itinerary format that treats Dixie — America's Deep South — as a destination in itself. Whether you're Southern yourself, or are making your travel debut in Dixie, I hope you'll find the approach I've taken in this book refreshingly different.

Discovering Dixie is not an inclusive guide that attempts to list everything in bewildering array, nor does it cater to a specific kind or class of traveler. It's not as superficial as some pocket-sized regional guidebooks that leave one hungering for more, but I won't overload you with description and history to the point you feel it's all right here and you don't have to leave your armchair. I think I've included just enough so that you'll feel well-informed and eager to go.

Although I'm using a day-by-day format, a specific (and wonderful!) travel route, and include a workable timetable for each Discovery Day of this three week adventure, there's plenty of latitude and sufficient information here for concocting any number of days in Dixie that will fit your interests and lifestyle — without your having to start from scratch. Whether you want to follow my timetables and sightseeing recommendations precisely, or use the book to invent your own tour(s), I'm *certain* you're going to have a wonderful time in the Deep South!

This part is for those who may have been fascinated by the magnetism of the South, yet felt reluctant to travel here. I was once one of you. The school history books and movies I grew up with came not from the South, but were produced in places like Chicago and California. Nearly all of them, I came to find, had an undeniable Yankee bias. If your image of Dixie comes from *Easy Rider* and Civil Rights era newsreels, you're in for some very pleasant surprises. All the good stuff you've heard is true, and most of the bad stuff isn't true now and some never was in the first place. (As a young man I was kidnapped by a Louisiana lady and stolen away to Dixie, then left to make these wonderful discoveries myself — but that's another story!)

Southerners, black and white, do see the world from a slightly different vantage point than maybe you're used to, however. On this adventure you're invited to appreciate that Southern ways of looking at things — whatever one's economic or social circumstances — can make life very rich, and full of humor and wisdom and grace. Once you're here, get set to do some listenin' and laughin', because there's no place else on earth where these ever-so-human diversions and the arts of conversation are as much a shared pleasure as in Dixie.

I'd like to apologize to the citizens of Virginia, Texas and Arkansas, which are also part of the Confederacy but don't fall on the Magnolia Trail route. And likewise to folks who live in Southern towns and cities not included here but which have so much to offer. I hope you'll understand that this book is intended as a sampling — a hearty one, but not the whole feast by any means!

Richard Louis Polese
Between Santa Fe
and New Orleans
March 1992

Introducing Dixie

HOW TO USE THIS GUIDEBOOK

IS IT TRUE what they say about Dixie? Do fragrant magnolias really blossom at everybody's door? Do folks laugh, do they sing — like it says in all those songs?

If you're heard that the Deep South is a land of easy days and dreamy nights, of live oaks on bayou banks laden with long tendrils of Spanish moss wafting gently in warm breezes, of succulent fresh seafood, of romantic and tragic stories nurtured like precious heirlooms, of charming small cities, graceful antebellum homes, exciting music, mysterious swamps, sugar-white beaches, quiet forest wildlands, and particularly kind and hospitable people of every station in life — then, *YES!*, it's all true — as you're about to discover on this three-week, 2,700-mile adventure through eight states in the heart and soul of the Confederacy.

Whether you're a Southerner yourself or have never ventured South before, I've written *Discovering Dixie* to provide you the most complete and enjoyable experience for the time you have — whether it's a weekend, a three-week vacation, or longer.

What's down the road? You'll learn to two-step with Cajuns in Louisiana, sleep in an enchanting antebellum mansion in Natchez, motor serenely along two scenic National Parkways (the Blue Ridge and the Natchez Trace), be part of the audience at a *Grand Ole Opry* broadcast in Nashville, relax in the quiet forests of Great Smoky Mountain National Park, venture out into the Okefenokee Swamp, and bask in the sun on Georgia's Golden Isles and along Florida's Emerald Coast. Along the way you'll have the opportunity to ride a sternwheeler on the Mississippi River, board a real Union ironclad gunboat in Vicksburg and NASA's orbital Skylab in Huntsville, sip she-crab soup at a Charleston tavern where time stopped in 1862, promenade the enchanting squares of old Savannah, and tap your feet with old and new jazz masters in New Orleans.

The *Magnolia Trail* travel route and itinerary is my personal dream trip, but I think you'll find that it includes much of the very best the South has to offer. If you follow my day-by-day timetables, seeing just the best of the *Best to See and Do*, you'll be assured of an unforgettable adventure. However, I encourage you to modify the itinerary and route to suit your own preferences and passions.

To help you plan your trip, I have arranged *Discovering Dixie* into twenty-two *Discovery Day* chapters in which you'll find:

• *"Getting to know you"* city orientations and descriptive overviews of every day's primary localities — including bits of culture and history that will help you feel more at home.

• A *Timetable Suggestion* for each Discovery Day's travel and sightseeing, to help you make the best use of your time.

• A detailed description of each *driving segment* along the Magnolia Trail.

• *The Best to See and Do* — Sightseeing highlights (including days and times when they're open, how to get there, and admission fees, if any), rated by me with one, two, or three blossoms, according to their significance and promise for a visitor's satisfaction:

    ❀❀❀ Don't miss it!
       ❀❀ Try hard to see this one!
          ❀ Worthwhile, if you have time.

• *Places to Dine, Places to Stay, Places to Camp* — Tried and true lodgings (often historic guest homes and inns), campgrounds, and restaurants for every Discovery Day. These are places I've been myself or which come with strong local recommendations.

• *Useful Tips* — Helpful bits of information (insights, shopping areas, key phone numbers, etc.) to help make your trip easier and more fun.

• *Linger Longer* and *Today's Shortcut* — Optional excursions for travelers with the inclination to linger awhile, as well as occasional route shortcuts to make up time or bypass places not of particular interest to you.

• Twenty-four user-friendly *city and route maps* to get you around town, locate highlights, and show you what the road ahead is like.

The *Magnolia Trail* route begins and ends in New Orleans, but you can pick your own starting point anywhere along the loop. If you have less than three weeks to wander, this tour route divides easily into convenient segments for exploring specific areas (such as the Gulf Coast or the Smoky Mountains) in a week or a weekend. If you find yourself slowing down to savor a particular area, the shortcuts will help get you to your next major destination quickly. If you have extra time or special interests (military forts? wilderness camping? heron-watching? ocean fishing?) you'll find some *Linger Longer* options inviting.

I've set up an easy driving schedule along the Magnolia Trail. On the seventeen travel days, you'll average 156 miles, or only about three hours on the road. (The longest drive is a pleasant 300-mile Interstate run through the pines from Asheville in the mountains of North Carolina to charming Charleston by the sea.) You will have one or more full days in New Orleans, Natchez, Nashville, Chattanooga, Charleston, and Savannah — Southern cities of special interest and fascination.

Dixie Is Different

You'll know you're in Dixie when you see red, white and blue Confederate flags displayed with pride, steamy grits or biscuits on your plate at breakfast, and meet folks who know January 19 is Robert E. Lee's birthday. If you haven't traveled in the South before, it's important to remember that Dixie was once, and in many ways still is, a *nation* — rich with national truths and traditions and tempered by three great freedom movements beginning with the American Revolution.

Contrary to what it says in yankee schoolbooks, people in the South know that the War Between the States (Civil War to some, though there wasn't much civil about it) wasn't waged over slavery as much as to prevent Southern states from leaving a union they had joined voluntarily. Before 1860, the South was at peace and prosperous, but going its own way. For a North that wanted to define America differently and centralize power in Washington, this wouldn't do. This difference of opinion broke into a four-year armed struggle that cost 600,000 lives. The outcome of that conflict determined so much about the destiny of the South, and it still does. The Civil War sites I've chosen for visits will help you understand the scope of this conflict and may give you a fresh appreciation for the Southern point of view. After the South lost the military struggle, just about everyone here was thrust into degrading poverty due to the exploitive "reconstruction" policies dictated by the North. And despite Abraham Lincoln's lofty words, black Southerners had to wait a hundred years more for real emancipation.

In 1955, a quiet black lady named Rosa Parks refused to sit in the back of a bus in Montgomery, Alabama, and the Civil Rights Movement (the South's third great revolution), with it's emphasis on nonviolent change, was under way. By almost every measure, it turned out a lot better for everyone than did the Civil War.

The way I've experienced it, relations between the races are generally better and more honest in the South today than elsewhere in America — testament to a people who, despite differences, find it surprisingly easy to forgive one another and live and let live. Blacks as well as whites take pride in their Southern past and traditions. Two recent popular bumper stickers express it well. One's a rebel flag with the motto: HERITAGE, NOT HATE. The other says simply, AMERICAN BY BIRTH, SOUTHERN BY THE GRACE OF GOD.

Southerners of all kinds are instinctively warm to respectful visitors and will invite you to enjoy their legacy. On Sunday mornings, though, most everybody's in church and beyond New Orleans you may find many businesses and attractions closed on Sundays until 1 p.m. Consider it a respectful invitation for you to pause and absorb life's deeper verities.

Discovering Dixie is unabashedly a tour of the Old South. It seems that ever since the first carpetbagger arrived during Reconstruction days there's been talk of a "New South." To me, the New South looks a lot like the everyday North. Comparatively speaking, the Old South is a lot more interesting and certainly a lot more fun. That's why boomtowns such as Atlanta, Charlotte and Jacksonville, though they have undeniable virtues, aren't emphasized in this book. Along the roads and in the cities and towns I've chosen, you may be surprised to find how much enchanting Old South culture, architecture and charm remains, just waiting for your discovery. Yet in between you'll see modern expressions of Dixie's values and spirit — from song-in-its-heart Nashville to the hands-on Space and Rocket Center in Alabama. *Discovering Dixie's* twenty-two Discovery Days are filled with an amazing variety of experiences, reflecting the breadth and depth of Southern culture, history, scenery, and things to do.

When to Go

I've designed the route for pleasant travel most of the year. Dixie's climate is generally warm and moist, but it does have seasons. Unquestionably the best time to go is during the South's long, gentle springtime, from mid-March to mid-June. You'll have delicate bouquets of dogwood and azalea blossoms along most of the route, and the air will feel fresh and sweet. Summer is predictably hot and steamy, yet you'll find it pleasant in the mountains (Discovery Days 12 through 15), with refreshing breezes near the coasts (Days 16, 17, 18, 20, 21, 22) — and people everywhere will show you how to slow down and enjoy even sultry days. Rainfall and humidity increase toward the end of summer. The hurricane season, which occasionally affects the coasts, peaks in August and September. If you hear of one on the way, call the hurricane hotline, (900) 410-NOAA. Autumn in Dixie is often pleasant, with changing colors in the Appalachian mountains, and beaches along the Gulf Coast swimmable into November. Southern winters tend to be short, with a mix of nice and nippy days. However, true winter conditions, including snow and subfreezing temperatures, can be expected north of Tupelo and in the mountains.

In making your plans, take into account peak seasons and special events you may want to take part in — or which may limit your accommodations choices. For instance, rooms will be in short supply during Mardi Gras and Jazz Fest in New Orleans, FanFair in Nashville, and the Spoleto Festival in Charleston. Natchez fills up with visitors for Spring Pilgrimage in March and April. The beaches are popular from Easter through Labor Day.

How to Get There

Major airlines, the Interstate highway system, and Amtrak make it easy to get to New Orleans as well as seven other convenient "entry cities" on or near the Magnolia Trail.

New Orleans: The Crescent City makes a sensible starting point particularly if you're coming from Texas or anywhere west of the Mississippi River. New Orleans is an easy day's drive (363 miles) from Houston on Interstate 10. Typical economy, advance purchase round-trip air fare from Los Angeles or New York to New Orleans is about $375 at this writing.

I've found **Amtrak** to be a fine, adventuresome way to scoot across the country. Take the legendary *City of New Orleans* overnight from Chicago ($156 round-trip), the *Sunset Limited* from L.A. ($303), or the *Crescent* from New York ($233). Amtrak trains also run to Atlanta, Charlotte, Savannah, Charleston, and Columbia, South Carolina. Call (800) USA-RAIL for schedules, reservations, and special discounts.

Nashville: If you're coming from the Midwest, Nashville *(Discovery Day 9)*, northernmost city on the Magnolia Trail, makes an excellent entry point. Music City is 470 miles due south of Chicago on Interstate 65 and is a major hub for American Airlines.

Atlanta: Gigantic Hartsfield Airport is the hub for Delta Airlines, with direct flights from everywhere in the East and South. If you start from Atlanta, take I-75 north 119 miles to join the Magnolia Trail in Chattanooga *(Day 12)*. Take time in Atlanta to see the Confederate tableau on Stone Mountain, Ebenezer Baptist Church where Dr. Martin Luther King, Jr. preached, his memorial and tomb at the Center for Nonviolent Social Change, semi-bohemian Little Five Points, and the Jimmy Carter Presidential Center.

Memphis: A good connection from Missouri, Arkansas and the Mid-South, Tennessee's delta city is just 107 miles on US 78 from Tupelo, Mississippi *(Day 7)*. You may want to check out Graceland and the blues clubs on Beale Street before heading out on the Magnolia Trail.

Charlotte: Convenient if you're coming in from the mid-Atlantic and New England states, Charlotte, North Carolina is the hub for US Air. Drive just 100 miles on I-77 to reach Columbia, South Carolina *(Day 15)*.

Charleston: Drive the Dixie Highway down the Atlantic seaboard and you'll meet the Magnolia Trail loop in Charleston *(Day 16)*. Charleston is 750 miles from New York via I-95 and I-26.

Tallahassee: The Magnolia Trail intersects here on *Discovery Day 20* with the Florida route of Richard Harris and Tamalyn Harris's *2 to 22 Days in Florida* guidebook. Tallhassee is a convenient junction for travelers coming north from the Florida peninsula.

Jacksonville: From this sprawling metropolis near Florida's far northeast Atlantic Coast it is only a 90 minute drive on Interstate 95 to Brunswick and Georgia's Golden Isles *(Discovery Day 18)*. The old St. Augustine of Ponce de Leon is 40 minutes south of Jacksonville via I-95.

How Much Will It Cost?

Calculate your expenses based on your travel lifestyle and mode of transport. If you take your own subcompact car, pack lunches and camp all the way, the entire three week Magnolia Trail adventure with two aboard can still done for a whisker over $1,000. If you rent a sedan or minivan and stay in an antebellum guest house or upscale bed and breakfast every night, figure on at least $160 a day or $3,500 for the whole trip for both of you. Most people should spend from $2,000 to $2,500.

You'll use about 140 gallons of gas on the route if your vehicle normally gets 20 miles per gallon. Whether you fly in or drive, don't forget to add in the cost of getting there from your home. There are no toll highways on the Magnolia Trail (even the Natchez Trace and Blue Ridge parkways are free). You'll pay only to get on the Lake Pontchartrain Causeway ($1), the bridges to the Georgia Sea Islands (35 cents and $1), and the ferry from Fort Morgan to Dauphin Island ($9). Parks in the Deep South are real bargains. Admission is free at Great Smoky Mountains National Park, all but one area of Gulf Islands National Seashore, all National Military Parks, as well as at some other historical sites you'll be visiting.

A key to economical and memorable travel in the South is to *let people help you.* Southern hospitality is no cliche. Putting other people's comfort first comes naturally for Southerners of every class, race and region. Make them happy — accept the generosity you're offered, whether it's help changing a tire or an invitation to come for dinner. They really mean it.

Prices shown throughout the book are current as of early 1992. Use them for comparison, but in these uncertain economic times don't expect them to be cast in stone.

Renting a Vehicle

For road travel satisfaction, minivans are taking over as the popular choice — with good reason. They give you stretching out room, a great view, decent economy, and (in the case of Chrysler and GM minivans and Mazda's MPV) car-like handling and driving ease. At this writing, you can rent a Voyager or Caravan in New Orleans from Spinato Chrysler's **Swifty Car Rental** for around $300 a week, plus 15 cents a mile beyond 700 miles. Call David Burridge at (504) 822-4400 or 822-RENT to have it delivered. **Thrifty Car Rental**, (800) 367-2277, will put you in a minivan with 1050 free miles for $250 per week, plus 25 cents for each additional mile.

One of America's best car rental secrets is **Agency Rent-a-Car**, which offers new compact and mid-size sedans starting at $150 per week with 1000 free miles. They will deliver the car to your door free, but are open only from 8 a.m. to 5:30 p.m. weekdays and to noon on Saturdays. Call Agency at (800) 321-1972 nationally, (504) 486-3723 in New Orleans, (615) 367-0698 in Nashville, or (404) 991-1274 in Atlanta. On a strict budget? Squeeze into an unlimited free miles subcompact for about $100 per week from **Avis**, (800) 331-1212, or **Hertz**, (800) 654-3131. You'll get something like Geo Metro or Toyota Tercel. Check with your insurance or credit card company or auto club to see if you're covered for rental vehicles — many travelers have been stuck for exorbitantly high add-on rental car insurance they did not need. Be sure to try out the air conditioner before you drive off.

If there are three or more of you, renting a motor home may make sense. In Slidell, Louisiana, 30 miles east of New Orleans, **Bayou Country RV**, (504) 641-9432, will put you in a 26-foot mini-motorhome for $595 per week (100 free miles, plus 20 cents each additional mile). From New Orleans airport catch the Coastliner shuttle bus to reach Slidell, (800) 647-3957 ($37 round trip). **CruiseAmerica** rents completely self-contained 24-foot RVs for $784 a week in Atlanta, Nashville and Jacksonville. Call CruiseAmerica at (800) 327-7778 for details and reservations.

What to Bring

Most of the year, light, loose, quickly washed clothing for day wear is what you'll need. In humidity, a cotton mix is more comfortable than synthetics. Bring along a jacket or sweater to keep you warm in the mountains, especially important if you're traveling in early spring or late fall. Since it's certain you'll encounter rain showers and probably a downpour, you'll appreciate having an umbrella or a rain poncho. Your umbrella (if it's a light color) will also make a nice parasol for sunny days at the beach. Sunglasses and swimwear are essential, since you'll be spending at least six days at or near the seashore. At least one outfit of dressy clothes will make you feel in place in church, at a fancy restaurant, and for Sunday brunches.

Bugs are a fact of life in the South. If you look forward to mosquito-free strolls after sunset in summer and fall, prepare yourself. I keep my trusty can of Hunter's Sta-A-Way insect repellant in the glovebox.

A small beer cooler serves as an excellent food box for travel snacks and picnics, and an onboard water supply or soft drinks will add to your comfort. Failed air conditioning can alter radically the pleasure of driving in Dixie, especially in summer. Have your A/C system checked out before you depart.

A Mini-Maglite flashlight, five-inch Vise-Grip pliers, and a Swiss Army knife are three small glovebox tools that have rescued me from numerous unexpected travel annoyances. Virtually everywhere along the Magnolia Trail help will turn up in minutes when you need it, however. Dixie is rife with Good Samaritans.

Places to Stay

Guest houses, bed and breakfast inns, and antebellum mansions that take in overnight visitors are wonderful places to experience the warmth of Dixie. I see no point staying at a comparably priced chain motel when you can sleep in a *tester* (canopied) bed in a cozy, antique-decorated room, then join your hosts in the morning for congenial conversation over a leisurely Southern breakfast. Expect to spend between $50 and $90 for two. There's such a hostelry waiting for you most nights of this trip. Bed and breakfast hosts are also the best sources of up-to-date local suggestions and information. I have provided a selection of recommended places to stay for each night, including phone numbers for reservations. I've also tucked in some exceptional bargain accommodations (such as New Orleans' Marquette House and coastal Georgia's Hostel in the Forest) for as little as $6 a night. In Asheville, on Georgia's Golden Isles, and along the Emerald Coast, you may want to stay at one of the luxury resorts I recommend.

Prefer the camping or RV lifestyle? Whether you drive a Class A motor home, pull a travel trailer, or tote a tent, you'll find at least one recommended campground for every night of the trip. Public (state and National Park) campgrounds run from $7 to $12 per vehicle and have nicer wilderness settings than most commercial counterparts. Many now have amenities (a store, showers, full hookups) not found a few years ago. If you're traveling in summer, make reservations well in advance for Cades Cove, Smokemont and Elkmont in the Smokies, and Grayton Beach on the Gulf Coast. Commercial campgrounds in Dixie charge from $10 to $17 on average. I recommend several for their convenience or particularly pleasant surroundings.

Life of all kinds abounds in Dixie's great outdoors, so be prepared for the annoyances of ticks (wear a hat), chiggers and mosquitos if you plan to camp out or walk in the wilds, and keep an eye peeled for the occasional cottonmouth snake in low, watery areas.

Dining in Dixie

The South was *made* for eating! Nearly everywhere you go, food is plentiful, fresh, inexpensive, and prepared for maximum enjoyment. Most seafood dinners in Charleston, Savannah, and along the Gulf Coast are so reasonably priced they'd make a Maine lobster blush. Don't be surprised to find full Southern or "plantation" breakfasts of grits, eggs, country ham, biscuits with gravy, juice and coffee for under $5. Such breakfasts are often so hearty that a snack may suffice for lunch. New Orleans, where food can be a full-time preoccupation, is a world-class restaurant city. Follow my neighborhood restaurant suggestions and even in the Crescent City you can eat like a king for very little.

You'll want to sample a number of regional specialties and variations — oysters Rockefeller and shrimp Creole in New Orleans, crawfish etouffee and hot boudin in Cajun Lafayette, catfish and hushpuppies in Mississippi, fried chicken and country ham in Tennessee, she-crab soup and Low Country cuisine in Charleston. Everywhere, the vegetables are fresh, delicious and skillfully prepared.

Every restaurant suggestion in this book is based on personal experience — I've either tried the place myself or it has been recommended to me by local friends who eat there regularly. I've made an effort to include not only the best dining experiences, but also the best ones for your dollar. Where reservations are in order (or where times or the menu might change) I've included the restaurant's telephone number. Casual, presentable clothes are acceptable nearly everywhere, but refined dress for dinner, particularly on Sundays, will often help make you feel you belong.

Service throughout the South is friendly and solicitous. "Enjoy your meal" is a heartfelt wish, not a hollow phrase.

Books and Movies

Dixie has poured forth a treasure trove of great literature about itself. Prime yourself by checking your library or bookstore for these:

In the Land of Dreamy Dreams by Ellen Gilchrist, *A Confederacy of Dunces* by John Kennedy Toole, *The House on Coliseum Street* by Shirley Ann Grau, *Queen New Orleans* by Harnett Kane, *All the King's Men* by Robert Penn Warren, and works by Grace King and Walker Percy will enliven New Orleans and Louisiana for you. William Faulkner *(Absolom, Absolom!)* and Eudora Welty *(The Golden Apples)* reflect Mississippi's literary greatness.

Paul Hemphill's *The Nashville Sound: Bright Lights and Country Music* and Michael Bane's *Willie Nelson* are my favorite books about Nashville and country music. Harper Lee's *To Kill a Mockingbird*, and *The Story of My Life* by Helen Keller give two very different reflections from Alabama. You'll get more out of your visit to Thomas Wolfe's home in Asheville if you read *Look Homeward, Angel* first. *Our Southern Highlanders* by Horace Kephart is a classic. Read Archibald Rutlege's *Days off in Dixie*, DuBose Heyward's *Porgy*, Ambrose Gonzales's *The Black Border*, and Ntozake Shange's *Sassafrass, Cypress and Indigo*, to catch flavors of the South Carolina Low Country. Joel Chandler Harris's *Uncle Remus* stories, Margaret Mitchell's *Gone With the Wind*, the St. Simons Trilogy of Eugenia Price, and *Cold Sassy Tree* by Olive Ann Burns all came from the wellspring of life in Georgia.

Shelby Foote's *The Civil War: A Narrative* stands out as a definitive and a very readable account of that great struggle. Booker T. Washington's *Up from Slavery* and Ely Green's *Too Black, Too White* are insightful black perspectives. Sense Dixie's soul in *Southern Families* by Gail Godwin, the novels of Carson McCullers, and the short stories of Flannery O'Connor. *Adventuring Along the Gulf of Mexico*, a Sierra Club book by Donald G. Schueler, and the Georgia Conservancy's *A Guide to the Georgia Coast*, are excellent guides to Dixie's two fascinating shores. The fine maps and regional Tour Books put out by the American Automobile Association (AAA) are well worth the price of membership, even if you never use the tow service. Keep abreast of places to visit and things to do by subscribing to *Travel South* magazine ($12 for four issues, 800/633-8628).

Southern stories translate particularly well to the screen, and filmmakers are forever trying to capture nuances of this nation within a nation. In fact, the first full length motion picture ever made, D.W. Griffith's *Birth of a Nation*, was about the Civil War. Check late-night listings or your video store for these movies:

Norma Rae (Sally Field), *In the Heat of the Night* (Rod Steiger and Sidney Portier), *Coal Miner's Daughter* (Sissy Spacek as Loretta Lynn), *Honeysuckle Rose* (Willie Nelson), greatly underrated *WUSA* (Paul Newman and Joanne Woodward), *To Kill a Mockingbird* (Gregory Peck), *Blaze* (with Paul Newman as Louisiana Gov. Earl Long), *Pretty Baby, Nashville, Inside Daisy Clover,* and the film versions of Tennessee Williams's *A Streetcar Named Desire* and *Summer and Smoke*. The critics derided them but there's a lot of Dixie in old Elvis Presley movies, particularly *King Creole*.

Driving Miss Daisy (Jessica Tandy and Morgan Freeman) and *The Long Walk Home* (Whoopi Goldberg, Sissy Spacek) are among the few modern films that have managed to explore the subtleties of relations between the races with depth and beauty.

Dixieland Delights

Nearly the whole year round, people in Dixie find all sorts of excuses for festivals, parties, and celebrations — invariably accompanied by great food and music, and a warm welcome for out-of-town visitors. Will one or more of these annual events fit into your plans?

❀ *Louisiana, the Pelican State:* **Mardi Gras** (New Orleans and nearly every town in the state, February or early March), **Jazz Fest** (New Orleans, April, May), **Breaux Bridge Crawfish Festival** (May), **Festivals Acadiens** (Lafayette, September), **Sugar Bowl** (New Orleans, New Years Day).

❀ *Mississippi, the Magnolia State:* **Natchez Spring Pilgrimage** (March and April), **Blessing of the Shrimp Fleet** (Biloxi, June), **Deep Sea Fishing Rodeo**

(Gulfport, July), **Natchez Fall Pilgrimage** (October), **Mississippi State Fair** (Jackson, October), **Heritage Music Festival** (Vicksburg, November).

❀ *Alabama, the Heart of Dixie:* **Sailboat Regatta** (Dauphin Island, April), **Bellingrath Gardens Rose Show** (May), **Alabama June Jam** (Fort Payne, June), **W. C. Handy Music Festival** (Florence, August), **National Shrimp Festival** (Gulf Shores, October).

❀ *Tennessee, the Volunteer State:* **Wildflower Pilgrimage** (Great Smoky Mountains, April), **Country Music FanFair** (Nashville, June), **Mountain Music Festival** (Pigeon Forge, June), **Italian Street Fair** (Nashville, September), **Tennessee State Fair** (Nashville, September).

❀ *North Carolina, the Tar Heel State:* **Festival of Flowers** (Asheville, April), **Grandfather Mountain Highland Games** (Linville, July), **Mountain Dance Festival** (Asheville, August), **Southern Highland Handicraft Fair** (Asheville, October), **Music in the Mountains** (Burnsville, September).

❀ *South Carolina, the Palmetto State:* **Black Heritage Tour** (Beaufort, February), **Heritage Classic PGA Golf Tournament** (Hilton Head Island, April), **Spoleto Festival USA** (Charleston, May and June), **South Carolina State Fair** (Columbia, October), **Taste of Charleston Food Fair** (September).

❀ *Georgia, Empire State of the South:* **St. Patrick's Day Parade** (Savannah, March 17), **Thomasville Rose Festival** (April), **Beach Festival** (Jekyll Island, July), **Pogo Fest** (Waycross, October).

❀ *Florida, the Sunshine State:* **Springtime Tallahassee** (March), **Fiesta of Five Flags** (Pensacola, May), **Billy Bowlegs Festival** (Fort Walton Beach, June), **Florida Jazz Festival** (Jacksonville, October).

Turn to *Fairs, Feasts and Festivals* at the back of the book to find a more complete list of public events and celebrations, with phone numbers you can call for specific dates, times and details. I've also included the tourism office phone number for each state in that section.

Stay in Touch

This is the first edition of *Discovering Dixie Along the Magnolia Trail*, and as far as I know it's the first travel guide of this kind available about the Deep South. I'd like to keep it the best and most useful. It has been a delight putting it together for you, and I consider it an ongoing project open to your input and suggestions. If you have recommendations you'd like to share, please write to me in care of Ocean Tree Books, P.O. Box 1295, Santa Fe, NM 87504, and they'll forward your letter to me wherever I am.

Meanwhile, I just know you're going to enjoy the people, the places, and your adventures in Dixie.

Show her your smile, and she'll smile right back!

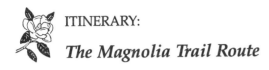

ITINERARY:

The Magnolia Trail Route

THE MAGNOLIA TRAIL is a grand highways and byways loop through eight Deep South states. Not only the destination cities and sights, but the road itself will bring Dixie to you in intimate and surprising ways. As described in this book, the trail begins and ends in New Orleans. The Crescent City makes an exciting beginning and climax for a pilgrimage through Dixie. However, you can have a pleasurable and complete adventure starting anywhere along the route, and it divides into interesting segments if you have only a week or a weekend.

Here's a quick look at what you'll experience on each day of discovery along the Magnolia Trail:

DISCOVERY DAY 1 Get to know mysterious, eccentric, fun-loving New Orleans with an exploration of the French Quarter, vibrant Riverfront, and glassy Aquarium of the Americas. Take a riverboat up the Mississippi to Audubon Park, then ride back beneath moss-draped oaks on the St. Charles Avenue Streetcar. Tonight, savor Creole cuisine, and tap your feet to jazz at its roots at Preservation Hall in the heart of the Vieux Carre.

DISCOVERY DAY 2 Explore New Orleans' fascinating Uptown neighborhoods, including the elegant Garden District. Venture out to the Museum of Art in City Park, the Cemeteries district, and Lake Pontchartrain. Find good things to eat everywhere, shop for antiques on Magazine Street, and check out the Crescent City's get-down music scene tonight at Tipitina's or the Maple Leaf Bar.

DISCOVERY DAY 3 You're on the road now, following the levees to graceful old sugar plantations along the Mississippi River. Drive along the Bayou Lafourche into swampy, romantic Cajunland. Follow serene, live oak shaded Bayou Teche through Jeanerette and New Iberia, and watch herons and egrets nesting on Avery Island. Savor tangy crawfish bisque in Lafayette, then two-step tonight to infectious Cajun *chank-a-chank* music in Breaux Bridge.

DISCOVERY DAY 4 Visit Evangeline's quiet shrine in St. Martinville this morning, then head out across the primeval waterscape of the Atchafalaya Basin on the Swampland Expressway. You'll see Huey P. Long's monumental art deco state capitol in Baton Rouge, reflecting his "every man a king" visions. After a pause in prim English colonial St. Francisville, follow the river north into Mississippi and settle into timeless Southern comfort tonight in a bed and breakfast mansion in Natchez.

DISCOVERY DAY 5   Spend the whole day a century back in time in dreamy Natchez, Mississippi's antebellum jewel. If your vision of the Old South is rich with the romance of Greek Revival palaces, fan-fluttering belles and courtly cotton barons, then you'll walk right into your fantasies at enchanting Longwood, Rosalie, Melrose, and Magnolia Hall. Sleep snugly again tonight in your tester bed among the heirlooms.

DISCOVERY DAY 6   Ramble a short distance on the Natchez Trace Parkway — ancient route of Indians, explorers and boatmen. At Vicksburg, you'll sense the calamity that befell the South when Union forces lay siege to the city for 47 cruel days in 1863. Step aboard the Union ironclad gunboat *Cairo*, raised virtually intact from the mud of the Yazoo River, where it lay undisturbed for a hundred years.

DISCOVERY DAY 7   Today's 200-mile drive north along the fabled Natchez Trace is a serene motoring experience: lovely forest, thought-provoking stops, and no trucks. It's a National Park all the way. Pause among the blossoming dogwoods (if it's spring) for a roadside picnic. In Tupelo, dine on catfish and hushpuppies and visit the humble two-room cottage where Elvis Presley was born.

DISCOVERY DAY 8   Along the Tennessee River in Alabama, visit the homes of two remarkable Southerners — inspiring Helen Keller and W.C. Handy, "Father of the Blues." Cross into the gentle hills of Tennessee and look forward to good times tonight in Nashville, America's Music City.

DISCOVERY DAY 9   Nashville! If you've come for the good-timing sounds and the glitter you won't be disappointed. Try your hand mixing recording tracks on Chet Atkins' console in RCA Studio B, where Jim Reeves, Jerry Lee Lewis, Dolly Parton and other legends created hundreds of country music hits. You're in the audience tonight at a live broadcast of the *Grand Ole Opry* or *Nashville Now*.

DISCOVERY DAY 10   Visit The Hermitage, Tennessee home of charismatic "Old Hickory" — President Andrew Jackson. Ramble on through the Tennessee hills to see good whisky being made the old fashioned way at the Jack Daniel Distillery in Lynchburg.

DISCOVERY DAY 11   Let your sense of wonder soar today at Alabama's Space and Rocket Center, the world's largest space science museum. Walk through an unlaunched Skylab, inspect a once super-secret SR-71 spy plane and a German V-2 rocket, and gaze up at a gigantic Saturn V moon launcher. Then follow the Tennessee River to Chattanooga, where you'll sleep tonight aboard a restored luxury railroad car.

DISCOVERY DAY 12   Relive Chattanooga's dramatic Civil War story atop Lookout Mountain, through Chickamauga Battlefield, and along Missionary Ridge. Inspect a modern engineering wonder at the TVA pumped storage generator atop Raccoon Mountain and discover the innocent enchantment of Rock City Gardens, the charming granddaddy of all tourist traps.

DISCOVERY DAY 13   Enter mist-mantled Great Smoky Mountains National Park near secluded Cades Cove, where you'll see how mountain people lived in bygone days. Pause to feel the peace and renewal of a woodland walk, then drive through spruce forests and carpets of wildflowers to Clingmans Dome on the ridge that separates Tennessee from North Carolina. In Cherokee, North Carolina, you'll encounter Native Americans whose ancestors refused to be exiled West.

DISCOVERY DAY 14   Asheville is North Carolina's pleasant mountain city. Take the morning to explore the 250 rooms and great gardens of palatial Biltmore Estate. Head out across the sky on the Blue Ridge Parkway — to Mount Mitchell, Linville Falls and Grandfather Mountain — then take back roads through slow-to-change towns in the heart of the Appalachian Highlands.

DISCOVERY DAY 15   Today's pleasant 300-mile drive takes you down from the mountains through South Carolina's lush pine forests to the Carolina Low Country and enchanting, colonial Charleston. Along the way, stop at Carl Sandburg's mountainside farm and take in the virgin wilderness of Congaree Swamp.

DISCOVERY DAY 16   Wake up this morning in charming Charleston, a deeply historic city proud of its "livin' in the past" style. Cross the Cooper River and board the aircraft carrier *U.S.S. Yorktown*, a floating maritime museum. Visit Fort Moultrie, which served the nation from the American Revolution through World War II. Shop for sweetgrass baskets in the City Market, or cruise Charleston Harbor and imagine the shot fired above Fort Sumter that kicked off the War Between the States.

DISCOVERY DAY 17 You'll want to take to foot to explore Savannah's 22 tranquil town squares, garden-like setting, well-preserved Old South neighborhoods, and lively River Street. Walk a drawbridge over the moat at Fort Pulaski, last and best-preserved of America's medieval-style forts. Gaze out to sea from the Tybee Island lighthouse.

DISCOVERY DAY 18 Island adventure day! Take the causeway across the Marshes of Glynn to discover history-rich St. Simons Island. Bicycle through the woods and soak in the sun at Jekyll Island. Or take the ferry to the unspoiled solitude of Cumberland Island National Seashore. Sleep tonight in the "clubhouse" of turn-of-the-century millionaires.

DISCOVERY DAY 19 Venture out into Georgia's vast Okefenokee Swamp. Here you'll find a mysterious wetland with floating islands in mirror-like waters, towering cypresses, slumbering alligators, quiet canoe trails, and maybe a possum named Pogo. Stay overnight Thomasville, one of the South's most elegant small towns.

DISCOVERY DAY 20 See Tallahassee, Florida's attractive capital, then picnic beside the clear, deep waters of oasis-like Walkulla Springs. This afternoon you'll arrive at the Emerald Coast on the Gulf of Mexico, a seaside empire of sea-oats covered dunes, warm waters, and the whitest sand beaches in the world.

DISCOVERY DAY 21 Drive along the dunes through Gulf Islands National Seashore. See the first plane to fly the Atlantic and 100 more historic aircraft at the National Museum of Naval Aviation in Pensacola, ferry across Mobile Bay to Dauphin Island, and wander through a floral Eden at Alabama's Bellingrath Gardens.

DISCOVERY DAY 22 Stop at Beauvoir, the beachfront mansion where Jefferson Davis spent his final years, then drive along the gentle (except during hurricanes) Mississippi Gulf Coast. Cross the Pearl River into Louisiana and make a make a dramatic re-entry into New Orleans on the 24-mile Lake Pontchartrain Causeway. Enjoy *lagniappe* (a little something extra) this evening in New Orleans, and celebrate your adventure in Dixie with a toast at the Top of the Mart, high above the Mississippi River.

One Week Trips

The Magnolia Trail route can be separated into three very complete one-week vacations, each one including historic cities, wilderness areas, important military sites, and a beautiful drive:

❀*New Orleans to Nashville (Discovery Days 1-8):* Enjoy the French Quarter and Uptown New Orleans. See River Road plantation homes, the Cajun country, primeval Atchafalaya Basin, Baton Rouge, antebellum Natchez and Vicksburg, then drive the serene Natchez Trace Parkway north through Mississippi and the Tennessee Valley to Music City.

❀*Nashville to Charleston (Discovery Days 9-15):* Visit Music Row, Opryland, The Hermitage, Jack Daniel Distillery, Alabama's Space & Rocket Center, and the battlefields of Chickamauga and Chattanooga, then enjoy the peace of Great Smoky Mountains National Park and the Southern Appalachian Highlands before descending through South Carolina to the sea.

❀*Charleston to New Orleans (Discovery Days 16-22):* Begin in an old city drenched in American and Confederate history, then wander Savannah's charming squares, explore the Georgia coastal isles, paddle out into the Okefenokee Swamp, and take in the sun along the Emerald Coast and Mississippi's beaches before a day of fabulous food and music in New Orleans.

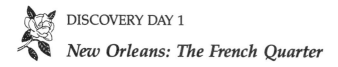

DISCOVERY DAY 1

New Orleans: The French Quarter

"SLOW DOWN, BOY — you're in Dixie!" my Louisiana friend cautioned with a gentle smile as I outpaced her on New Orleans' Decatur Street. I relaxed and found that an easier gait brought me into step with a fabulous city I was just beginning to discover. She smiled again. Smiles come easily in the Crescent City.

Magnetic, mysterious, sensual New Orleans isn't really typical of the South (or anywhere else, for that matter), yet a lot about Dixie begins and ends here — including your three-week Deep South adventure. She's where the Louisiana Purchase came to be and where the Confederate President Jefferson Davis died. She's the birthplace of jazz, the dreamed-of destination of French "casket girls" seeking husbands and frontier Kaintucks seeking fortune and adventure, and the first and final port on America's mightiest river. A feast for the eyes and senses, fun-loving New Orleans is one of the great visitor cities of the world.

Timetable Suggestion

8:30 a.m.	Coffee and beignets at Cafe du Monde.
9:30 a.m.	Stroll Jackson Square and the French Market.
10:30 a.m.	Take the National Park Service's free walking tour of the French Quarter.
12:15 p.m.	Lunch at Rita's on Chartres Street.
1:30 p.m.	Aquarium of the Americas.
3:30 p.m.	Board the *John James Audubon* riverboat for a ride up the Mississippi River to Audubon Park.
5:30 p.m.	Survey St. Charles Avenue from the streetcar as you ride back downtown beneath the live oaks.
7:00 or so	Dinner at Galatoire's or Commander's Palace.
9:00 p.m.	Hear jazz at its roots at Preservation Hall.

Arriving in New Orleans

New Orleans International Airport (MSY) hugs the edge of a cypress swamp in Jefferson Parish, ten miles from Canal Street, but this city's very accommodating attitude will make it easy for you to get in to your French Quarter or Uptown guest house. Airport limousine shuttles will stop at or near your destination for $7 per person (**Airport Rhodes Limousine** 469-4555), or take a taxi from the airport directly to your front door for a standard $18 charge (**United Cab**, 522-9771). **Louisiana Transit**'s express bus leaves the airport about every 15 minutes for Tulane Avenue and Elk Place, two blocks from the French Quarter, for just $1.10 (exact change).

If you're driving into the city, stay on **Interstate 10** until you're close to the Superdome and the high-rises of the Central Business District (CBD). Coming in from the east take the Vieux Carre exit. From I-10 West/Pontchartrain Expressway, follow the signs toward the Crescent City Connection (Mississippi River) bridges, and take the St. Charles Avenue exit just after you pass the Superdome. If plan to camp at Bayou Segnette State Park, continue across the bridge to the West Bank Expressway.

Most highlights of this human-scale enchantress of a city are best discovered on foot, by streetcar, bus, taxi, or boat. If you plan to rent a vehicle, wait until *Discovery Day 2* to pick it up — or even the morning of *Day 3*, when your motor tour along the Magnolia Trail begins.

Getting to know New Orleans

New Orleans is a place of a thousand traditions and mysteries that run as deep and obscure as the Mississippi River itself. She reflects both Mediterranean and Caribbean roots, yet she's a swamp critter with a life and style of her own. Moated in by Lake Pontchartrain on the north and the Mississippi on the south, with formidable swamps to the east and west, this improbable city is the antithesis of puritanism — unashamedly feminine, seductive, more than a little dangerous, and devoted to the pursuit of life's most basic pleasures. The Crescent City's many contradictions may come from the fact that life here has always been both abundant and tenuous: if the giant pumps on Broad Street stopped, the city would go underwater with the next rain. Parts of New Orleans are as much as four feet below the mean level of the silted-up Mississippi, a fact astonishingly clear as you walk along the top of a levee.

New Orleans was founded in 1718 by LeMoyne, Sieur de Bienville, who picked an unlikely mosquito and alligator-infested site a hundred miles upriver from the Gulf of Mexico. Through the centuries, New Orleans was swapped by France to Spain, back to France for a month, then sold to the U.S. in 1803 to float some cash for a bankrupt Napoleon. Among her colorful settlers were gambler-speculator John Law, derelicts and "correction girls" imported from France, Irish canal-diggers, and a Spanish general named Alexander O'Reilly. Despite (or perhaps because of) unpredictable politics, floods, fires, and deeply tragic yellow fever epidemics stretching into the late nineteenth century, the people of the "Isle of Orleans" cooked up a culture all their own, with special *toujours gai* attitudes toward life, death, sex, food, and a way of welcoming visitors to their ongoing party that fascinates and delights everyone.

From red beans and rice on Mondays, to jazz funerals, dark chicory coffee, and a secret code for pronouncing certain street names (Burgundy Street is *B'GUN-dy,* Chartres is *CHAW-dis*), New Orleans is steeped in charming, oddball traditions. Look around and you'll see streets named for Greek muses (Urania, Terpsichore, Clio), as well as hopes and emotions (Felicity, Treasures, Abundance, Desire, Piety). There's even a saint unique to New Orleans. A religious statue once arrived in port with the word "expedite" stamped across the crate. It was duly installed in a parish church and years passed before embarrassed priests realized their error. Yet St. Expedite is still venerated by some as the Crescent City's special patron.

Many New Orleanians, black as well as white, are proud to claim Creole roots — which means they have French and/or Spanish ancestors. But the accent you hear won't be French or plantation Southern. It's a peculiar urban patois called *Yat.* Although it came from white blue-collar neighborhoods like the Irish Channel, even the city's blacks and patricians sometimes talk yatty or use yat expressions. What's it like? Some claim that folks in Brooklyn learned how to talk in New Orleans. (*"You got dat rite, dollin.' Nat'ly's makin' groceries, but dez nice ersters in da zink. Dey fo' yo' momma."*)

And just how does one say New Orleans? You're OK with *Noo OR-luns,* *N'WALL-ins,* and *New AWL-yuns.* Just don't say *New Or-LEENS* — except in a song. However, it is *Or-LEENS* Street and *Or-LEENS* Parish. Don't ask why. Consider this just another of the Big Easy's little eccentricities.

Getting around New Orleans

Set aside assumptions based on normal experience while getting your bearings in New Orleans. Quirks produced by the river's deep bends make evidently parallel streets mysteriously cross at right angles, and you'll wonder why you drive due east across the bridge to reach the West Bank of the Mississippi River. Forget east and west. Accept the four cardinal directions as: *toward the river, toward the lake, uptown* (upstream), *downtown* (downstream). Downtown is a direction, rather than a place. Uptown is both a direction and the general name for the neighborhoods upriver from the Central Business District.

Lively **Canal Street**, which runs to the river, is the great commercial dividing line of the city. Along its median (always called a "neutral ground" in New Orleans), Creoles of the French Quarter traded (or fought) with the Americans who were building the new Uptown neighborhoods in the early nineteenth century. The **French Quarter**, also called the *Vieux Carre* (pronounced *Voo Ca-RAY*), forms a rectangle along the river from Canal Street down to Esplanade Avenue and back to Rampart Street. The compact **Cen-**

NEW ORLEANS

tral Business District (CBD) is a wedge of old and new skyscrapers between Canal Street and the Pontchartrain Expressway from the Superdome to the river. Along Loyola Avenue you'll find the main post office, library and civic center. The Pontchartrain Expressway leads to the double **Crescent City Connection** (Greater New Orleans) bridges across the Mississippi to the West Bank. Many folks just call it the Mississippi River Bridge.

Uptown New Orleans really begins at Lee Circle's handsome, towering monument to General Robert E. Lee. From this point, St. Charles Avenue swings uptown, following the river's curve past the Lower Garden District, **Garden District**, University section and **Audubon Park**. Head "toward the lake" on Canal Street, Esplanade or Carrollton avenues to reach **City Park**, the Cemeteries district, and tranquil Lakeshore Drive along **Lake Pontchartrain**.

New Orleans has a good transportation system of buses, two streetcar lines, and the Vieux Carre minibus in the French Quarter. The fare on all lines (except Riverfront Streetcar) is 80 cents, plus two nickels for a transfer. The **Riverfront Streetcar** line gives excellent access to the attractions blossoming along the water; fare is $1 each way. Call the RTA at 569-2700 to find out which line or bus takes you where you want to go. Stick with the black and white **United Cabs**, 522-9771, for quick, dependable taxi travel. The drivers know the city and love to share their insider tips.

Forever part of New Orleans' allure is its mingling of the pleasurable with the shady, even dangerous, side of life. To minimize the risks, keep your money and credit cards in more than one place and don't wander beyond the main streets at night. (Under Catholic as well as voodoo influences, the city's vibrations respond positively to short prayers and invocations.)

The French Quarter (Vieux Carre)

The Vieux Carre (Old Square) — the 70 city blocks where New Orleans began — remains today its lively, alluring heart. Most often called the French Quarter (or simply the Quarter), the version you visit today was brick-built by the Spanish, following fires in 1788 and 1794 that wiped out all the wooden French structures. As you walk beneath the lacy iron galleries (not balconies, please), peer through arched passageways to the lush fountain courtyards within that still seclude residents from whatever may be going on in the streets. Despite the tourist-oriented hotels, shops and restaurants you'll first see in the blocks from Canal Street to Jackson Square and from the river to Bourbon Street, most of the Quarter is a proud, living residential neighborhood. Daily life goes on here amidst the ghosts of privateer Jean Lafitte, voodoo queen Marie Laveau, French casket girls seeking soldier husbands, mixed-race *quadroon* maidens courted as mistresses by wealthy Creole swains, Confederate General P.G.T. Beauregard, playwright Tennessee Williams, novelist Frances Parkinson Keyes, and a thousand other dreamers great and small who were (and still are) drawn to the Vieux Carre's vortex of charm, drama and romance.

Explore **Chartres**, **Royal**, and **Bourbon** streets along the eight blocks from Bienville Street down to St. Philip Street to find most of the Quarter's highlights. Things get even prettier and quieter the deeper you go into the Quarter:

St. Philip, Ursulines and Governor Nicholls streets are especially inviting.

Since there are so many things of fascination, it's best to take a guided tour first. One stands out among the dozens that depart from Jackson Square. It's the National Park Service's 90-minute **History of New Orleans** walking tour, and it's absolutely free. This walk departs daily at 10:30 a.m., 1 p.m. and 3 p.m. from the Jean Lafitte National Park visitor center in the French Market between Decatur and North Peters streets. (The visitor center will be at 419 Decatur Street in 1992.) It's best to get your ticket a half-hour early because the rangers take only 30 people on each walk. Call 589-2636 to find out about their informative **City of the Dead** (9:30 a.m.), **Tour de Jour** (11:30 a.m.), and Garden District (2:30 p.m.) tours.

Window shopping the fabulous antique stores along **Royal Street** beats many a museum experience. They are among the finest in the world, and to gaze at the many wonders of Old World craftsmanship on display at Manheim Galleries, Waldhorn's and Dixon & Dixon costs nothing. As you'd expect, the French Quarter is also home to a few occult and voodoo shops, oriented toward both tourist and practitioner, replete with musty interiors and a dark cat. Get a Tarot reading at the Bottom of the Cup Tea Room at 318 and 732 Royal Street. There's also The Witchcraft Shop, 521 St. Philip Street, and the Voodoo Museum/Shop at 724 Dumaine Street, where you'll find gris-gris potions and a live boa constrictor (admission $2, open until midnight). Hand-blended scents can be procured at Bourbon French Perfume, 525 St. Ann Street (open to 10 p.m. for that late date). Lose a button on Granny's wedding dress? You'll find it a Zula Frick's Button Shop, 328 Chartres Street.

Don't park on the street in the French Quarter if you can help it. The cops ticket and tow very quickly. Stash your car in a parking garage; one I use often is Economy Parking at Iberville and Dauphine streets ($4 all day). A car in the Quarter isn't a convenience.

The Best to See and Do

The French Quarter itself is one big sightseeing highlight, with something of interest and fascination every few steps along the flagstone sidewalks. Here's what to look for:

❀ ❀ ❀ **Jackson Square** — Alive day and night with street musicians, artists, tourists, and streetside vendors, this famous square fronting on Decatur Street near the Mississippi River is the historical gathering place of the city and the logical starting point for exploring the Vieux Carre. It used to be the Place d'Armes, until Andrew Jackson became the city's hero at the Battle of New Orleans. The equestrian statue of Jackson at the center of the square is as much a symbol of New Orleans as the crescents on the water meter covers and the *fleur-de-lis* on the Saints' football helmets.

FRENCH QUARTER AND RIVERFRONT

The **Pontalba Buildings**, apartment blocks built in 1849 by the Baroness de Pontalba, flank Jackson Square's upriver and downriver sides on St. Peter and St. Ann streets. Delicately symmetrical **St. Louis Cathedral**, gift of a Spanish benefactor in 1794, is the spiritual centerpiece of the square and the city. Step inside to sense New Orleans' soul. At its shoulders are the Mansard-roofed **Presbytere** and **Cabildo**, once powerful symbols of church and government authority in Louisiana and now units of the Louisiana State Museum. Both contain treasures of art and history, but tend to be open sporadically (call 568-6968 for current days and times). In the Presbytere, as of this writing, you can see War of 1812 and Uptown New Orleans exhibits, and Napoleon's death mask. Open 10 a.m. to 5 p.m. Wednesday through Sunday; adults $3, students and seniors $1.50, children under 12 free.

Check out the artists' offerings mounted all around the iron fence surrounding the square. Crave a snack? The curbside Lucky Dog vendors are another time-honored New Orleans tradition.

❀❀❀ **The Moon Walk** — A stroll along this riverfront boardwalk and park is the best way to introduce yourself to the charms of the mighty Mississippi. It's right at the front door of the French Quarter, across Decatur Street from Jackson Square and up the steps over the flood wall. New Orleanians and tourists alike come here to relax, gaze at the colorful paddlewheel riverboats and massive barge tows, listen to the steam calliope aboard the *Natchez*, and enjoy a refreshing breeze on a muggy day. You also get a great view of the bridges, the World Trade Center, and Algiers Point on the West Bank. Walk down the steps and dip your tootsies in the Big Muddy. The Moon Walk is free and fun, and you can feel fairly safe here night or day. It's named for a popular mayor, Moon Landrieu.

❀❀ **French Market** — There are really three markets here: an open-air produce market, a series of indoor shops, and a flea market. The fruit and vegetable vendors between Ursulines Street and the Old U.S. Mint open their stalls early, and you'll find a few still operating into the wee hours. French Quarter denizens have come here to "make groceries" as long as anyone can recall. It's a great place to pick up a fresh apple, banana or alligator pear (avocado) after exploring the Quarter.

The French Market begins across from Jackson Square at Cafe du Monde, the renowned New Orleans meeting place where you can have coffee or chocolate milk and puffy deep-fried beignets (pronounced *BEN-yays*) around the clock. Follow the colonnaded French Market buildings (housing boutiques and praline shops) down Decatur Street and duck through a passageway into the pedestrian promenade where you'll see some amusing sculptures: my favorite is the real-looking cat on the lip of a fountain eyeing bronze birds pecking at bronze salt crackers. Down North Peters Street you'll encounter the popular flea market: check out colorful baubles offered by Rastafarians from an old VW van.

❀❀ **Historic New Orleans Collection** — You might find nineteenth-century Mardi Gras ball invitations, Storyville photographs, old maps, or Vieux Carre architectural plans among the thoughtful and frequently changing exhibits at this fascinating cultural research center at 533 Royal Street. Visit the front gallery for free, $2 for the complete tour which includes the Williams Residence and adjacent buildings. The front gallery is open daily except Sundays from 10 a.m. to 4:45 p.m.; tours of the whole complex are given Tuesday through Saturday from 10 a.m. to 3:15 p.m., (504) 523-4662.

❀❀❀ **Preservation Hall** — Completely unpretentious (its sign is an old trombone case), this renowned shrine is a nightly living museum of New Orleans jazz and an experience no visitor to New Orleans should miss.

You cram into an intimate room and stand (unless you're in the front row) to hear aged black musicians play the music they learned from Scott Joplin, Louis Armstrong and other immortals. Nothing is served but music, but you can buy tapes and albums of the six authentic groups that play here. Preservation Hall is at 726 St. Peter Street, just off Bourbon Street next to Pat O'Brien's saloon. Doors open at 8 p.m., $3 donation. Phone 523-8939 to find out who's playing.

❀ **New Orleans Pharmacy Museum** — Examine ancient apothecary and medical tools, voodoo potions, an 1850s soda fountain, and a garden of medicinal plants. This building at 514 Chartres Street was built in 1823 by America's first licensed pharmacist. Open 10 a.m. to 5 p.m. daily except Mondays, donation $1.

❀ **Gallier House Museum** — Architect James Gallier designed many of the city's finest homes, including this one for himself at 1118-32 Royal Street. You'll see how it looked at the peak of his influence in the 1860s, plus an exhibit of long-lost house building crafts. Open Monday through Saturday at 10 a.m., last 30-minute tour at 3:45 p.m.; adults $4, seniors $3, children $2.25; 523-6722.

❀ **U.S. Mint** — Not only a U.S. mint, this was also the Confederacy's only mint, for a few months in 1861. Inside is the **Jazz and Carnival Museum**, with fine exhibits tracing New Orleans music and Mardi Gras. In the courtyard is a streetcar from the old Desire Street line. The Mint is at the corner of Decatur and Esplanade at the downriver end of the French Market. Open Wednesday through Friday from 10 a.m. to 6 p.m.; adults $3, seniors $1.50, kids free; 568-6968.

❀ **Beauregard-Keyes House** — Confederate General P.G.T. Beauregard lived at 1113 Chartres Street and the place was later restored by novelist Frances Parkinson Keyes. In Beauregard's bedroom and Keyes' study you'll see mementos of their families. Open 10 a.m. to 3 p.m. daily except Sundays; adults $4, seniors $3, students $2, kids $1; 523-7257.

❀❀ **St. Louis Cemetery Number 1** — Those chalk Xs you see on Marie Laveau's tomb are there to ward off hexes or, in some cases, to draw on the power of this legendary spell-caster. Here you'll read gravestones hinting of the sorrowful tragedies that stuck whole families during the yellow fever epidemics of the nineteenth century, but you'll also get a fine sense of the multi-ethnic history of the city. Don't go here after dark — Marie won't harm you, but werewolves from the adjacent bad neighborhood prey on nocturnal tourists. St. Louis Cemetery is on Basin Street, toward the lake from Rampart Street.

The Riverfront and Beyond

❀❀ **River Tours** — At the foot of Canal Street and down toward the Moon Walk, no less than eight boats — ranging from the humble *Voyageur* and the free Algiers Ferry to the steamboat *Natchez* — stand ready to take you out on the river where you can wave to Soviet, Chinese and Scandinavian sailors aboard ships anchored midriver in America's second busiest port. You need to be on the river to appreciate the port's enormous size and scope.

The **Zoo Cruise** aboard the *John James Audubon* is ideal for launching your exploration beyond the Quarter. Departing from the Riverwalk dock, this riverboat runs seven miles upriver to Audubon Park at 10 a.m., 1 p.m. and 3:30 p.m. every day. You can return on the boat or, better yet, stroll through this beautiful urban park and catch the St. Charles Avenue Streetcar for a dreamy 80-cent ride along one of America's great boulevards back to the French Quarter. Along the way, pick out places (Tulane University, Garden District mansions) you'll want a closer look at tomorrow. The one-way run on the *John James Audubon* is $6.50, children $3.75 (round trip $9.50 and $5.25); (504) 586-8777.

The *Voyageur* is merely an old tugboat decked out to resemble a riverboat, but its two very inclusive daily cruises give you the most for your money. The **River, Plantation, Locks and Bayou Cruise** departs from the end of Canal Street at 10 a.m. and comes back at 3 p.m. This five-hour voyage goes all the way to the Bayou Barataria and costs just $11.50 for adults, $5.75 for children over 6; 523-5555. The *Voyageur*'s very satisfying two-hour **Harbor and Battlefield Cruise** leaves the same dock at 3:30 p.m., adults $7.50, children $3.75. Ride the magnificent *Natchez*, a real 265-foot sternwheel steamboat, through the harbor on a two-hour cruise from the Jackson Brewery dock at 11:30 a.m. and 2:30 p.m., adults $12.50, children $6.25; 586-8777.

❀❀❀ **St. Charles Avenue Streetcar** — The oak-shaded loveliness of Uptown New Orleans slips around you as you clack easily along St. Charles and Carrollton avenues in a streetcar that's served this route since the 1920s. (It's a "streakcaw" in New Orleans, never a trolley.) The line itself dates from 1835 and is America's oldest continuously operating city railway. Use it tomorrow for your Uptown neighborhoods adventure, as well as for today's return downtown from the Zoo Cruise. The streetcar runs seven miles from Canal Street (pick it up at Carondelet Street, just across Canal from Bourbon Street), through the CBD, around Lee Circle, and the length of St. Charles Avenue to the end of the line at Carrollton and Claiborne avenues. Cars run every 10 to 20 minutes until midnight, then hourly. Fare: 80 cents (exact change).

❀❀ **Aquarium of the Americas** — New Orleans is constantly coming up with new pleasures, and the glassy, 16-acre Aquarium of the Americas is the very latest. You'll walk through Caribbean Reef, Amazon Rainforest, Gulf of Mexico, and Mississippi Delta habitats. The African penguins and spectacular shark tank are visitor favorites. It's right on the Riverfront at Woldenberg Park, between the end of Canal Street and the Jackson Brewery. The aquarium opens daily at 9:30 a.m. and closes anywhere from 5 p.m. to 9 p.m., depending on the day and season (call 565-3006 for current times); adults $8, seniors $6.25, children 2-12 $4.25.

Places to Stay

The bed and breakfast guest houses of the Lower Garden District are reasonably priced, have great access by streetcar to attractions and nightlife both in the French Quarter and Uptown, offer wonderful New Orleans ambiance and very informative hosts, and you can park your car nearby. Although I prefer the Uptown hostelries, a first night in the French Quarter can be fun. If you'll be in New Orleans for Mardi Gras or Jazz Fest, expect higher rates and make reservations well in advance.

French Quarter: **Lafitte Guest House**, (504) 581-2678, just beyond the noisy section of Bourbon Street, offers antique-furnished rooms starting at $70. **Lamonthe House**, (800) 367-5858, is a Victorian "double" with a courtyard on lovely Esplanade Avenue, from $80. **St. Peter House**, (800) 535-7815, and **A Creole House**, (800) 535-7858, are guest houses on Burgundy Street with rooms from $50. Pleasant and reasonable is **Villa Convento**, 616 Ursulines Street, (504) 522-1793. **Soniat House** at 1133 Chartres Street, (800) 544-8808, is a deluxe small hotel with rooms from $115; you'll receive a silver service breakfast in the courtyard. Tennessee Williams wrote *A Streetcar Named Desire* in room #9 at **Maison de Ville**, a fine small hotel at 727 Toulouse Street, (504) 561-5858, $85 to $130. The French Quarter from Canal to Toulouse Street is packed with larger hotels (such as the Royal Sonesta and Monteleone), but with all the great guest house possibilities, why bother?

Add 11 percent to all rates for the city hotel tax.

Lower Garden District/Uptown: **The Columns**, 3811 St. Charles Avenue, (504) 899-9308, is a beloved local gathering spot and engaging place to stay. Its aging, high-ceilinged rooms made The Columns an ideal set for the Victorian bordello in the steamy film *Pretty Baby*. The Garden District and streetcar line are at your doorstep. Rooms with private bath from $75 to $125, with hall bath $55. **St. Charles Guest House** at 1748 Prytania Street (it runs parallel to St. Charles Avenue) has a quiet, shady courtyard with a pool where you can relax and share your day's adventures. Rooms for two range from about $45 to $65; for backpackers there's a hostel-style setup for just $30 per couple. Call Dennis and Joanne Hilton at (504) 523-6556 for reservations. Also on Prytania Street in the same Lower Garden District neighborhood is **Longpre Guest House**, 581-4540, a favorite of young travelers, private rooms from $40. **Old World Inn**, 566-1330, where you're welcome to practice ragtime on the piano, is on Prytania near Thalia Street, $45 to $55. The same folks operate **The Hideaway** across the street, rooms and suites from $65. On the edge of the Garden District is **Josephine Guest House**, (800) 779-6361, $75 to $130. A little farther Uptown you'll find **Jensen's B&B**, 897-1895, a Victorian at 1631 Seventh Street that's a stone's throw from the streetcar, with rooms from $50. Quietly elegant **Park View Guest House**, 861-7564, overlooks Audubon Park at 7004 St. Charles Avenue, $60 to $95. **The Dusty Mansion**, 891-6061 is neither dusty nor a mansion but has three cozy upstairs rooms ($35 and $45) which are often available when other guest houses are booked, and Cynthia will give you a homey welcome. On a strict budget? **Marquette House** (523-3014) is New Orleans' world-class youth hostel. It's in an antebellum house at 2253 Carondelet Street, one block from St. Charles Avenue. Share insights and tips with intrepid young travelers from all over the world. Dormitory rate $13 per person, private room $30 (even less if you're an American Youth Hostels member).

If you'd like to stay in a private home, contact **Bed & Breakfast Inc.**, (504) 525-4640, or **New Orleans Bed & Breakfast**, (504) 822-5038. Most New Orleans guest houses and B&Bs offer a simple continental breakfast (coffee, juice, fresh pastry), but sometimes also afternoon tea or evening wine.

Places to Camp

At last there's a public campground within striking distance of the city — and it's a beauty. Thoughtfully developed and maintained, spacious **Bayou Segnette State Park** is on a quiet West Bank bayou only 20 minutes from the French Quarter. Here you will find 100 first-rate campsites ($12), clean restrooms/showers, plus 20 fine new cabins ($50) perched on the edge of the bayou. The gates are locked at 10 p.m., but once you've signed in the ranger will give you the lock combination (it's changed daily) so you can let yourself back in after a night carousing in the Quarter. The only drawback here might be the occasional swarm of mosquitoes — pack your repellant. Take the Crescent City Connection across the Mississippi and follow the West Bank Expressway to Westwego and the well-lit entrance on the left just past Louisiana Street, (504) 342-8111. A tour boat outfit right next door (Bayou Segnette Tours, 561-8244) will take you down the bayou to nearby swamps and marshes at 9:30 a.m. and 1:30 p.m.

Food: Jamabalaya, Gumbos and Etouffe

Eating occupies more attention in Louisiana even than politics. The Gulf and the bayous and a climate that grows almost everything make for a delicious abundance. My Cajun chef friend David Aubin claims Louisiana cuisine is "like jazz — improvisation within generally agreed upon processes." That leaves room for a lot of invention and taking full advantage of what's come in on the boat this morning. You'll learn that a *gumbo* is a darkly rich soup often served over rice, delicious anytime, and *jambalaya's* a stew made from everything on hand. Don't be dazzled by the French names: *etouffe* merely means your crawfish or shrimp are stewed or smothered in a tasty roux and tomato-based sauce. Crawfish *bisque* means stuffed crawfish, a *remoulade* is a cold mustard sauce, *grillades* are beef cubes or strips, and so on. The best Creole cooking isn't fancy, just skillfully and lovingly prepared to send your taste buds into orbit.

Try at least once: ***Red beans and rice*** — Leave it to New Orleanians to turn so prosaic a dish into something exquisite; it's traditional and widely available on Mondays, but delicious anytime. *Po-boy sandwich* — "Got somethin' fo' a po' boy?" How about a loaf of French bread with slices of beef or fried shrimp, dressed with shredded lettuce, tomatoes and a tangy sauce? A mere submarine sandwich may never suffice again!

The best restaurant in this city of great restaurants isn't in the French Quarter. It's **Commander's Palace** at Washington and Coliseum streets in the Garden District, a short ride from the Quarter by taxi or streetcar. Call (504) 899-8221 a couple of weeks in advance for reservations; if you can't get in for dinner, lunch at Commander's is also a wonderful experience, especially in the Garden Room. Start with the Creole turtle soup, try an innovative fish entree, and sample the heavenly pastries. Commander's is expensive, but you won't care. (If you're there for lunch, step across the street to stroll through fascinating, crypt-lined Lafayette Cemetery — very New Orleans, in that it is quite old and still in use.)

Cajun style cooking has a lot in commom with Creole but it isn't native to the city; wait until you're in Lafayette *(Discovery Day 3)* to sample an authentic Cajun restaurant.

Places to Dine: The French Quarter

In the French Quarter you'll find five old Creole restaurants whose names are associated far and wide with New Orleans cuisine. Generations of tradition and interesting settings make each of these a culinary event, although some tend to rest on their laurels. Classy, cavernous **Antoine's**, 713 St. Louis Street, (504) 581-4044, is the oldest family-owned restaurant in America; try Oysters Rockefeller (invented here) and the *tournedos marchand de vin*. Consistently good Creole seafood at a reasonable price is the attraction of **Galatoire's**, 209 Bourbon Street, which takes no reservations and is closed Mondays. Try the stuffed eggplant with crabmeat and the pompano dishes. To avoid the agony of standing in a long line, arrive at Galatoire's by 11:30 a.m. for lunch and before 6 p.m. for dinner. Surrounding a lush courtyard, pricey **Brennan's** at 417 Royal Street is sometimes overwhelmed with tourists for its famous hours-long Creole breakfasts. Call 525-9711 for reservations. I like the eggs Sardou with grillades (beef strips in a roux with onions and green peppers, served over grits with cheese). Pleasantly elegant with it's cut-glass wall and pressed-tin ceiling, **Arnaud's** at 813 Bienville Street (523-5433) is best known for its weekend jazz brunches. The game bird entrees are very good at **Broussard's**, 819 Conti Street (581-3866), and you'll love the pretty courtyard.

If I had to pick just one Quarter restaurant to take a date for dinner, it might be **Cafe Sbisa** at 1011 Decatur Street (561-8354). It feels like old New Orleans and their grilled fish dishes are near perfection. Cafe Sbisa and **Le Jardin**

(566-7006) on the 11th floor of Canal Place are among the best places for Sunday Brunch, a lavish New Orleans food-and-jazz tradition that can go on and on into the afternoon.

Dozens of small restaurants with doors open to the sidewalk dot the Quarter, waiting to be discovered. **Rita's** at 945 Chartres Street dishes up such tasty concoctions as a chicken beignet appetizer ($3.75) and seafood-stuffed porkchop ($11.95), prepared before you with soulful flare; reservations not needed. Nearby at the corner of Chartres and St. Philip is **Miss Ruby's** (523-3514), a good place for home-style Creole cooking. You'll find huge delicious crepes as well as Creole seafood specialties every day at **Petunia's Restaurant**, 817 St. Louis Street (522-6440). For fresh oysters, follow the beaten path to the **Acme Oyster House**, 724 Iberville Street, or **Felix's** at Iberville and Bourbon streets. **Buster Holmes** in the Jackson Brewery (524-5234) built its reputation on soul food and red beans and rice. **Feelings Cafe D'Aunoy** on Chartres Street down from Esplanade is a treat for fine chicken dishes; dinner only Thursday through Saturday, plus Sunday brunch (945-2222). Muffalettas, giant round Italian sandwiches with slices of everything, were invented at the **Central Grocery**, 923 Decatur Street, and are good also at the **Napoleon House** on Chartres Street. The **Hummingbird Grill** occupies the street floor entrance of a seedy hotel at 804 St. Charles Avenue in the CBD, but its varied and extremely inexpensive menu (including melt-in-your-mouth cornbread) makes it a 24-hour favorite that crosses all class lines. It's hard to beat the red beans and rice served every day at **Popeye's**, a fast food chicken chain with outlets Uptown on St. Charles Avenue and elsewhere. **Mother's Restaurant** at 401 Poydras in the CBD is legendary for its inexpensive, overflowing seafood po-boys.

Drinking in the Big Easy

Friendly, funky, easygoing little bars are everywhere. Their well-worn, overhead-fan homeyness welcomes you to stop in for a beer — often for a dollar or less. And you *can* take it with you — as long as it's in a plastic "go-cup" which your barkeep has in plentiful supply. Closing hours? Whenever everyone gets sleepy, usually very late. Many bars also serve po-boys or gumbo (food's rarely out of anyone's mind for more than an hour). **Abita Beer,** from across Lake Pontchartrain, contends with **Dixie Beer** as the city's favored local brew. Several cocktails (Ramos Gin Fizz, the Hurricane, the word "cocktail" itself) are New Orleans inventions.

Napoleon House on Chartres Street is my favorite watering hole in the French Quarter, an agreeable mix of dignity (classical music) and decay (cracks in the plaster). It is said that the exiled Bonaparte's New World sympathizers plotted to rescue him from St. Helena and settle him in this house. At **Pat O'Brien's**, 718 St. Peter Street, you slip through a mixed mob of tourists and New Orleanians, but almost everybody's smiling and singing along with the piano player. Congenial **Old Absinthe House**, 240 Bourbon Street, reputedly served real absinthe until the stuff was outlawed. Potions served there today, beneath zillions of calling cards dating from the 1930s, are far safer. **Top of the Mart** is a revolving lounge high atop the graceful World Trade Center at the foot of Canal Street. It offers an unparalleled nighttime panorama of the city in a romantic setting, open daily to 2 a.m., Sundays until midnight. Another great above-it-all experience is the **Rain Forest** on the top floor of the Hilton Hotel, where huge bay windows let you to look down on the river traffic far below.

New Orleans Music and Evening Fun

The get-down jazz and syncopated ragtime sounds so original to New Orleans were born in back of Rampart Street on Congo Square, where slaves and free people of color came to dance and jam, and in the opulent "sporting houses" of the Storyville red light district. Jazz and it's blues and rock offspring have spread throughout the world, but in New Orleans — home of Professor Longhair, Louis Armstrong, Fats Domino, Wynton Marsalis, Clifton Chenier, Allen Toussaint, Irma Thomas, The Meters, and the Neville Brothers — the hypnotic, seductive rhythms go on and on. Let's go find some!

Preservation Hall on St. Peter Street, where the founders of jazz and their immediate inheritors play every night, is the place to start (see *The Best to See and Do*). The **New Storyville Jazz Hall**, 1104 Decatur Street near the French Market, features everything from Dixieland to contemporary jazz and Southern rock, cover charge, (504) 525-8199. Listen to gospel sounds from 8:30 p.m., then stick around for blues after 10 p.m. at **The Gospel and Blues Tent**, 227 Bourbon Street, 523-3800. Charmaine Neville and others on the cutting edge of New Orleans music can be heard at **Snug Harbor**, 626 Frenchman Street in the Faubourg Marigny, 949-0696. Clarinetist Pete Fountain is showcased on the third floor of the Hilton Hotel. He usually plays from 10 p.m. Tuesday through Saturday, $16.50, reservations required, 523-4374.

Bourbon Street at night is a Disneyland of temptations, with joints calculated to play to popular fantasies about New Orleans. Fascinating and often quite amusing are the female impersonator strip shows. It's amazing what can be accomplished with makeup, wigs and silicone. You'll see a music bar with $7.50 beers and a big sign that declares, "Dedicated to the Preservation of Jazz"— but Preservation Hall it ain't. On Bourbon Street things are often not what they seem. Hold on to your wallet.

Mardi Gras

Intoxicating Mardi Gras is America's biggest free-for-all party, and you're invited. Carnival season starts in early January with countless "king cake" parties, then builds into non-stop parades and pageantry during the two weeks before Ash Wednesday. Some 70 *krewes* (Mardi Gras clubs) spend lavishly on floats, costumes, private balls and millions of bead necklaces and souvenir doubloons (specially minted coins) that are tossed generously to parade-watchers.

Try to see **Endymion** and **Comus**, two grand nighttime parades, and be on St. Charles Avenue when **Rex**'s krewe rolls, followed by hundreds of lesser, flatbed truck krewes tossing out even more give-away bounty. Be prepared for sometimes chilly pre-spring weather. Call (504) 566-5011 for the dates.

Book your room at least four months in advance, then lose yourself in bacchanalian madness.

Riverfront Shopping

Shopping can be fun at three locations along the Riverfront: **The French Market**, **Jackson Brewery** and in the **Riverwalk**. When the Jackson Brewery between Decatur Street and the river folded in the 1970s, the building was converted into six floors of specialty shops of amazing diversity — from a music box store to gift shop where every item has a hearts design theme. Just as lively and even larger is the Riverwalk, which runs along the Mississippi from near Canal Street up to the New Orleans Convention Center. It's a short trip from Jackson Square via the Riverfront Streetcar line. Nearby along Julia Street are many art galleries in the awakening old **Warehouse District**.

Useful Tips

The New Orleans visitor center at 529 St. Ann Street on Jackson Square is a good place to stop for the latest in-depth information about the French Quarter and beyond. Find out who's playing where and what's going on in *Gambit*, a popular free weekly tabloid, or check the *Lagniappe* section of Friday's *Times-Picayune*.

The telephone area code for New Orleans and nearby parishes is (504). Reach tourist and events information by calling 566-5031 or 566-5047. Reach the cops at 821-2222. If you get your car towed in the Quarter, call 525-3990 to get it back. If you get turned around, remember that New Orleanians delight in helping a visitor understand their incredible city (they've spent a lifetime trying to figure it out themselves). If you can't find a place to stay (you've arrived a week before Mardi Gras), the Greater New Orleans Hotel and Motel Association, 423-2264, can usually come up with a room.

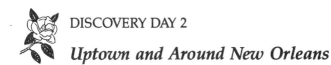

DISCOVERY DAY 2

Uptown and Around New Orleans

SO MUCH THAT'S DELIGHTFUL about New Orleans is found beyond the French Quarter. Spread your wings today in the enchanting old Uptown neighborhoods. Wander through the comfortably elegant Garden District, poke around for antique bargains on Magazine Street, and drop in at Parasol's Bar in the Irish Channel (where you'll hear pure *yat*, dollin').

Stroll Audubon Park or the University section, then venture out to the Cemeteries (a neighborhood also, despite the fact all the residents are dead). See City Park's great art museum, take a drive along Lake Pontchartrain, and get down tonight at the Maple Leaf or Tipitina's for more shake-it-loose New Orleans music.

Timetable Suggestion

9:00 a.m.	Breakfast at the Camellia Grill or La Madeleine.
10:30 a.m.	Get off the St. Charles Avenue streetcar at First Street and wander through the Garden District.
Noon	Have a po-boy sandwich at Parasol's or Domilise's, or leisurely lunch at Copeland's Restaurant.
Afternoon	Stroll Audubon Park, then visit Metairie Cemetery and the New Orleans Museum of Art. Enjoy the tranquility of City Park and Lake Pontchartrain.
8:30 p.m.	Dinner Uptown at Brightsen's or Clancy's, or seafood on Lake Pontchartrain.
9:30 p.m.	Head for Tipitina's or The Maple Leaf for music.

Getting to know Uptown New Orleans and the Lakefront

Use the streetcar and your feet to explore the Uptown neighborhoods this morning. Then drive (or take a taxi or RTA bus) to City Park, the Cemeteries and the Lakefront.

Uptown New Orleans opens like a fan along mansion-lined **St. Charles Avenue**, Magazine Street and Tchoupitoulas (pronounced *Choppa-TOO-lis*) Street, upriver from Lee Circle and the CBD. Here you'll discover a treasure trove of New Orleans diversity. The **Lower Garden District** is a recovering neighborhood with many of the city's oldest American-built homes. It's mostly on the river side of St. Charles Avenue from just below Melpomene

Avenue to Jackson Avenue. The genteel **Garden District** is next, bounded by St. Charles Avenue, Magazine Street, and Jackson and Louisiana avenues. Across Magazine Street toward the river is the **Irish Channel**, with its hundreds of nineteenth-century shotgun and "camelback" houses. They're narrow and tall with ornate millwork fronts, French doors along the porch, and rooms that march in a line from front to back. Once the city's great working class neighborhood, the Channel is now peopled by a racial and economic mix, but still features wonderful old yat characters who refused to move to the suburbs. Farther up the streetcar line you come to the **University/Audubon Park** section — prosperous, pretty and intellectually stimulating. St. Charles Avenue ends at the river near where it crosses Carrollton Avenue, which heads toward the lake. The streetcar makes the turn into the **Carrollton** neighborhood, yet another pleasant urban environment for dining, shopping and living. Oak Street's music spots are a few blocks up from Carrollton Avenue.

Carrollton Avenue, City Park Avenue, West End Boulevard, and/or Wisner Boulevard are the arteries you'll use to get from the Uptown neighborhoods to **City Park**, the **Cemeteries** and the **Lakefront**.

The Best to See and Do

The wonderful St. Charles Avenue "streakcaw" is your chariot for exploring Uptown New Orleans. Get on at Canal Street or at convenient stops all along St. Charles Avenue, pay the conductor 80 cents, and enter the land of dreamy dreams.

❀ ❀ ❀ **The Garden District** — Beneath moss-draped live oaks in a heaven of floral lushness stand the gracefully ornate mansions and cottages of the Garden District, a wonderland of urban comfort and elegance. Built by Americans, not Creoles, on cotton, sugarcane and importing wealth from 1840 to 1880, Garden District homes are celebrated for the detail of their columns, ironwork, galleries, and grounds — much of which you can see on an hour's walk.

Step off the St. Charles Avenue streetcar at First Street and walk one block to Prytania Street. You will find the best of the Garden District in the three blocks between Prytania and Camp streets, and from Philip Street up to Washington Avenue. Let temptation and your own architectural taste be you guide — or follow my favorite Garden District route (see the map). Pause outside the graceful home at **1134 First Street** where Jefferson Davis, the Confederacy's only President, lay dying in 1889. Search the fences fronting this and a few other mansions for small signs with tidbits of house history. Chestnut Street's corners with Third and Fourth streets are among the loveliest and most elegant in the whole city. Notice the amusing ironwork cornstalk fence at Fourth Street and Prytania. One more block up along Prytania or Coliseum streets will bring you to Washington Street and high-walled **Lafayette Cemetery** (open to 2:30 p.m. weekdays). Commander's Palace, New Orleans' finest restaurant experience, is across from the cemetery at the corner of Washington Avenue and Coliseum Street. There's a convenient streetcar stop at Fourth Street and St. Charles Avenue.

❀ ❀ ❀ **Audubon Park/University Section** — Lush Audubon Park, facing the campuses of Tulane and Loyola universities along St. Charles Avenue, is a fabulous urban park experience. It's place to see and be seen, heaven for joggers and walkers. A loop drive, now closed to traffic, winds through Audubon Park. If you're on foot, come through the stately main entrance on St. Charles Avenue, go left and follow the loop along the lagoon to Magazine Street, which bisects the park. Signs there will point you to **Audubon Zoo**, one of the finest in the South. A free **Zoo Shuttle** runs between the St. Charles Avenue entrance and the zoo every 15 minutes from 9:30 a.m. to 5:45 p.m. Noted for its walk-through tropical aviary, Louisiana Swamp Habitat and the world's only known white alligators (all nine of them), Audubon Zoo is open Monday through Friday from 9:30 a.m. to 4:30 p.m. (weekends to 5:30 p.m.); adults $6.50, seniors and children $3. If there's time after your zoo visit, enjoy the prospect of the Mississippi from Riverview Drive.

Tulane University and adjacent **Loyola**, a Catholic university, are two of the South's premiere institutions of learning. Their lovely campuses across

St. Charles Avenue from the park are worthy of a stroll. Along the upriver side of Tulane's campus is **Audubon Place**, the most exclusive street in the city. Peer through its gates into a lane of fabulous mansions.

❀❀ **The Cemeteries** — From Interstate 10/Pontchartrain Expressway, the view of thousands of family crypts seems at first a vision of a vast alabaster city — and it is, except all the residents are dead. Everyone is interred high and dry in this city where the water table may be just a foot below ground. The individual styles and inscriptions on these homes lovingly built for dead people make for interesting "neighborhood" strolls and an intimate look at New Orleanians' unique acceptance of death. If you're lucky, the Olympia Brass Band may be strutting by from a funeral. Feel free to strut along in the "second line."

Go toward the lake on Canal Street to where it meets City Park Avenue and Metairie Road — you'll be at the heart of the thirteen cemeteries that make up the district. The largest (7,000 tombs and still growing) is **Metairie Cemetery**. Among its famous residents: Jefferson Davis, who later "moved" to Virginia, bordello madam Josie Arlington, nine Louisiana governors, and 49 kings of Mardi Gras. Free. (If you're on Canal Street downtown, you can get there by taking any RTA bus with a "Cemeteries" destination sign.)

❀❀ **City Park/New Orleans Museum of Art** — Once a plantation, sprawling City Park follows Bayou St. John from the end of Esplanade Avenue almost to Lake Pontchartrain. It's wonderful for lazy, timeless afternoons. Its centerpiece is the Greek Revival **New Orleans Museum of Art**, noted for its Renaissance paintings, Faberge collection, and precolumbian artifacts. NOMA is open Tuesday through Sunday from 10 a.m. to 5 p.m., adults $4, children and seniors $2. Call (505) 488-2631 to find out about world-class traveling exhibits that appear here frequently. Nearby are the **Duelling Oaks**, where hot-tempered young Creoles once settled scores over some insult, real or imagined, or over the affections of a quadroon beauty.

A lagoon meanders through the park, and you can launch yourself in a rental canoe or paddleboat (482-4888) to float quietly along with the swans beneath overhanging, moss-draped cypresses. Snacks and hot dogs are sold in the Casino. To get to City Park, take Carrollton or Esplanade avenues to Beauregard Circle and follow lovely DeLong Drive around the museum.

❀❀ **The Lakefront** — The Lake Pontchartrain shore between the City Yacht Harbor near West End Park and the Inner Harbor Canal is a pleasant getaway right in the city. Drive along **Lakeshore Drive**, then pick a pleasant spot to jog, or stroll over the levee for a peaceful picnic while you gaze out across the broad but shallow lake. It's often dotted with sailboats in pleasant weather, and families have come here to fish and set out crab traps since anyone can remember. Along Lakeshore Drive, **Mardi Gras Fountain** dances to lights of green, purple and gold, the traditional Carnival colors. From Uptown, take Carrollton Avenue to City Park and follow Wisner Boulevard along Bayou St. John to the lake. New Orleans' Lakefront restaurants, built over the water on pilings, are all clustered in one spot adjacent to the yacht harbor at the outlet of the 17th Street Canal.

❀ **Louisiana Superdome** — Appearing like a gigantic mother ship from some far-flung galaxy, the silvery Superdome swallows up some 80,000 people for star-spangled concerts and gatherings of the Saints — of the National Football League. It anchors the north end of the CBD between Poydras Street and the I-10 interchange. Park at the Poydras Street entrance lot to take a one-hour odyssey through this most spacey of American indoor stadiums. Tours daily (except during events) at 10 a.m., noon, 2 p.m. and 4 p.m.; adults $5, kids and seniors $4; (504) 587-3810.

❀ **Confederate Museum** — Begin your appreciation of the 1861-1865 era of the Confederate States of America here. You'll see many things that once belonged to President Jefferson Davis, donated by his widow, plus uniforms, flags, documents, and weaponry. The museum is an old brick building just off Lee Circle at 929 Camp Street. Open 10 a.m. to 4 p.m. daily except Sunday; adults $2, students and seniors $1, children 50 cents.

❀ **Louisiana Nature Center** — This 86-acre wilderness park on the edge of the suburban sprawl of New Orleans East offers a refreshing, informative look at the critters and creepers of Louisiana's swamps. There's a planetarium here too. Take I-10 east over a "highrise" across the Industrial Canal to Read Boulevard (exit 244). Open weekdays 9 a.m. to 5 p.m.; adults $2, seniors and children $1 (weekends from noon to 5 p.m., with slightly higher admission); call 246-5672 to find out about nocturnal canoe trips and 246-STAR for the $1 planetarium shows. Nearby is the vast 22,770-acre **Bayou Sauvage National Wildlife Refuge** — all of it within the city limits of New Orleans!

Uptown Shopping Hints

The antique stores on **Magazine Street** between Jackson and Louisiana avenues have fascinating variety and much lower prices than you'll find on Royal Street in the French Quarter. Pleasant shops line **Maple Street** between Carrollton Avenue and Lowerline Street in the University section. Rhoda Faust, who always has an eye out for the latest and best from Louisiana writers, holds court at **Maple Street Book Shop**, 7523 Maple Street. Browse awhile, then stop for coffee and dessert at P.J.'s Coffee & Tea Co. up the street.

The most authentic voodoo shop in the city may be **Divine Light** at 3316 Magazine Street near Napoleon Avenue. Surrounded by magical candles and potions with not a single tourist trinket in sight, you'll quickly feel you're not in Kansas anymore.

Places to Dine

Uptown (breakfast and lunch): The Avenue-view tables are festive and the dishes imaginatively New Orleanian and inexpensive (Creole lunches from $5 to $7) at **Copeland's** on the corner of St. Charles Avenue and Napoleon Avenue, (504) 734-1867. I've had pleasant breakfasts in refined atmosphere at the **Pontchartrain Hotel**, 2031 St. Charles Avenue (close to the Lower Garden District guest houses). Brightly efficient **Camellia Grill** is a breakfast and lunch legend at 626 Carrollton Avenue, but it's often cramped and noisy. **La Madeleine Bakery and Cafe** across the street is a more tranquil alternative; for lunch they serve wonderful caesar salads and tasty deli sandwiches.

I can't imagine anything better for lunch than an overflowing po-boy on a fresh loaf of French bread and a cold Dixie Beer at a neighborhood hangout. Bring the kids, too. **Parasol's Bar** at Third and Constance streets is the heart and soul of the Irish Channel. You'll hear Channel yat *("Heaz yo' sammich, dollin', srimp an' it's dressed.")* at its most fluent. Parasol's is closed Tuesdays and Sundays. Fabulous po-boys are made right before your eyes at **Domilise's**, on the corner of Annunciation and Bellecastle streets. You won't pay more than $4 for the sandwich, and a draft beer in a frosty glass is just 90 cents. Savory red beans and rice, gumbo, and fresh shrimp are frequently available at friendly, unheralded little bars, such as **Martin's** at 4416 Magazine Street near Napoleon Avenue (atmosphere and prices from another time: red beans and rice with salad, $2.95; specials under $4, beer 75 cents). **Audubon Tavern II** at 6100 Magazine Street is a good, inexpensive lunchtime choice after your visit to Audubon Park.

Uptown (dinner): See *Discovery Day 1* for my remarks about incomparable **Commander's Palace** in the Garden District. (It's also wonderful for lunch, when you can sometimes get in on short notice.) At **Brigtsen's Restaurant**, 723 Dante Street, look for duck a l'orange with angel hair pasta and soft shell crawfish; open Tuesday through Saturday for dinner, (504) 861-7610 (expensive but good). Discover smoked soft-shell crab and pasta with crawfish at **Clancy's**, 6100 Annunciation Street (895-1111). The menu is creole and soul (beef pot pie, fried catfish) and inexpensive at **Mais Oui** on Magazine Street near Nashville Avenue (897-1540). **Pascal's Manale**, 1838 Napoleon Avenue (897-1540), is famous for barbecued shrimp, but bring a full wallet. The **Upperline Restaurant**, 1413 Upperline Street (891-9822), is a quietly sophisticated bistro featuring nouvelle New Orleans dishes, such as trout lacombe. You'll find spicy-boiled peel 'em yourself shrimp and crawfish and interesting things on the jukebox at **Franky and Johnny's**, 321 Arabella Street near Audubon Park (899-9146). **Vera Cruz** at Maple and Hillary streets (866-1736), is a pleasant Mexican restaurant.

The Lakefront: I'll get an argument, but **Fitzgerald's** is my favorite Lakefront seafood restaurant. The prices are fair, dishes palatable, service is friendly and family-like, and the view out across the lake serene. Fitzgerald's is open for lunch and dinner every day, no reservations, pay with cash or traveler's checks (282-9254). **Bruning's** has a window wall overlooking the lake and is especially renowned for the way they prepare flounder (282-9395). To get to the cluster of Lakefront restaurants, take I-10 west, then follow West End Boulevard all the way to the City Yacht Harbor; turn left on Lake Marina Avenue and follow the signs to the restaurant parking area. The boiled crawfish are simply wonderful at **Sid-Mar's** (831-9541), a down-home tavern in Bucktown, the old fishing village just across the 17th Street Canal from West End Park (take Robert E. Lee Boulevard across the canal bridge and turn right to 1824 Orpheum Avenue).

How to Eat Crawfish:
A few deft moves, and that succulent "mudbug" is down the hatch. Pick a critter off the tray and break him in two at the middle. Now hold the end of the tail with one hand while you use thumb and forefinger of the other to peel off the first two "rings" of his shell. Pinch the end of the tail and the meat should pop right out. It's considered correct to suck out the savory juices left inside the head.

As they say in New Orleans, *"Pinch dem tails, suck dem heads!"*

Uptown Music and Evening Fun
Originally set up as a venue for Professor Longhair, the beloved New Orleans piano man, **Tipitina's** is a showcase for Louisiana's best native talents. Tip's has a great dance floor too. Find Tip's where Napoleon Avenue meets Tchoupitoulas Street at the river. Call (504) 897-3943 to find out who's playing and the evening's cover charge. Funky, fun, and a real New Orleans experience, **Benny's Bar** at Valence and Camp streets (895-4905) is where the city's best unknown musicians come to jam into the night.

The Oak Street neighborhood off Carrollton Avenue is a lively area centering on the inviting **Maple Leaf Bar**, with several other music clubs a few steps away. They finally closed the laundromat at the Maple Leaf, 8316 Oak Street (866-9359), but you can still find classical selections on the juke box and at night after 10 p.m. the place is jumpin' with bluegrass, blues, Cajun, or Zydeco rock. (Once I saw folk-blues legend Odetta step out of the audience to jam with a group of Tulane professors playing long-lost ragtime tunes). When things get too lively, take your Dixie Beer out back to the romantic patio. Step across Oak Street for more great sounds (mainly blues) at **Muddy Waters** (866-7174). For rock music, there's **Jimmy's** at 8200 Willow Street (861-8200). Tucked into nearby side streets are a few seemingly nameless rock clubs.

Jazz Fest

Hundreds of jazz, blues and gospel performers — from Miles Davis to Chuck Berry, Buckwheat Zydeco and Sun Ra — turn out to play on a dozen outdoor stages set up at the Fair Grounds racetrack for two rousing three-day weekends in late April and May. Started in 1969, the **New Orleans Jazz and Heritage Festival** is now so wildly popular (300,000 came in 1990) that it spills over into a Riverfront venue. Have your soul stirred in the gospel singers tent. As with Mardi Gras, make room reservations three or more months ahead. Advance adult tickets are $7, children $2; the music workshops are free. Call (504) 522-4786 to find out who'll be performing.

Useful Tip

Here's an easy, unadvertised loop tour of the city you can take for only 90 cents, due to the oddball geography. Get on the St. Charles Avenue Streetcar at Canal Street and buy a ten-cent transfer. Ride to the end of the line at Carrollton and Claiborne avenues, then get on the Tulane Avenue bus with your transfer and ride along through part of Mid City. It's considered a one-way trip by the RTA, but you'll be returned downtown to the CBD, not far from where you first stepped aboard the streetcar.

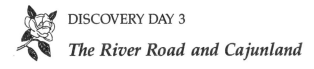

DISCOVERY DAY 3

The River Road and Cajunland

TIME TO HIT THE ROAD! Begin your Magnolia Trail adventure through Dixie with a visit to Louisiana's enchanting old plantation homes along the fabled Great River Road between New Orleans and Baton Rouge. Each one has a different, often curious story. Cross the Sunshine Bridge and drive down along Bayou LaFourche, where Cajun influences begin.

Beyond the Atchafalaya River, take time to absorb the serenity of sweet, live oak-shaded Bayou Teche. Visit the egrets, herons, alligators, and a hot sauce factory on an island that isn't what an island usually is. After dinner in Lafayette, capital of modern Acadiana, put on your dancin' shoes and *laissez les bon temps rouler* with a Cajun chank-a-chank band in Breaux Bridge.

Timetable Suggestion

8:30 a.m.	Quick breakfast in Uptown New Orleans.
9:00 a.m.	Head west on I-10 over the Bonnet Carre Spillway.
10:00 a.m.	Arrive at Tezcuco or Belle Helene Plantation.
Noon	Lunch at The Cabin or Lafitte's Landing.
2:30 p.m.	Drive along the Bayou Teche.
3:15 p.m.	Avery Island Jungle Gardens, Bird City sanctuary, and Tabasco factory tour.
6:15 p.m.	Arrive in Lafayette for savory Cajun feast.
9:00 p.m.	Stomp and clap into the night at Mulate's.

Magnolia Trail: New Orleans to Lafayette (200 miles)

Find a ramp to Interstate 10 west (near Lee Circle or from Tulane or Carrollton avenues) and head west out of New Orleans. Just past the airport you'll cross a wild cypress swampland — the **Bonnet Carre Spillway**. When the Mississippi threatens to inundate the city, floodgates here open up and the muddy river waters gush across the spillway into Lake Pontchartrain — to the consternation of the lake's fish population. Be sure your fuel tank is full — this elevated freeway drive is fun, but it's a long walk back if you run out of gas. When you're 51 miles west of New Orleans take exit 182 to Burnside. Follow Louisiana Road 22 two miles to LA 44 and turn left to reach the **River Road** — designated LA 942/LA 75 upriver (right) and LA 44 downriver (left). Turn right to visit Houmas House and Belle Helene; turn left to

SOUTH LOUISIANA

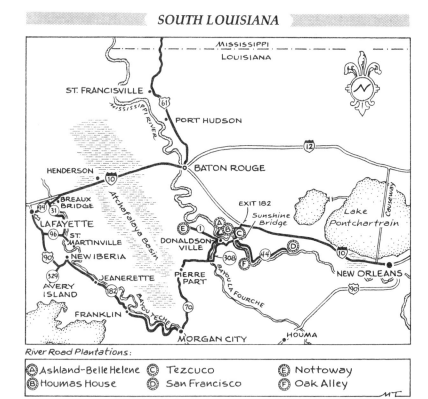

River Road Plantations:

Ⓐ Ashland-Belle Helene	Ⓒ	Tezcuco	Ⓔ	Nottoway
Ⓑ Houmas House	Ⓓ	San Francisco	Ⓕ	Oak Alley

see Tezcuco and San Francisco, and to cross Sunshine Bridge to see Nottoway or Oak Alley and to continue on the travel route.

In Louisiana politics, it always pays (sometimes quite well) to be colorful. Some say Governor Jimmy Davis sang his way into the Louisiana statehouse, so **Sunshine Bridge** is an appropriate reflection of his most famous song, *You Are My Sunshine*. Sing a few bars as you cross the Mississippi, continue three miles on LA 70, then turn right onto the four lane bypass into **Donaldsonville**. Turn left on LA 308 or LA 1 and drive south about ten miles along the **Bayou LaFourche**, keeping an eye out for interesting old plantations (Belle Alliance, Madewood), and historic St. Elizabeth's Church. When you reach LA 70 again near Paincourtville, turn right and head out on a fascinating, watery, rural drive through sugarcane fields and past cypress swamps laced with bayous for the next 33 miles into **Morgan City**. Along the way you'll see clues to how bayou folks draw a good living from their bounteous environment ("Catfish Traps $15," "Crawfish Wire For Sale," "Scully's Swamp Tours"). Along your left will be the Belle River and Lake Verret; to your right over the big levee runs the Bayou Maringouin Alternate Route — part of the Intra-coastal Waterway shipping lane. Just beyond it you'll see the tall, moss-draped cypresses of the wild and dark **Atchafalaya** (pronounced *ah-CHAF-ah-lye-uh*) **Basin**. Take a closer look by turning right at Adams Boat Landing for a levee-top view.

The mighty Mississippi has been trying to change course into the Atchaf-alaya for decades. When one day it finally breaks the dikes upriver and comes this way, Morgan City (if it survives the flood) gets to be the next New Orleans. Today the town is a major supply point for Louisiana's offshore oil industry. Stay on the main route (LA 70) through downtown and take the US 90 bridge across the Atchafalaya River. About five miles farther, take LA 182 along the **Bayou Teche** through Patterson and back briefly to US 90. From here to New Iberia (about 40 miles) US 90 is a freeway shortcut, while LA 182 and LA 87 wind along the Teche, mile-for-mile the loveliest bayou in Louisiana. Stay on LA 182 through Garden City into **Franklin**. You'll pass in-viting Frances and Arlington manor homes (open for visits Tuesday through Saturday). For an intimate look at the bayou, drive behind Franklin's impos-ing 1950s-style courthouse and take the little bridge across the Teche (a left turn on LA 87 will put you on a quiet winding drive along the Teche and return you to LA 182 at Baldwin or Adeline). To avoid the shopping mall sprawl coming into **New Iberia**, pick a left turn off LA 182 at Baldwin or Jeanerette, follow the signs to US 90, and head north toward Lafayette. Look for the turnoff south on LA 329 to **Avery Island** as you approach New Iberia. (If you drove into New Iberia on LA 182, turn left at Center Street/LA 14 and follow the signs to LA 329.) After the 16-mile round-trip to Avery Island, continue north on US 90.

If you're traveling in early spring, you may see people putting down set nets for crawfish in the shallow water of the highway median. US 90 becomes the **Evangeline Throughway** as you come from the south into **Lafayette**.

Lafayette's organic street pattern can be confusing. Vermilion Bayou mean-ders south and east of town. As you're coming in on Evangeline Throughway, you'll cross Pinhook Road, location of several of this evening's restaurant choices. Downtown is west of the Throughway via Johnston Street. Keep going north through the motel gauntlet and you'll meet Interstate 10.

Land of the Cajuns

Bergeron, Broussard, Delcambre, Guidry, Hebert, Labadie, Trahan, Quebe-daux are surnames you'll find in long columns in the Lafayette phone book. Their progenitors came down from French Canada, driven out by the British more than 200 years ago. Isolated in the surrounding food-rich swamps and bayous, the adaptable, industrious, life-loving Acadians (the blacks later called them Cajuns) held fast to their Catholic roots and created a particularly flavor-

ful culture, peppered with lively traditions like the frequent street *fais-do-do*
(dances) which are held for any number of excuses. The words may be French,
but the sounds of the language, beat of the music, and tang of the food are
distinctly *Cajun*.

Fancy mixes with fact in Henry Wadsworth Longfellow's epic poem *Evangeline*, but this tragic Acadian heroine really existed, and the true story of
Emmeline (Evangeline) Labiche and Louis (Gabriel) Arceneaux is even more
poignant than the poem. You'll see lots of references to this Cajun creation
myth particularly in Lafayette and nearby St. Martinville, where Emmeline
died of a broken heart. Spreading out from St. Martinville, Acadians embraced
the roadless, swampy realm of southwest Louisiana, poling out in *pirogues*
(narrow boats still seen here) to trap nutria, hunt waterfowl, fish the shallow
waters, and later grow sugarcane and pump oil. Today, Cajunland stretches
from the Bayou LaFourche virtually to the Texas line and from well north of
Interstate 10 to the Gulf of Mexico.

The Best to See and Do

❀❀❀ **Great River Road Plantations** — The great Creole plantations up from
New Orleans made the lower Mississippi a river of riches for nearly a century. Oilfields have gradually moved in on the sugarcane plantations along
the Great River Road, which refers these days to the Louisiana highways
hugging the levee on both sides of the Mississippi. Pull off on one of the shell
lanes leading to the top of the levee and walk up for a very different view
above the riverscape. A half dozen great antebellum homes — each with a
very individual character and history — are within easy reach of today's route.
Choose two or three to view in detail. All are open daily.

East Bank: My favorite and probably the most memorable is **Ashland-Belle
Helene**, precisely because it looks its age and shows all it's bones. Galleried
on all four sides with 28 towering, time-tattered square columns, 1841 Belle
Helene is only now feeling the stirrings of a real effort at restoration. Still,
it'll take a lot more money to finish the job, and you'll feel that your $3 tour
fee will be put to good use. Step up on the brick first-floor gallery to the table
that serves as a makeshift reception point for visitors. Here you'll likely meet
a descendant of Helene herself, for whom the placed was renamed in 1889.
Remnants of filmmaking *(Mandingo, Band of Angels)* lie about. That monstrous
iron kettle, big enough to boil an elephant, was once used to process sugarcane. Lovingly restored, **Houmas House** is actually two houses — the original
eighteenth century Spanish-style building is linked by a carriageway to the
1840 Greek Revival mansion in front. Curious features include two hexagonal
garconnieres (young men's quarters), a still-functioning colonial kitchen, and
a three-story spiral staircase. Bette Davis's *Hush, Hush Sweet Charlotte* was
filmed here. Tour: adults $6, students $4, kids $3.50, (504) 473-7841. **Tezcuco** is

built of bricks fired in this plantation's own kilns and cypress cut on the property — then woodgrained to look like a more fashionable wood. The clusters of plantation outbuildings and a labyrinthine antique shop under the main building add to the delights. Tour: adults $5, seniors $4, students $3.50, children $2.50 (562-3929). Fanciful **San Francisco**, with it's peach and blue shutters and five elaborately-decorated cypress ceilings, was originally named *Sans Fruscins* ("without a penny to spare") — a humorous reference to its high cost. Tour: adults $5.50, children $3.75, (504) 535-2341.

West Bank: Let your jaw drop as **Nottoway** comes into view. At 53,000 square feet in 64 rooms on three rambling stories, this white Italianate and Greek Revival palace is the largest plantation home in the South. Builder John Randolph needed room for his eleven kids. Unusual nineteenth century high-tech features include indoor bathrooms and an intercom system using silver bells in every room. Lunch and dinner are served at Nottoway's dining rooms. Tour: adults $8, children $3, (504) 545-2730. **Oak Alley** lures visitors because of it's stunning setting: an enchanting archway of 28 huge, 250-year-old live oaks runs from the river to the Greek Revival mansion. Tour: $5.50 — but the view is the best part.

❀❀❀**Avery Island Jungle Gardens / Bird City Sanctuary** — Gaze out at thousands of snowy egrets and herons perched on specially-built nesting platforms above the water in this far-sighted family-developed preserve established in 1892. Alligators snooze in the lake, a serene 1,000-year-old Buddha rests in the beautifully tended Chinese Garden, and hundreds of irises and camellias bloom winter through spring. This "island" is really a salt dome uplift above the surrounding flat prairie and cane fields. If you arrive before 3:30 p.m., take the free Tabasco pepper sauce factory tour first; you'll still have time for an hour or more in the Jungle Gardens. Avery Island is at the end of LA 329, eight miles south of US 90 at New Iberia. Bridge toll onto the island is 50 cents. Open every day 9 a.m. to 5 p.m. (you'll be able to visit the gardens and sanctuary even if you're there just before 5 o'clock); adults $4.50, children $3.50.

❀❀ **McIlhenny Tabasco Factory** — A blend of red capsicum peppers grown in South America, vinegar and salt, Tabasco brand hot sauce has been bottled by this Louisiana company since 1868. A free half-hour factory tour departs every 15 minutes Monday through Friday from 10 a.m. until 3:30 p.m., and Saturday mornings until 11:45 a.m. The plant is next to Avery Island Jungle Gardens on LA 329; call (318) 365-8173 for more about both.

❀ **Bayou Teche Homes** — Through Franklin, Jeanerette and New Iberia you will pass several elegant sugarcane plantation homes along the Bayou Teche, some of which are open for a peek inside. **Frances Plantation** (1820) and **Arlington** (1830) are on your right on LA 182 as you enter Franklin. **Oaklawn**

Manor (1837) on Irish Bend Road has a haunting grove of oaks that probably predates the discovery of America. All are open Tuesday through Saturday from 10 a.m. to 4 p.m., admission from $3 to $6. The two gems of New Iberia are **Mintmere/Broussard House** and **Shadows-on-the-Teche**. The Broussard House is a very early (1790) Acadian manor house of *bousillage* (mud and moss) construction. There's lots of movie and literary history (H.L. Mencken and Henry Miller were guests) connected with Shadows, open daily 9 a.m. to 4:30 p.m.; adults $4, children $2, (318) 369-6446.

❀ **Konrico Rice Mill** — Tour the oldest operating rice mill in America and see a film on Cajun culture. The Konrico Mill is at 307 Ann Street in New Iberia; hourly tours from 10 a.m. to 3 p.m. daily except Sundays; adults $2.75, seniors $2.25, children $1.25.

❀ **B.F. Trappey's Sons Factory** — If you can't make it to McIlhenny's at Avery Island, enjoy this free pepper sauce plant tour at 900 East Main Street in New Iberia, weekdays 9 a.m. to 3 p.m.

❀ **Acadian Village** — A cluster of restored nineteenth-century attic-over-the-porch Acadian houses furnished with period south Louisiana household items recreates a Cajun lifestyle that persisted into the 1930s. The village was developed to train and employ the talents of Lafayette's handicapped citizens. From Evangeline Throughway take Johnston Street/LA 167 southwest to Ridge Road. Open 10 a.m. to 5 p.m. daily except holidays and early December, adults $4, children $1.50, (318) 981-2364.

❀ **Chitimacha Reservation** — Tucked away on a bend of the Bayou Teche, a small band of Indians have coexisted with the Cajuns for generations. There's a cultural center, trading post and a small museum here, operated by Jean Lafitte National Historical Park as one of its Acadiana units. From Baldwin, drive LA 326 five miles east to Charenton. Open 8 a.m. to 4:30 p.m. daily; free. Other Jean Lafitte Acadiana units are opening up in Thibodaux, Lafayette, and Eunice. Call (318) 264-6640 for updates.

❀ **Vermilion Queen** — Cruise Vermilion Bayou past the elegant homes and gardens of Lafayette's **Millionaire's Row** on this two-deck tour boat. The Queen departs from the Pinhook Road Bridge on daily two-hour tours at 11 a.m. and 2 p.m., adults $8.50, kids $4.50. Call (318) 235-1776 to make reservations for the 7 p.m. dinner cruise ($24 with dinner, $9.50 without).

❀ ❀ ❀ **Mulate's** — More Cajun lore and liveliness is stuffed into this famous Breaux Bridge restaurant and dance hall than you'll find anywhere else. Even if you dine in Lafayette this evening, come here and surrender cheerfully to the fiddle and accordion *chank-a-chank* of Dewey Balfa, Beausoliel, the Breaux Bridge Playboys, or other top Cajun bands — there's one here every night. You won't be able to keep your feet still and you'll pick up the traditional two-step in no time. Mounted above the dance floor are bronze-gilt shoes from the feet of the best regulars, but kids and grannies will be dancing, and the same band may have a 20-year-old playing drums while white-haired *grandpere* pumps a mean squeeze box. It's wild and happy. Go ahead and gawk at the ceiling (held up by cypress trunks) and the walls: there's a stuffed alligator in a *pirogue*, paintings by the Cajun artist George Rodrigue, and notes and photos from which you'll learn a lot about today's Cajuns. There's a souvenir counter with a great selection of books about Acadiana. The food's good, too. Try the Zydeco salad with *andouille* sausage. From Lafayette take Pinhook Road east to Carmel Drive/LA 94, turn right and go about five miles to the outskirts of Breaux Bridge. Mulate's phone number is (318) 322-4648.

Places to Dine

Make your River Road lunch stop at one of these restaurants: **The Cabin** at the intersection of LA 44 and LA 22 is an experience in plantation history as well as a good restaurant (most lunches under $6); the building was pieced together from slave dwellings moved to the site from three River Road plantations. **Hymel's Seafood** along the road on the East Bank serves an eggplant, crabmeat and shrimp plate for $5. Next to Tezcuco is **The Pilot House**. Good choices on the West Bank are **Lafitte's Landing**, just across Sunshine Bridge, and **First & Last Chance** in Donaldsonville.

Bring an appetite when you're in Cajunland! You can hardly go wrong tonight at any of the established restaurants in Lafayette, and they won't break the bank either. When they're in season (January through maybe July), savor crawfish bisque or etouffe, or just crawfish boiled in wonderful spices, and sample juicy hot *boudin* (a tangy Cajun sausage) with rice. **Mulate's** in nearby Breaux Bridge is a special treat that shouldn't be missed, so I've included it in *Best to See and Do.*

Popular for steamed seafood with just-right Cajun spices is **Randol's Greenhouse**, 2320 Kaliste Saloom Road, off Pinhook Road south of Vermilion Bayou, (318) 981-7080. **Prejean's**, 3480 LA 167 north of I-10 (896-3247), tempts you with crawfish — prepared bisque, etouffe and six more ways — fresh oysters for just $4.95 a dozen, and a big alligator dinner at $9.77. Randol's and Prejean's both feature live Cajun and sometimes Zydeco (black Cajun) music seven nights a week. My favorite for Cajun-style eating in a friendly family atmosphere is the **Old Ice House**. Far warmer in spirit than its name implies, the Ice House is at 325 Pinhook Road, a left turn off the Evangeline Throughway (237-7884). Reservations are a good idea at **Cafe Vermilionville** in an historic house at 1304 West Pinhook Road (237-0100), **Chez Pastor** at 1201 West Pinhook (234-5189), and time-honored **Don's Restaurant** at Vermilion and Sixth streets downtown (235-3551) — all of them dependable for satisfying Cajun (what else?) seafood. For something extra special, try the shrimp-stuffed Snapper Daniel at **Angelle's** on LA 167 four miles north of I-10 (896-8416), or Snapper Mamou at **The Landing** on Vermilion Bayou (233-8640).

Places to Stay

Bois des Chenes Inn, at 338 North Sterling Street just off the Evangeline Throughway, is a 1890s carriage house behind the columned, Acadian-style 1820 Charles Mouton Plantation Home. You get a bottle of wine, a tour of the Mouton House, and a Louisiana-style breakfast in the morning; $65 and $75 for two, $95 for a suite. Call Coerte or Marjorie Voorhies at (318) 233-7816 for reservations. **Til Frere's House**, 1905 Verot School Road, 984-9347, has gained notoriety for its mint juleps. **Evangeline Oak Corner** on the Bayou Teche in St. Martinville (tomorrow morning's first destination) is a splendid Acadian bed and breakfast experience, 394-7675.

Lafayette's franchise strip, with all the modern chain motels you'd ever need, is on Evangeline Throughway from Cameron Street north to the I-10 interchange. Find **Hotel Acadiana** at 1801 West Pinhook Road just across Vermilion Bayou, rooms from $50, (800) 826-8386. **Acadian Motel**, 120 North University Avenue, 234-3268, offers budget rooms from about $20.

Places to Camp

There are no public campgrounds near Lafayette, but these commercial ones are convenient to tomorrow's travel route. Not far from Mulate's and right on the Bayou Teche in Breaux Bridge is **Pioneer Campground**, (318) 322-3502. It's just off I-10 at exit 109, $10 per night. Farther away but more of an experience is **Frenchman's Wilderness**, 20 miles west of Lafayette in the middle of the wild Atchafalaya Basin; full hookups, laundry, store, nature trails, 228-2616. Close in are **Acadian Village Campground** at 200 Greenleaf Drive, 981-2489, and **Acadiana Park Campground** off East Alexander, 234-3838.

Useful Tips

Lafayette's visitor center is on 16th Street in the short block between the northbound and southbound routes of the Evangeline Throughway. Telephone area code along the River Road is (504); throughout Acadiana it's (318).

Vermilionville is a new Cajun/Creole theme park replica of a 1765-1890 Acadian village. Costumed guides make crafts, play music, and cook for you. It's off US 90 south of Lafayette near the airport. Open daily 9 a.m. to 5 p.m.; adults $8, seniors $6.50, students $5; (318) 233-4077.

Linger Longer

Houma Route: From New Orleans' West Bank, US 90 dips low into Terrebonne Parish and passes through lovely **Houma** (pronounced *HOME-uh*, population 32,000), a Cajun city at the crossroads of seven bayous, including Bayou

Blue (thank you, Linda Ronstadt!) and the Intracoastal Waterway. Nearby, several tour operators will take you out into the coastal swamps and bayous, but legendary **Annie Miller's Terrebonne Swamp and Marsh Tours**, (504) 879-3934, is a favorite. It's about 60 miles from the Crescent City Connection bridges to Houma, then 37 miles from Houma to Morgan City, where you can pick up today's travel route along the Bayou Teche to Lafayette.

River Rest: Take your time along the River Road, then head for Cajunland tomorrow. Three river plantation homes on the *Best to See and Do* list take overnight guests. A third-floor room overlooking the river at Nottoway, (504) 545-2730, is $115 with a full plantation breakfast. Quiet cottages with kitchens at Tezcuco, 562-3929, start at $65. Oak Alley, 265-2151, also offers cabins.

Fais-do-do: A half hour's drive west and north from Lafayette will bring you to **Eunice** on US 190, where you can grab a seat at the *Rendezvous de Cajun* radio show at the Liberty Theatre; Saturday nights from 6 p.m. to 8 p.m., $2 donation, (318) 457-7389.

Today's Shortcut
After a visit to the River Road plantations, you can return to I-10 and continue northwest 27 miles into Baton Rouge, where you'll pick up the *Discovery Day 4* travel route north to Natchez.

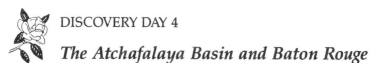

DISCOVERY DAY 4

The Atchafalaya Basin and Baton Rouge

THE SPRAWLING PRIMEVAL WATERSCAPE you cross today on Interstate 10 is America's second largest swamp (half a million acres — only the Okefenokee is bigger) and the most dynamic. Eons ago, the mighty Mississippi came through here to the Gulf of Mexico, then changed its mind and went southeast via present-day New Orleans. Now it wants to come this way again, which set up a battle of titans that has raged here since 1929: Mother Nature and the Father of Waters versus the Army Corps of Engineers. North near Morganza, the Corps poured a lot of concrete keep the Mississippi where it is, yet the Atchafalaya insists on doing things its own way. Who will win in the end? Nobody's betting on the engineers.

But credit them for the wonderful drive you have across the breadth of this superswamp on the I-10 Swampland Expressway, an environmentally sound elevated highway many folks believed could not be built. On the other side, visit Huey Long's magnificent capitol, then drive through flowery West Feliciana Parish to Natchez — Mississippi's antebellum dream.

Timetable Suggestion

8:00 a.m.	Early start, head for St. Martinville.
8:20 a.m.	Pay homage to Evangeline at St. Martin of Tours Church; breakfast in St. Martinville.
10:00 a.m.	Atchafalaya Basin swamp tour at Henderson.
12:30 p.m.	Lunch at Ralph and Kacoo's in Baton Rouge.
1:30 p.m.	See Huey P. Long's fabulous Louisiana State Capitol and the Pentagon Barracks.
3:00 p.m.	LSU Rural Life Museum.
5:00 p.m.	Cruise St. Francisville's Royal Street.
6:45 p.m.	Arrive in Natchez, dine at Natchez-Under-the-Hill.
8:00 p.m.	Snuggle into your antebellum tester bed in an elegant Natchez mansion.

Magnolia Trail: Lafayette to Natchez (170 miles)

Take the Evangeline Throughway south out of Lafayette, exit at LA 96, and drive seven miles into **St. Martinville**, a lovely town and the spiritual heart of Acadiana. After your audience with dear Evangeline at St. Martin of Tours

Church, have breakfast on the square and head north 13 miles along the Bayou Teche on LA 31 to Breaux Bridge and Interstate 10 east. Latch on to the Interstate and soon you'll be lifted onto the **Swampland Expressway**, a concrete ribbon high above an absolutely magnificent swamp wilderness — the untameable Atchafalaya Basin. This route across the Atchafalaya wilds into Baton Rouge is among the most exhilarating stretches of freeway in America. Get off at exit 115/Butte La Rose to reach **Henderson** for a close up look at the swamp on one of the recommended boat tours.

Baton Rouge, with it's towering monument to the passions of Huey Long, looms ahead at the eastern edge of the Atchafalaya Basin and across the Mississippi River. Take the Nicholson Drive exit to reach the city's downtown highlights along the riverfront. Depart Baton Rouge on Interstate 110, which runs about ten miles north and delivers you to US 61. For miles this highway is lined by huge chemical plants but then becomes rather scenic as you approach **St. Francisville**. Turn left and drive down St. Francisville's Royal Street for a look at English Louisiana. Return to US 61 and continue north across the Mississippi state line and on into **Natchez**, an hour's drive from St. Francisville. Take Junkin Drive/US 84 and Homochitto Street (or Melrose Avenue and John Quitman Parkway) into the heart of Natchez.

Getting to know Baton Rouge

As wild and arcane as the Atchafalaya, convoluted as the Mississippi, and spicy as gumbo, Louisiana politics are a source of endless merriment. From W.C.C. Claiborne in 1812 to Edwin "Fast Eddie" Edwards in the 1980s, Louisiana's governors have frequently been colorful and charismatic, and none more so than Huey Pierce "Kingfish" Long, who ousted complacent Creole bluebloods by hook and crook and in the depths of the great depression declared, "Every man a king!" Through controversial (some say dictatorial) but effective means, Long built roads, bridges, hospitals, and a fabulous new capitol building (in just 14 months), established a family political dynasty, and changed the face of Louisiana. His populist appeal was growing nationally and he had the Presidency in mind when he was gunned down in 1935. Fifty-five years later, you still see the Long legacy everywhere in Louisiana.

The only true political sin in Louisiana is to appear boring. The nation was aghast in 1988 when Jefferson Parish elected David Duke, a blow-dried ex-Ku Klux Klan wizard, to the legislature — but Duke won largely because, in contrast to his moribund opponent, he was at least lively.

Baton Rouge (which simply means red stick) is on the first relatively high point of land upriver from New Orleans and thus it was an important square on the eighteenth-century France vs. Spain vs. England monopoly board. It became Louisiana's capital when the hinterlands up from New Orleans began to be settled. Most Baton Rouge highlights are conveniently clustered north

BATON ROUGE TO VICKSBURG

of I-10 between **Catfish Town** and the **State Capitol**. Take the Nicholson Drive exit, then cross back north under the freeway to reach the Nautical Historic Center, Old State Capitol, and Catfish Town. Then go north a few blocks on River Road or Riverside Mall to the State Capitol and Pentagon Barracks. **Louisiana State University**'s park-like campus is a just south of downtown via either Highland Road or Nicholson Drive.

The Best to See and Do

❀ **St. Martin of Tours Church Square** — St. Martinville is where most Acadian refugees first arrived in 1765, and its quiet church square is still the jewel of Cajunland. Behind the left wing of St. Martin of Tours Catholic Church, Mother Church of Acadiana, is the grave of Emmeline Labiche, who the world knows as Evangeline. Step around the side of the church to the tiny graveyard and the seated statue of Evangeline, given to St. Martinville by actress Dolores del Rio, who played her role in a 1929 feature film. Next door is the **Petit Paris Museum**. After bluebloods from Europe found refuge here during the French Revolution, St. Martinville got nicknamed *Le Petit Paris*. Walk the square's tranquil grounds on your own, or take a tour of the museum and church from 9 a.m. to 5 p.m.; adults $2, seniors $1.50, children $1, (318) 394-7334.

❀ **Longfellow-Evangeline State Park** — An original Creole raised house of brick and mud-and-moss bousillage construction and, just inside the park entrance, a fine little Cajun frame cottage with porch-mounted stairway leading to its attic are the best features of this little park just north of St. Martinville on LA 31. Open 9 a.m. to 5 p.m.; adults $2, children $1.

❀ ❀ **Atchafalaya Boat Trips** — Get down on the water for a close-up look at the critters and cypress trees in this vast swampy realm. You'll be shown how crawfish are caught and learn about the engineering miracles that built the amazing Swampland Expressway. Take exit 115 off Interstate 10 (or drive LA 347 directly from Breaux Bridge) and turn east on LA 352 through Henderson's row of restaurants (all are quite good); cross the Henderson Canal and turn right on the levee road to reach the tour boat landings. **McGee's Atchafalaya Basin Tours**, (318) 228-8519, departs from Henderson Levee on 90-minute trips at 10 a.m., 1 p.m. and 3 p.m.; adults $7.50, children $4. **Basin Boat Tours** at Whiskey River Landing, 228-8567, sends the pontoon *Bayou Boss* out on the same schedule, plus an earlybird 8 a.m. excursion; adults $7, children $4. Both outfits also do 5 p.m. Sundowner trips during Daylight Savings Time.

❀ ❀ ❀ **Louisiana State Capitol** — "Nazi Deco" might be the apt name for the unique style of this fabulously-detailed 34-story fantasy, the largest state capitol in the United States. You can't help but react to it strongly. It speaks volumes about it's creator, Huey P. Long, whose legendary populism and political skills both stirred and scared a nation in the early 1930s. Walk up the 48 marble steps, each named for a state of the Union (plus Alaska and Hawaii at the top), intended as a welcome for visitors from across the land. Little surprises are everywhere: bas-relief pelicans on the friezes, and nickel-plate art deco moon, stars and lightning bolts on the tower.

Did young Dr. Carl Weis assassinate Governor Long in the Back Gallery, or were the Kingfish's own bodyguards involved? Nobody's talking. But you can touch some of the many bullet holes in the marble and wonder. Don't fail to peer into the majestic pink and gold-trimmed legislative chambers (Benito Mussolini, eat your heart out!). A trip up to the 27th-story observation deck affords a terrific view of the port of Baton Rouge. The capitol is at the north end of downtown; take Riverside Mall to State Capitol Drive, open 8 a.m. to 4 p.m. daily, free.

❀❀ **Pentagon Barracks** — Built in the 1820s to impress the locals with the permanence of American authority, this once-five-sided building (the river took the missing side) was the first home of Louisiana State University. Its fine little museum has enlightening photographs from Huey Long's era. Open Tuesday through Saturday from 10 a.m. to 4 p.m. and Sundays from 1 p.m., free.

❀❀ **Old State Capitol** — Fortunately, the budget crunch has not yet forced the closing of this beloved and newly-restored Gothic castle. It's spiral grand staircase and stained-glass skylight make it well worth a brief visit. The Old Capitol is adjacent to **Riverfront Park** at North Boulevard and River Road, eight blocks south of the Capitol; open Tuesday through Saturday 9 a.m. to 4:30 p.m., free.

❀ **Nautical Historic Center/*U.S.S. Kidd*** — A World War II destroyer and a wonderful P-40 "Flying Tiger" airplane are highlights of this small, modern maritime museum that highlights the achievements of native son and war hero General Chennault. It's on the Mississippi River just up from **Catfish Town**, an admirable but still struggling mall/restoration at the old riverfront railroad depot. The ship and museum are open daily from 9 a.m. to 5 p.m.; adults $4, seniors $3, children $2.50.

❀❀ **LSU Rural Life Museum** — At this living demonstration project of Louisiana plantation and country life you will see yesteryear's everyday tools, an open kettle sugar mill, and a plantation commissary among the 20 authentic buildings moved to the site. Take I-10 east to Essen Lane. Open weekdays 8:30 a.m. to 4 p.m., (504) 765-2437; adults $2, children $1.

❀ **Jimmy Swaggart Ministries/Family Worship Center** — Always intense and dramatic, Jimmy Swaggart is still the most effective of the evangelical television preachers despite his well-publicized "fall." Jimmy's gospel singing and piano can stir even the most hardened soul. Here you'll see the tangible results of all those dollars Brother Swaggart asks you for every week, including a four-year Bible-based liberal arts college. Take Highland Road south from downtown and turn left on Bluebonnet Road. Weekday tours (hourly until 3 p.m.) of the **Family Worship Center** from which the telecast originates are free. Sunday services at 10 a.m. and 6 p.m., Wednesday service at 7 p.m. Call 768-6113 to find out which days Pastor Swaggart will be preaching.

❀ **Port Hudson** — Walk six miles of wooded paths through this important Civil War site where the Confederacy lost, at Fort Desperate, its last stronghold on the Mississippi River. Port Hudson is 14 miles upriver from Baton Rouge off

US 61; open daily until 7 p.m. from April 1 through September 30, free.

❀ ❀ ❀ **St. Francisville** — As you turn off US 61 and ease down Royal Street, you may think for a moment you're somewhere in New England — and with good reason. The English first settled this area when West Florida, a vast territory that stretched from here to Pensacola, went from Spanish to British hands in 1763. Left out of the Louisiana Purchase, West Florida became its own nation for 74 glorious days in 1810, with St. Francisville as its capital. Stop at the **Barrow House**, 524 Royal Street, and ask for the mimeographed walking tour guide to the town. Peer down Prosperity Street. Turn right when you reach Ferdinand Street to return to US 61. Round out your visit with stops at lovely **Afton Gardens** and **Catalpa Plantation**, both just off US 61 as you head out of town. See *Linger Longer* below if you'd like to spend extra time in West Feliciana Parish.

Places to Dine

Head for **Ralph and Kacoo's**, arguably the best Cajun restaurants east of the Atchafalaya, for lunch in Baton Rouge. The ones at 6110 Bluebonnet Road (near Jimmy Swaggart Ministries) and 7110 Airline Highway are large and friendly but often crowded. Try the softshell crawfish topped with sauteed crabmeat. Across the street from the Old State Capitol downtown is **Original New Orleans Po'Boys and Seafood**, 105 Third Street. Try the inexpensive roast beef po-boy with Cajun curlicues. If you're hungry right after your Atchafalaya swamp excursion, I suggest **Pat's Fisherman's Wharf**, **Crawfishtown USA**, or **Landry's Cajun Village** in Henderson.

See *Discovery Day 5* for evening dining suggestions in Natchez.

Places to Stay

For the next two nights, pamper yourself in antebellum gentility and splendor. With more than a dozen very convenient old homes and inns, Natchez is bed and breakfast heaven. Some of the places suggested here are also in tomorrow's *Best to See and Do*, so check *Discovery Day 5* to learn more about them. Lower priced rooms may be in a dependency, not the main house. Nearly all serve a Southern plantation breakfast so fabulous you may want to take most of the morning to enjoy it. **Natchez Pilgrimage Tours**, (800) 647-6742 or (601) 446-6631, acts as a reservations clearinghouse for more than 20 antebellum homes.

At **Linden**, you step through the doorway used in *Gone with the Wind* and will stay with the sixth generation of the Conners family. Every room ($75 to $110 for two) is furnished with heirlooms and has a private bath, (601) 445-5472. **Dunlieth** fulfills ultimate antebellum fantasies with colonnaded galleries surrounding the house on two levels and a forty-acre landscaped park, $85 to $130, (800) 443-2445. The swimming pool is a nice plus at **The**

Burn, $75 to $125, (800) 654-8859. Greek Revival **Weymouth Hall** perches on the bluff overlooking the Mississippi a mile upriver from the city, $70, 445-2304. **Monmouth Plantation** was General John Quitman's home, but it can be yours tonight, $85-$130, (800) 828-4531.

Ravennaside was the socially lively home of "Sweet Annie" Byrnes, famous for her efforts to preserve the Natchez Trace. It's post-bellum Victorian, but a fine parquet floor makes it special, $65, (601) 442-8015. Built in 1775, **Hope Farm** is one of Natchez' earliest mansions, yet you'll find a hot tub there, $80, 445-4848. All rooms are downstairs in the main house at **Pleasant Hill Bed & Breakfast** on Pearl Street, $85, 442-7674. **Lisle House**, a two bedroom cottage across State Street from Natchez Pilgrimage Tours, is available for $85, 442-7680.

If you don't make reservations early, you may have difficulty finding a bed and breakfast room in Natchez during the Spring and Fall Pilgrimages. Procrastinators can opt for the restored and added-to **Natchez Eola Hotel**, about $55, (800) 235-6100 or (601) 445-6000. A budget choice is the **Natchez Inn Motel** on the Mississippi Bridge bypass, from $27, 442-0221.

Places to Camp

This is one night when even dedicated campers should splurge on a cushy testered bed and a languorous plantation breakfast at an antebellum mansion. Tomorrow night, stay in the woods at **Natchez State Park**, 13 miles northeast of Natchez just off US 61. Next morning, get picnic supplies at nearby Mamma's Store. You're less than two miles from Emerald Mound (see *Discovery Day 6*). Natchez State Park is near the southern terminus of the Natchez Trace Parkway, so you'll have a head start on the *Discovery Day 6* drive to Vicksburg. The park is open all year, sites $5.50 and $11, call (601) 442-2658 if you think you'll arrive after 4 p.m. Stay a little closer to Natchez at **Whispering Pines** on US 61 north, full hookups, 442-3624.

Useful Tips

Area Code for all of Mississippi is (601); for Baton Rouge and St. Francisville it's (504). From Baton Rouge on, until you reach the Gulf Coast *(Discovery Day 20)*, you will find many attractions closed on Sundays until 1 p.m. since everyone's supposed to be in church. Why not join them? There's a Southern Baptist church around the corner in even the smallest towns and usually other protestant and Catholic options. If you've never been to an African Methodist Episcopal (A.M.E.) church, get set to receive a warm welcome and lift to your spirit from soul-stirring preaching and full-throated gospel singing.

Linger Longer: West Feliciana Parish

Tarry overnight in St. Francisville for in-depth exploring of the unusual plantation estates of flowery West Feliciana Parish. **Oakley Plantation**, where naturalist John James Audubon tutored and worked on *Birds of America*, is now a museum containing many of his first edition prints; adults $2, children and seniors free. Lavishly restored **Rosedown** is an elegant treasure inside (Federal and Empire period heirlooms) and out (camellias, azaleas and rare trees planted a century ago); adults $5, or $3 if you'd just like to stroll the gardens. The real treasure at **Catalpa** is Mamie Thompson, who will entertain you through five generations of family history, $3.50. The house at **Afton Villa Gardens** burned in 1963, but a winding avenue of live oaks and intricate landscaping are meticulously maintained; open spring and fall, $2. Stay in town at the **Barrow House** on Royal Street, $35 to $55, (504) 635-6502, or five miles north off US 61 at **The Cottage Plantation**, which includes Mattie's House Restaurant, all rooms $75, 635-3674.

DISCOVERY DAY 5
Natchez

TURN BACK THE CLOCK — at least 130 years. Nestled in handsome Natchez is the finest gathering of enchanting antebellum mansions in the entire South. If the Dixie of your imagination is rich with visions of the genteel life of the plantation aristocracy before The War — columned Greek Revival palaces, crinolined and fan-fluttering belles, courtly and very wealthy landowners — Natchez will fulfill your dreams.

Take most of today to wander through Longwood, Rosalie, Magnolia Hall, Monmouth, and other stately homes. After your day here you may wonder: What was so important about the twentieth century, anyway?

Timetable Suggestion

8:30 a.m.	Leisurely plantation breakfast with your hosts.
9:30 a.m.	Visit Longwood, then Magnolia Hall or Rosalie.
12:00 noon	Lunch at The Carriage House.
Afternoon	See Melrose, Monmouth, Stanton Hall, Grand Village of the Natchez Indians.
7:00 p.m.	Dine at Natchez-Under-the-Hill or across the bridge in Vidalia, Louisiana.
9:00 p.m.	Conversation with your hosts, then retire when you feel like it in antebellum splendor.

Getting to know Natchez and Mississippi

Cotton, white gold of the South, made Natchez a town of wealth and aristocracy in the 60 years after Mississippi became a U.S. territory in 1798. Here the barons of fertile plantations that stretched a hundred miles up the Mississippi River made their urban homes and created an exquisitely genteel society. By the grace of God, say some Natchezians, the city's hundreds of antebellum architectural treasures have survived both the war and the ravages of time virtually intact.

Natchez (pronounce it *NATCH-is*) is a compact, easy-to-get-around-in city of 25,000. The simple downtown grid, pleasant for walking, runs eight blocks from Pine Street on the east to Broadway on the bluffs above the river, and ten blocks from Oak Street on the north to Orleans Street on the south. Many of the most impressive antebellum homes are along graceful feeder routes

NATCHEZ

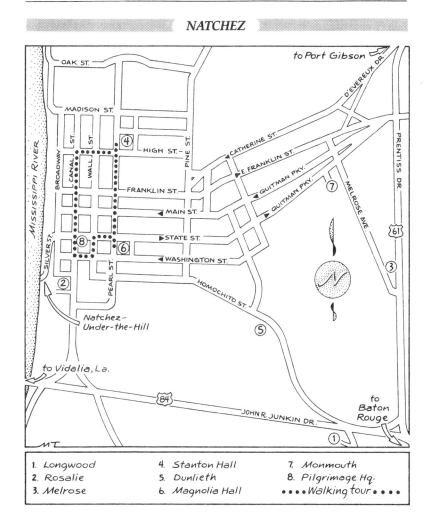

1. Longwood	4. Stanton Hall	7. Monmouth
2. Rosalie	5. Dunlieth	8. Pilgrimage Hq.
3. Melrose	6. Magnolia Hall	••••Walking tour••••

(Homochitto Street, Melrose Avenue, Quitman Parkway, D'Evereux Drive) that run between US 61 and the start of the town grid at Pine Street. Silver Street descends from Broadway to **Natchez-Under-the-Hill**, the intriguing remnant of a once-rowdy community right on the riverbank.

Southern Carriage Tours and a couple other horse-drawn outfits depart on 35-minute downtown tours from the **Natchez Pilgrimage Headquarters** at Canal and State streets starting at 8:30 a.m. (adults $7, children $4). Better yet, pocket the seven bucks and do this easy walking tour that takes you past most of downtown's historic homes: From Canal and State streets go south one block and turn left on Washington Street. Turn left again one block later (you'll see *Texada* and *Dixie* on the corner) at Wall Street. Turn right on State Street, pass the Natchez Museum, then turn left onto Pearl Street. Shortly, you'll encounter a cluster of smaller historic homes and imposing Stanton Hall at High Street. Go left toward the river on High Street where you come upon *White Wings*, *Cherokee* and *Choctaw* on the corner at Wall Street. Continue on High Street one more block and turn left at Canal Street. You'll pass the *House on Ellicott Hill* and the U.S. Post Office on your way back to State Street.

This is your first full day in Mississippi, a land of delicate natural and manmade beauty, where the distance between past and present seems to disappear. (What might dreamlike, magnolia, pine and kudzu-covered Mississippi have in common with far-away Vermont and New Mexico? I think of these three as the "museum states" — lands apart where rich histories nurtured ways of living so valid and appropriate that there's a natural resistance to the insults and "improvements" of modern times.)

A drive through Mississippi is an invitation to let go of Hollywood's twisted images of this lovely state and absorb a deeply rewarding, almost spiritual travel experience.

The Natchez Pilgrimages

If you come for Natchez' famous Spring or Fall Pilgrimage — a wondrous, city-wide antebellum open house — you're considered a pilgrim, not a tourist. In 1932, the ladies of the Natchez Garden Club thought it would be nice to honor a treasured heritage by opening their homes and gardens to visitors who also appreciate the lifestyle, history and heirlooms that bind the South together. Half a century later, spring pilgrimages have spread throughout Dixie, but Natchez still does it best.

The month-long **Spring Pilgrimage** usually runs from the second full week in March through the first full week in April, at the height of the azalea and dogwood blossom season. A similar **Fall Pilgrimage** runs two weeks in October. Natchez Garden Club and Pilgrimage Garden Club cooperate in the Natchez Pilgrimage Tours enterprise, which coordinates six five-house tours. The homes named in *The Best to See and Do* are on the tours, plus at least 22 more you can't see any other time of the year. Call ahead to Natchez Pilgrimage Tours, (800) 647-6742, to get the tour schedule and secure tickets. Although thousands come for Pilgrimage, they've worked it out so you won't feel you're part of a mob. *Green Leaves* is my favorite home that can only be visited during Pilgrimage. It's a fantastic living family museum, with curious memorabilia everywhere and a 500-piece collection of handpainted Audubon china. The nicks and scratches on the fine furniture and mildew on the clippings make you feel privy to a precious family scrapbook. *Linden, Hope Farm,*

Montaigne, and *D'Evereux* are other outstanding homes on the Pilgrimage list. Take in the evening Cofederate Pageant, where costumed young people relive old Southern traditions.

The Best to See and Do

Natchez' foremost highlights are, of course, the dozens of magnificent antebellum mansions. Each one has a distinct personality — you won't be repeating yourself. The great houses suggested here receive visitors all year (except Christmas Day). All are open from 9 a.m. to 5 p.m. and charge $4 for adults and $2 for children. Call or drop by **Natchez Pilgrimage Tours** at Canal and State streets, (601) 446-6631, early in your day for information on all except Weymouth Hall. Each home tour lasts about 30 minutes, but you can linger to ask questions and stroll the gardens.

❀ ❀ ❀ **Rosalie (1820)** — An early stop at Rosalie will give you a good perspective of Natchez history. It stands on the bluff very near the site of Fort Rosalie, where Natchez began in 1716. It served as a Union post during the Civil War and is today headquarters for the Mississippi Daughters of the American Revolution. Find Rosalie on Canal Street, looming above Natchez-Under-the-Hill.

❀ ❀ ❀ **Longwood (1861)** — Here you will find an enchanted fantasy of almost overwhelming beauty and sadness. Indeed, you can feel the whole history of the South in this one house.

Young, cotton-rich Dr. Haller Nutt imagined a six-story, octagonal dream palace for his growing family. Most of the exterior was completed, and rare mosaic floor tiles, marble statuary and other lavish furnishings were on their way from Europe when the War broke out. Despite his Union sympathies, Dr. Nutt saw his cotton fields worth millions burned by the Yankees. The means to complete Longwood were suddenly gone with the wind. Dreams shattered and his fortune vanished, Dr. Nutt died before the war ended. His wife Julia and their eight children lived on in the nine-room basement, the only interior part of Longwood to be finished. Dr. Nutt's descendants continued to occupy the basement for the next 100 years, until this National Historic Landmark was given to the Pilgrimage Garden Club in 1970. Today, the interior remains as it was at the outbreak of the War. Louise Burns, who has lived in the basement apartment for 20 years now, will take you upstairs: a workbench, scaffolding, and paint buckets undisturbed since the Civil War lie about in the cavernous interior, yet it's easy to envision the grandeur that would have been there, given only a few more months of work. Above you, scaffolding winds upward into the magnificent clerestory and huge Byzantine dome. Yes, you will hear stories of ghosts.

Take Homochitto Street or John R. Junkin Drive to Lower Woodville Road to enter Longwood's winding garden drive.

❀❀❀ **Melrose (1841)** — Surrounded by a vast English-style garden with huge old moss-draped oaks, a fanciful gazebo and a tranquil lagoon, impeccable Melrose contains almost all of its original furnishings — brocatelle draperies, a Cornelius chandelier and lamps, ever-so-chaste sweetheart sofa, four-post tester (pronounced *TEE-ster*) beds, and above the dining table is a carved mahogany *punkah* (shoo-fly fan), an innovation borrowed from India and operated manually by servants at dinnertime. Because of its pristine authenticity, Melrose is now operated by the National Park Service; (504) 446-5790.

❀❀ **Monmouth (1818)** — General John A. Quitman, Mexican War hero and Mississippi governor, made his home at Monmouth and you can see many of his personal belongings in this fully restored mansion. Delights include the parlor fountain, fairy lamps, a wig dresser, wallpaper printed with early American scenes. In the garden are rare rose species that date from when the house was built. Monmouth is at Quitman Parkway and Melrose Avenue.

❀❀ **Magnolia Hall (1858)** — This Greek Revival "brownstone" with its high, fluted columns, is a favorite of mine, perhaps because it still shows evidence of the many transitions it has gone through over the years. Upstairs is a museum of historical gowns and Confederate Pageant costumes. Owned by the Natchez Garden Club, Magnolia Hall is right in town at Washington and South Pearl streets.

❀❀ **Stanton Hall (1857)** — Covering virtually a whole city block, palatial Stanton Hall has become a gathering place for antiquities from all around Natchez, thanks to the efforts of the Pilgrimage Garden Club. On the grounds is the pleasant Carriage House Restaurant.

❀ **More antebellum homes** — Galleries supported by 26 Tuscan columns completely surround **Dunleith** at 84 Homochitto Street, making it appear like a Greek Revival temple; pre-1850 furnishings and French Zuber wallpaper are inner attractions. **The House on Ellicott Hill** (1798) overlooks the river on North Canal Street at the site where Major Andrew Ellicott, on orders from George Washington, raised the American flag for the first time in the lower Mississippi Valley in defiance of Spanish authority. Three-story **Weymouth Hall** (1850) stands above the river north of town on Cemetery Road, an extension of Maple Street; call 445-2304 to let the owners know you're coming.

❀ **Grand Village of the Natchez Indians** — The native Natchez people were here first and co-existed with the French for some time until they decided to thin out the newcomers in a massacre at Fort Rosalie in 1729. The French retaliated with a massacre of their own, which spelled curtains for the Natchez tribe. An excavated mound, artifacts, and reconstructions illustrate what life may have been like at the central village. Take US 61 south to Jeff Davis Boulevard; open 9 a.m. to 5 p.m. daily and from 1:30 p.m. Sundays, free.

✽ **Jefferson College** — Mississippi's first school, Jefferson College endured from 1802 until 1964. Several of its buildings are now under restoration; you can see cypress shingle-making and other demonstrations weekdays. Northeast of Natchez off US 61, open daily 9 a.m. to 5 p.m., free.

Places to Dine

At least once, slip down Silver Street to Natchez-Under-the-Hill for a casual dinner by the river at **Natchez Landing** (442-6639), specializing in ribs and catfish, or **Cock of the Walk** (446-8920), which serves wonderful broiled catfish as well as chicken dinners. Both are open from 5 p.m. to 10 p.m.

The Carriage House Restaurant on the grounds of Stanton Hall at High and Pearl streets (445-5151) features a very nice baked ham with raisin sauce ($5.95 lunch, $7.25 dinner) and lemon tarts or pecan pie for dessert. **King's Tavern and Steakhouse** at 619 Jefferson (446-8845) occupies one of the oldest buildings in the territory. Friendly, funky and distinctly Southern, the **Corner Bar** at State and Canal streets has a $4 steak special on Monday nights. For a little elegance there's the **Pompous Palate** at 211 North Pearl Street (445-4946) serving continental cuisine for lunch and dinner. Downstairs is pub-like **Pearl Street Cellar**. **The Parlor Restaurant** at 116 Canal Street, kitty corner from Pilgrimage Tours, has something for everyone (from burritos to chicken breasts and steaks), for lunch and dinner.

For extra fun, drive across the Mississippi River Bridge to Vidalia, Louisiana, for seafood at **West Bank Eatery** or the **Sandbar Restaurant**, where you'll hear tales of a wild 1827 duel involving frontiersman Jim Bowie.

Places to Stay

See *Discovery Day 4.*

Linger Longer

Had your fill of aristocracy? From Natchez, take the Mississippi Bridge across the river and drive 15 miles on US 84 to humble **Ferriday, Louisiana**, boyhood home of three famous cousins: primal rocker Jerry Lee Lewis, honkytonk star Mickey Gilley, and televangelist Jimmy Swaggart. You'll see the little First Assembly of God Church where Jimmy's daddy preached. It was there, as well as from musicians in Ferriday's black bars, that the lads picked up their remarkable musical skills.

Drive this evening to lovely **Port Gibson**, 40 miles up the Natchez Trace toward Vicksburg, and stay at Oak Square. The quiet pace there invites you to appreciate and savor many of the sweet virtues of a devotedly Southern way of living (see *Linger Longer* for *Discovery Day 6*).

DISCOVERY DAY 6

Vicksburg

ALTHOUGH SIMILAR IN SIZE and only 73 miles apart, Vicksburg and Natchez are markedly different in character. Here the fewer elegant homes often stand next to quite humble dwellings. Natchez was almost unscathed by the war. Vicksburg was re-defined by it.

"The Gibraltar of the Confederacy" stood at a commanding, strategic site on the Mississippi, backed by formidable bluffs and moated to the north and south by a maze of swamps and bayous. But to Abraham Lincoln, Vicksburg was the key to victory. "The war can never be brought to a close," Lincoln wrote, "until that key is in our pocket."

Attacking from the river and through the swamps, Union forces were repulsed time and again. Then in the spring of 1863, General U. S. Grant switched strategy and crossed the Mississippi several miles downstream, looped around inland, and advanced on Vicksburg's bluffs from the east. Vicksburg was too well defended for a direct attack, so Grant's forces laid siege to the city, cutting off supplies and shelling the homes and factories below. For 47 days the citizens of Vicksburg held out, rationing food and taking shelter in caves cut in hardpacked earth; along the front above the city thousands of young soldiers were fighting and dying. On July 4, the Confederate army could hang on no longer and General Pemberton surrendered Vicksburg. From Illinois to the Gulf of Mexico, the vital Mississippi came into Federal hands. A day earlier, far away at Gettysburg, Robert E. Lee's army also suffered defeat. Dark days lay ahead for all of Dixie.

Timetable Suggestion

9:00 a.m.	Head up the Natchez Trace toward Port Gibson.
10:00 a.m.	Visit Emerald Mound, Windsor's ruins, Grand Gulf Military Park, or Waterways Experiment Station.
11:30 a.m.	Driving tour of Vicksburg.
1:00 p.m.	Lunch, then tour Vicksburg's battlefields.
2:00 p.m.	Climb aboard Union ironclad *U.S.S. Cairo*.
3:00 p.m.	See Cedar Grove, McRaven Home or Old Court House.
6:00 p.m.	Early dinner, then relax at your bed & breakfast.

Magnolia Trail: Natchez to Vicksburg (73 miles)

Begin today's journey on the Natchez Trace, an old frontier trail that is now a serene parkland highway, then drive through lovely old Port Gibson to Vicksburg, where you'll explore the full fury of the War Between the States.

From downtown Natchez, take Franklin Street and D'evereaux Drive to US 61. About eight miles from town, leave 61 for the **Natchez Trace Parkway** at its present southern terminus. Half a mile later you will see a section of the original Natchez-to-Nashville track, once the most important route of discovery and commerce on the southwestern frontier. (Learn more about this famous 500-mile road when you travel the greatest part of its length in *Discovery Day 7.*) If you camped at Natchez State Park, you'll join the Trace this morning where it intersects with MS 553 near Emerald Mound. Stop at **Mount Locust** (Milepost 15), a venerable 1780 "stand" (inn) and the last survivor of 50 stands that once lined the route, and pick up the National Park Service's free detailed map and guide to highlights along the Natchez Trace. Five miles up the Trace, MS 553 again crosses your path, leading to Springfield, Oak Grove, Lagonia and other plantation homes near Church Hill. Cruise on through the nicely-tended alley of evergreens, kudzu vines and dogwoods and take the US 61 exit into **Port Gibson** at Milepost 38. You'll find yourself on Church Street, lined with well-kept large old homes and churches.

Nobody's certain whether General Grant actually called tiny Port Gibson "the town too beautiful to burn," but today it is one of the finest antebellum small towns in the South. The centerpiece, majestic *Oak Square* mansion, is on your right at 1207 Church Street; stop here for directions if you plan to see the Windsor Plantation ruins or Grand Gulf Military Park. Stay on US 61 across the Little Bayou Pierre and 26 miles onto **Vicksburg**. As you approach the city, take the well-marked exit for I-20 West/Washington Street/Mississippi River Bridge; get in the right hand lane and pull off at exit 1-A. The excellent **Mississippi Visitor Center** here will orient you with a very clear free map. Take Washington Street north into town; drive east on Clay Street to the top of the hill to reach Vicksburg National Military Park.

Vicksburg Driving Tour

The best way to survey Vicksburg and check out places you might like to visit later is to take a little driving tour through town on your way up to Vicksburg National Military Park. Follow the dots on my map.

At the second stoplight on Washington Street, turn left down Speed Street, then right onto Oak Street. One of Grant's schemes to isolate Vicksburg was to divert the Mississippi by digging a ditch across the bend in the river. What Grant failed to accomplish the Father of Waters itself achieved just 13 years later, leaving the Port of Vicksburg riverless. The waterway you see fronting downtown Vicksburg today is the manmade **Yazoo Diversion Canal**, dredged out in 1902 to make Vicksburg again a river city.

Pass **Cedar Grove Estate** and take in the view across the canal, then dip down Clay Street and Levee Street to the **Port of Vicksburg**, where the *Spirit of Vicksburg* tour boat and *Mamie S. Barrett* showboat restaurant are tied up. The port has a relaxed, almost sleepy small-town feel. (The *Spirit* departs most days at 2 p.m. for a two hour canal and Mississippi River tour, $6.) Take brick-paved Grove Street up the steep hill and turn right onto Washington Street, where shortly you'll drive through a semi-malled section called **Old River Market**, an admirable effort at reviving the heart of town. Turn left when you reach Speed Street again and zigzag your way across Drummond and Cherry streets to reach Harrison Street, which dead-ends at the strange but fascinating **McRaven Home**. Hand-lettered signs tell you you're in for a different experience here: *"Visitors see every room including the 18th century kitchen totally unchanged since Civil War days, with battle scars inside and out!"*

Driving north on Cherry Street, you'll pass the house that served as Lieutenant General Pemberton's Confederate headquarters during the siege, and next to it on Crawford Street the home of Emma Balfour, who kept a remarkably detailed diary of the 47-day blockade. Farther along Cherry Street are the **Toys and Soldiers Museum**, the sprawling **Old Court House Museum** grounds (see *Best to See and Do*), and the **Warren County Courthouse**, a nifty fantasy in marble for Art Deco fans. Turn right at First East past Anchuca, where Jefferson Davis once spoke from the Greek Revival balcony, then follow the map past Duff Green and the Martha Vick House to Clay Street. A left onto Clay Street takes you to the top of the hill and the entrance to **Vicksburg National Military Park**.

The Best to See and Do

❀❀ **Emerald Mound** — Silent in the forest, this 770-foot long grassy mound, which you can climb, was the scene of Indian ceremonials a hundred years before Columbus. Built by the ancestors of the Natchez people, it is the second largest Indian mound in the United States. Emerald Mound is about a mile west of Milepost 10 on the Natchez Trace, free.

❀ **Windsor Plantation Ruins** — Windsor was once the most lavish mansion of antebellum Mississippi. Even though the magnificent four-story plantation house was destroyed in an accidental fire a quarter century after the Civil War, Windsor's 23 stately Greek Revival columns that still stand seem particularly poignant monuments to a time gone with the wind. Drive 12 miles west of Port Gibson on Carrol Street/MS 552, no charge.

❀ **Grand Gulf Military Park** — The town of Grand Gulf and two Confederate forts here were in the path of Grant's advancing army. Confederates put up

VICKSBURG

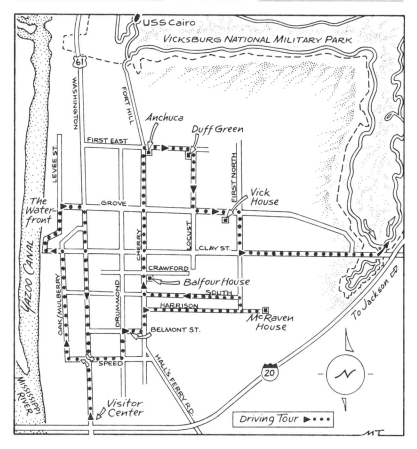

fierce resistance but finally had to abandon the site. A carriage house, water-mill, fine old church, cemetery, observation tower and a boardwalk out to the old Mississippi river bed add variety to this historical excursion. Grand Gulf, (601) 437-5911, is seven miles northwest of Port Gibson on a rural extension of Walnut Street. Admission to the park is free, $1 to get into the museum.

❀ ❀ **Waterways Experiment Station** — Watch engineering marvels in miniature at the Army Corps of Engineers' largest research and testing laboratory. Harbor, river, and flood control projects are studied here using fascinating scale models (New York harbor and the lower Mississippi, for example), some with little boats and barge tows, others with artificial wave- and tide-making devices. Two miles south on Hall's Ferry Road from I-20, the Waterways Experiment Station, (601) 634-2502, is open weekdays from 7:45 a.m. to 4:15 p.m. with guided tours at 10 a.m. and 2 p.m., free.

❀ ❀ ❀ **Vicksburg National Military Park** — Along this ridge east and north of the city, some 30,000 Confederate defenders dug in while Grant's even larger army bombarded Vicksburg unrelentingly for more than six weeks. Plunk down $4.50 to rent a tour tape and player at the visitors center and head out on a 16-mile drive through history, first along the Union lines and then through Confederate defensive positions. Numbered stops will help you understand the moves and countermoves. Of the 100,000 men and boys who fought here, nearly 20,000 would become casualties. Five Confederate generals lost their lives.

To the victors go the spoils — and the means to build statues, memorials and formal cemeteries. About 1,600 monuments are scattered throughout the park; the oldest, largest and most numerous honor Union military units, among them the 202-foot **Naval Obelisk** saluting Civil War era admirals including Admiral Porter, who contributed to the siege by bombarding the city from boats on the river. Across from the *U.S.S. Cairo* museum is **Vicksburg National Cemetery**, where 17,000 Union soldiers lie buried, making it second only to Arlington in size. Confederate soldiers wound up in the nearby city cemetery.

The visitor center, (601) 636-0583, is open daily 8 a.m. to 5 p.m.; there's a $3 per car charge to drive through the park.

❀ ❀ ❀ **U.S.S. Ironclad *Cairo* and Museum** — This is the finest shipwreck exhibit I've ever seen. On display under a broad outdoor canopy is the intact and painstakingly stabilized wreck of the *Cairo*, a steam-powered, 175-foot-long ironclad gunboat pulled from the mud of the Yazoo River. You can climb aboard and inspect its twin engines, giant paddlewheels, iron deckhouse, cannons, armor, structural timbers and laminated white oak flanks.

The story of the *Cairo*'s sinking and its recovery a hundred years later is as remarkable as the ship itself. In December 1862, inventive Confederates floated a five-gallon jar filled with explosives out into the Yazoo River to meet a Union flotilla and set it off by a wire from shore. It blasted a huge hole below the waterline of the 880-ton *Cairo* and sent her straight to the bottom. The first ship in history sunk by an electrically-detonated mine was quickly sealed up in the swirling mud of the Yazoo. It was raised to the surface, virtually intact, in 1964. Preserved inside was a time capsule of naval life in the mid-nineteenth century. At the adjacent museum you'll find details of its construction, sinking and recovery, and hundreds of artifacts — shoes, personal gear, tools, tinware, weapons — recovered when it was raised.

You come upon the *Cairo* at about the midpoint of your motor tour of Vicksburg National Military Park (or can reach it directly from downtown via

Cherry Street/Fort Hill Drive). The museum is open to 7 p.m. June through August, and until 5 p.m. the rest of the year, free.

❀❀ **Vicksburg Tour Homes** — Nine historic homes in the city are open for visits the year round and, except for two, you can spend the night in any of them (see *Places to Stay*). I suggest you pick one or two to visit, whichever seem the most intriguing to you. (You'll pass nearly all of them on my recommended driving tour of the city.) Most are open daily from 9 a.m. to 5 p.m. with $4 adult admission charge for tours of approximately half an hour each (except at McRaven Home, open to 6 p.m. in the summer, where the tour lasts an hour and a half).

Grey Oaks, on Rifle Range Road across I-20 from the Mississippi Visitor Center, was originally built in Port Gibson in 1834, then dismantled in 1940 and rebuilt on this site. It's sometimes called Vicksburg's *Tara*, because the front facade was redesigned to resemble that of the famed mansion in *Gone with the Wind*. Gas chandeliers, fountains in the formal gardens, and a Union cannonball still stuck in the parlor wall are features of **Cedar Grove** at 2200 Oak Street. **The Corners**, 601 Klein Street, was built as a wedding gift for a belle of Cedar Grove and has a commanding view of the rivers from its 68-foot-long gallery. **Tomil Manor** at 2430 Drummond Street is an interesting, if faded, expression of the Prairie style of the early 1900s, with Spanish touches and stained glass windows that make the interior glow warmly. Tucked away in the trees at the dead end of Harrison Street, looking for all the world like a perfect setting for some ghastly murder (which it was), the **McRaven House** bares its secrets colorfully in a comprehensive "way of life" tour that courses through the history of the South. The 1862 Christmas Eve ball at **Balfour House**, 1002 Crawford Street, was interrupted by news that federal gunboats had been sighted in the river above Vicksburg — words that brought the war to the city. It has a three-story elliptical staircase. **Anchuca** is an opulent, fully restored 1830 Greek Revival house at 1010 First East Street. Nearby at 1114 First East Street stands **Duff Green**, a 12,000 square foot slave-built Paladian style mansion. Duff Green became a hospital for Confederate and then Union wounded. The **Martha Vick House** mini-mansion at 1300 Grove Street contains many paintings by French post-expressionist Frederick Ragot.

❀ **Downtown Highlights** — Some 25,000 toy soldiers, from the Napoleonic era to World War II, stand ready for miniature mock battle at the **Toys and Soldiers Museum**, on the corner of Cherry and Grove streets, adults $2, children $1.50. **Biedenharn Candy Company and Coca-Cola Museum** is the old soda fountain and candy store at 1107 Washington Street where Coke was first bottled (and we always thought it was in Atlanta!). Have a homemade ice cream float and see antique bottling equipment; adults $1.75, kids $1.25. French and German bisque dolls, some life-size and wearing their original costumes, and a history of the Alexander doll your grandmother used to play with are on display at **Yesterday's Children**, 1104 Washington Street, across from Biedenharn's; tours from 10 a.m. to 4:30 p.m. Tuesday-Saturday; adults $2, children $1.

Slave-built in 1858, the **Old Court House Museum** on Cherry Street is a favorite of scholars and amateur historians for its Civil War and antebellum relics; open 8:30 a.m. to 4:30 p.m. (Sundays from 1:30 p.m.); adults $1.75, seniors $1.25, students $1.

Places to Dine

For lunch in Vicksburg, I suggest the sandwiches, soups and salads at **Walnut Hills Restaurant**, 1214 Adams Street; excellent Southern cooking at **The Old Southern Tea Room** in the Vicksburg Hotel at 801 Clay Street; or the luncheon buffet at **Eddie Monseur's**, 4702 Clay Street, just east of the cluster of franchise motor inns. Eddie Monseur's is also a good dinner choice for steaks and seafood. **Rowdy's Restaurant** is a family style place with good-and-plenty "Mississippi seasoned" Southern cooking, open for breakfast at 6 a.m. daily (7:30 a.m. Sundays); drive east on Clay Street until it becomes US 80 and intersects with Highway 27 just past the I-20 interchange.

These three are standouts for seafood or catfish this evening: **The Lucky Fisherman** (634-1040) on US 61 toward Port Gibson (sea and swamp buffet, $8.95); **Top o' the River** (636-6262) at 4150 Washington Street, a catfish lover's mecca; and **The Dock Seafood Buffet** (634-0450) on East Clay Street /US 80 near I-20, where the $10.95 all-you-can eat buffet includes blackened fish and crabmeat au gratin. All three open at 5 p.m.

Delta Point (636-5317) is a continental restaurant in the Magnolia Inn near the bridge, with a romantic river view and live classical music. **Velchoff's Corner & Miller's Still Lounge** (638-8661) at Washington and Grove streets serves up oysters, po-boy sandwiches and steaks in a lively, informal atmosphere.

Places to Stay

Vicksburg's most pleasant accommodations are in historic homes. **Grey Oaks** near the Mississippi Bridge, (601) 638-2704, has three rooms at $75. In town, **Cedar Grove**, (800) 862-1300 or (601) 636-1605, has seven rooms in the mansion, two poolside rooms and eight suites in the carriage house, $75 to $130, with a full Southern breakfast served in the formal dining room. **The Corners**, (800) 444-7421, is a relaxed bed-and-breakfast with rockers on the porch overlooking the river, from $65. Choose between the antebellum elegance of a full tester, eight-foot-wide "family bed" or an 1830s American Empire summer bed at **Balfour House**, (601) 638-3690, $75 with continental breakfast. Opulent **Anchuca**, (800) 262-4822, pampers its guests with a pool, hot tub, plantation breakfast, and a mint julep when you arrive, $75-$125, children and small pets welcome. **Duff Green Mansion**, (601) 636-6968, has antique-filled guest rooms and suites, $75 to $140. Less expensive are **Tomil Manor**, 638-8893, where you can sleep in a tester double bed for $40 (includes Southern breakfast), and **Cherry Street Cottage**, 636-7086.

Places to Camp

Vicksburg Battlefield Kampground on the I-20 frontage road is a full-service campground conveniently close to the park entrance, $9 to $12 for full hookups. Take Clay Street east past the entrance to Vicksburg National Military Park and turn at the "camping" sign just before the I-20 interchange, (601) 636-2025. An alternative is **Indian Hills Campground**, seven miles east of Vicksburg on I-20, 638-5519.

Useful Tip

Vicksburg's Spring Pilgrimage runs for two weeks in late March and early April. You get to see four additional homes not open to the public the rest of the year. Call Vicksburg visitor information, (800) 221-3536, for details.

Linger Longer: Port Gibson

Take an extra day to explore antebellum Mississippi plantation life at its heart in the fertile lands between Natchez and Port Gibson. Leave the Natchez Trace at Milepost 10 and take MS 553 back in time past *The Cedars*, *Lagonia*, *Oak Grove*, *Richland*, and *Springfield* plantation homes near Church Hill. Stay on MS 553 as it crosses the Trace again and take the US 61/Fayette Bypass north to Lorman to visit *Rosswood Plantation*, whose freed slaves helped found Liberia. Venture out to *Windsor* or **Grand Gulf Military Park**, then return to Port Gibson and treat yourself to a night at *Oak Square* in the company of Bill and Martha Lum, whose Mississippi roots go back some 200 years. Leisurely conversation with the Lums at breakfast will have you convinced that 1860 and "The Late Unpleasantness" (the War) were only yesterday. Call (601) 437-4350 to reserve a room, $65 to $85.

Campers will find full-hookup facilities at Grand Gulf Military Park.

Today's Shortcut

Bypass Vicksburg and stay on the Natchez Trace route all the way to Tupelo, your destination at the end of *Discovery Day 7*. It's a six hour, 272-mile drive from Natchez to Tupelo; if you leave at 9 a.m., you should arrive just in time to visit Elvis Presley's Tupelo birthplace.

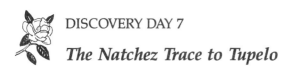

DISCOVERY DAY 7

The Natchez Trace to Tupelo

THE GENTLE TERRAIN, lush surroundings of pine and hardwood forest, complete absence of the usual highway annoyances, and often thought-provoking points of interest make the Natchez Trace Parkway the most serene long parkland drive in America. It now runs nearly its original length — almost 500 miles from Natchez to Nashville.

Treat yourself to a relaxing country drive as you cruise effortlessly northward along the Trace for four hours or so. A lone postrider will guide you to frequent convenient pull-outs where you can stretch your legs, enjoy the scenery close up, and learn about the people who traveled this historic road.

Your journey for the day ends in Tupelo, where you'll step inside a tiny two-room cottage that's become something of a shrine — the birthplace of a poor Mississippi boy named Elvis, who grew up to be the best known and best-loved entertainer of his generation.

Timetable Suggestion

8:30 a.m.	Breakfast, pack lunch, head towards Jackson.
9:50 a.m.	See Governor's Mansion and old and new capitols.
11:00 a.m.	Rejoin the Natchez Trace Parkway at Ridgeland Crafts Center, head north.
12:45 p.m.	Lunch in Kosciusko or picnic at Jeff Busby.
3:45 p.m.	Visit Elvis Presley birthplace and chapel.
5:00 p.m.	Sweep out the car. Get ready for supper.
6:00 p.m.	Check into a motel or Tombigbee State Park, go out for catfish and hushpuppies.
8:30 p.m.	Dance at a downhome Tupelo nightspot.

Magnolia Trail: Vicksburg to Tupelo (215 miles)

Your first stop today is in **Jackson**, 44 kudzu-lined miles east of Vicksburg on Interstate 20. Just after crossing the Pearl River near downtown Jackson, take I-55 north and get off at Exit 96B/High Street to see the capitols, old and new, and the Governor's Mansion, classical buildings of great grace and dignity. (But don't expect to see much antebellum splendor here — Sherman was quite proud of the torch-and-hatchet job he did on the city in 1863.) The rest of today's journey will be a relaxing 171-mile rural and forest

JACKSON TO TUPELO

drive northeast along the Natchez Trace. Check your fuel gauge! There's only one place on the entire Trace where you can buy gas: Jeff Busby, 90 miles north of Jackson (although Kosciusko is an easy exit about 60 miles from Jackson).

From downtown Jackson, return to I-55 north via High Street or Fortification Street. Nine miles north on I-55, take the **Natchez Trace Parkway** ramp. If you didn't pick up the National Park Service's Natchez Trace map yesterday, get one from the map box you'll see in the breezeway near the door at the Ridgelands Crafts Center. With this map, and keeping an eye open for the handy milepost and postrider markers along the road, you'll always know where you are on the Trace and what's just ahead. The pleasant shoreline of **Ross Barnett Reservoir** will be on your right for about 15 miles. **Kosciusko** (pronounced *Kozi-YES-co*) is one of the few towns close to the Trace and makes for a convenient lunch stop, unless you prefer a roadside picnic. Once called Redbud Springs, it was renamed for Thaddeus Kosciusko, the young Polish patriot who fought with George Washington. Jeff Busby, a couple of hours from Jackson, is a handy place for an afternoon picnic lunch. There's a convenience store here for provisions.

Leave the Trace for the day at **Tupelo**, a prospering little city dear to the heart of every Elvis fan. If you'd like a glance at the **Tupelo Battlefield** site, get off where the sign directs you to Main Street/MS 6. Main Street goes past the battlefield, crosses under US 45, and takes you to Elvis Presley Drive and the humble birthplace of the King of Rock n' Roll. (If you've dallied along the along the Trace, an easy thing to do, and arrive in Tupelo after 4:30 p.m., plan to visit the birthplace tomorrow morning.)

The Natchez Trace Parkway

The first quiet steps along this road were those of the Chickasaw and Choctaw people. After the American Revolution, the Natchez Trace became a main artery of the westering spirit. Rough Kentucky frontiersmen (dubbed "Kaintucks" by the French) floated flatboats down the Ohio and Mississippi rivers to Natchez and New Orleans. They sold these one-way barges for the lumber value, then set out for home on foot or horseback up the Trace. Widened in 1803 to handle wagons, the Trace carried a victorious Andrew Jackson back to Tennessee from the Battle of New Orleans. The road faded with the advent of steamboats and the railroads, and lay silent until heritage-conscious Daughters of the American Revolution began placing markers along the Old Trace in 1909. The beautifully maintained two-lane parkway you drive today was built during the past 30 years and is part of the National Parks system.

As a "freeway," the Natchez Trace Parkway is a wonder. Its manicured shoulders run out to meet walls of wilderness on either side, graced in springtime with mile after mile of delicate white dogwood blossoms. There are no towns and, except for the concession at Jeff Busby, no businesses on this pike. Commercial trucks can't use it. Intersecting roads pass under or over the Trace; no stoplights or stop signs hinder your progress. The speed limit is an easy 50 miles per hour, yet you'll make surprisingly good time. To enrich your journey, the National Park Service maintains more than 100 well-marked points of interest along the way. Best of all, there's no toll and no fee at any highlight. This is driving as it was meant to be!

As you peer down a section of the silent, sunken Old Trace, imagine a Kaintuck boatman of 1810 walking these miles through the forest back to his Ohio Valley home. Flush with cash from goods sold in New Orleans, he keeps an eye peeled and counts his steps. Will he be waylaid by highwaymen? Or will he rest tonight in the rumored friendly stand he hopes to reach by nightfall...?

The Best to See and Do

❀ ❀ **Mississippi State Capitols (old and new)** — The New Capitol isn't all that new; this gracefully-proportioned beaux-arts style building became the seat of Mississippi's government in 1903, but it has a recent $19 million facelift. You'll see it on your left as you come into downtown Jackson on High Street (free tours hourly every day 9 a.m. until 3:30 p.m., open at 1 p.m. Sundays). Turn left on Congress or West Street, then left again on Capitol Street to get a fine prospect of the dignified Old Capitol, built in 1833 at the height of Greek Revival passion. It's now the State Historical Museum, with exhibits tracing Magnolia State history from Hernando DeSoto's discovery of the Mississippi River through the poignant Civil Rights era of the 1960s. Open Monday through Friday 8 a.m. to 5 p.m. and Saturdays until 4:30, free.

❀ **Russell C. Davis Planetarium** — One of the most elaborate sky theaters anywhere, Davis Planetarium is on Pascagoula Street next door to the **Mississippi Museum of Art**, which has a large Americana collection including works by O'Keeffe and Rauschenberg and hands-on art stuff for kids. Call (601) 960-1550 for planetarium times; adults $3, seniors and children $2. The art museum is open daily from 10 a.m. to 5 p.m. (noon to 4 p.m. Sundays); adults $2, children $1.

❀❀❀ **Natchez Trace Highlights** — Just beyond Jackson is the **Ridgelands Crafts Center** (Milepost 102) where you'll find quilts, Choctaw baskets, pewterware and leaded glass for sale by the Craftsman's Guild of Mississippi (open 9 a.m. to 5 p.m. daily; call 856-7546 to find out about weekend demonstrations). **West Florida Boundary** (Milepost 108) marks the northern extent of the territory England got from Spain in exchange for Havana, Cuba, as part of a complicated eighteenth-century monopoly game. Stop at **Upper Choctaw Boundary** (Milepost 128) to learn the shameful story of the Choctaw's loss of a third of their lands here in 1820.

From **Beaver Dam** (Milepost 145), where there's a ten-minute nature trail, through Kosciusko, you may notice the handiwork of the industrious, flat-tailed critters. Another threat to trees, a tornado, cut a still-visible swath across the Trace in 1988 about five miles north of Kosciusko. You'll find out how well stand owners and the Choctaws got along in the early days at **French Camp** (Milepost 180). Take the five-minute drive at Jeff Busby (Milepost 140) to **Little Mountain**, at 603 feet one of the highest places in the state. At Mileposts 199 and 222 nice stretches of the **Old Trace** lead off into the forest; walk a few steps and imagine what it must have been like to be that Kaintuck boatman walking home through the wilderness. An ancient culture built the burial complex at **Bynum Mounds** (Milepost 232) a thousand years ago. The Chickasaw people and U.S. government frontier agents at **Chickasaw Agency** (Milepost 241) cooperated admirably to preserve the peace until the late 1820s, when settlement pressures upset the fragile balance. Postriders between Nashville and Natchez would get fresh ponies at **Tockshish** (Milepost 249) on their twelve-day ride from Natchez to Nashville; two miles north there once stood a council house that served as the capitol of the Chickasaw nation.

❀❀❀ **Elvis Presley Birthplace** — You will find no Cadillacs, no gaudy costumes, no Graceland opulence here. This place reflects instead simplicity and sincerity, sides of the King of Rock n' Roll that endear him to thousands of lifelong fans. Elvis's daddy borrowed $180 for the materials to build this little frame house where Elvis and his twin brother Jesse were born in 1935. A bed crowds the front room and a fireplace shares the wall with the humble kitchen behind it; the Presleys had neither electricity nor inside plumbing. Even so, they couldn't keep up their meager payments and lost the house two years later. When Elvis sang about being "just a po' Mississippi boy" he sang from his soul.

Stroll up Lisa Lane (named for Elvis's daughter) to the tiny, modern memorial chapel, built by the Elvis Presley Fan Club of Mississippi in 1979. Nearby there's a small gift shop of Elvis records, tapes and souvenirs. The house, chapel and gift shop are at a 15-acre children's park and youth center made possible by proceeds from a benefit concert Elvis gave in 1957. Elvis Presley Birthplace is on Elvis Presley Drive left off Main Street/US 6 east of downtown Tupelo; open Monday through Saturday from 9 a.m. to 5:30 p.m. from May through September (10 a.m. to 5 p.m. the rest of the year), Sundays from 1 p.m. to 5 p.m.; $1 donation suggested, (601) 841-1245.

One of the best things about this special place is the fans you'll encounter — both those who work here and those who've driven in from Minnesota with their kids and sometimes grandchildren in tow. You may feel you've met some of the gentlest hearts in the land.

On the ridge just behind the park, there's a little parking area by a pond and water tower. Picture yourself in the '50s, parked there with a sweetheart on a moonlit summer night, listening to *Don't Be Cruel* and *Loving You* on the car radio. It's very easy to imagine here.

Places to Dine

When hunger strikes in downtown Jackson, I head for the delightfully old-fashioned **Mayflower Cafe**, 123 Capitol Street, and order the Greek salad with crabmeat. The **Elite Cafe**, 141 East Capitol, has good food at prices much more reasonable than the name implies. **Keifer's**, 120 North Congress, and **Jackson Bar & Grill** on Fortification Street near I-55, are good bets too. If you're having lunch in Kosciusko, find **T.J.'s Battle House** on the town square to enjoy downhome fare at decent prices and a downright amusin' menu.

Catfish with hushpuppies should be sampled in Tupelo, where both are considered delicacies. **Estes's Restaurant**, (601) 842-5599, on SR 6 at State Park Road serves all-you-can-eat catfish with absolutely flawless hushpuppies for $6.95 from 4:30 until 10 p.m. Tuesday through Saturday. The following are all on Gloster Street, not far from the suggested motels: **Fisherman's Bay** south of Main Street, **Rebecca's** for very good country cooking, **Quincy's Family Steak House**, and a lively place boldly named **S.O.B.** (for Shrimp and Oyster Bar) at 1721 North Gloster. Try the cornbread and homey blue plate specials at **Rita's Gum Tree Cafe**, 206 North Spring Street (842-2952). For someplace a little more refined (you may need a reservation), there's **Jefferson Place**, 823 Jefferson Street (844-8696), and **Gloster 205** (at 205 Gloster, naturally, 842-7205). Tomorrow morning, fill up on **Shoney's** all-you-can-eat breakfast, next to the Comfort Inn where North Gloster Street crosses over McCullough Boulevard.

Places to Stay

The modern motels on North Gloster Street just off McCullough Boulevard/Old Highway 78 make for convenient, no-hassle overnight accommodations and a return to the twentieth century after your past three nights in the 1850s. **Comfort Inn**, (601) 842-5100, offers a light breakfast with your room ($38-$42). A **Ramada Inn** (844-4111) and **Econo Lodge** (844-1904) are nearby. Just off the Natchez Trace Parkway on Main Street/MS 6 is the **Natchez Trace Inn** (842-5555), from $40. Sorry, no guest mansions (yet) in Tupelo, but if you're not yet ready for modern times, there's **Nisbet House** (489-8484), a bed and breakfast sixteen miles west of Tupelo on MS 6 in the town of Pontotoc.

Places to Camp

The best choice is **Tombigbee State Park**, secluded on an emerald-green lake surrounded by peaceful woods. Clean and hot showers, hookup sites $10, plus air conditioned cabins with fireplaces from $27. Tombigbee is about six miles southeast of town off SR 6 (turn left at State Park Road in Plantersville), (601) 842-7669. City-run **Elvis Presley Lake and Campground**, 841-1245, requires $2 per person (children $1) to get in, plus $8 for a full-hookup site or $4 for primitive site. There's a sand beach, marked swimming area, and water skiing at this lake. From Main Street/MS 6 take Canal Street north and follow the signs for about four miles. Fishing (catfish, largemouth bass) is a temptation at both lakes.

Evening Amusements

For a city of 25,000, Tupelo has a surprising number of places where you'll find bands playing danceable country and rock six or seven nights a week. These three are all close to each other: **Tadpole's**, adjacent to the Holiday Inn at 923 North Gloster Street (842-8811); **Guy's Place**, 825 North Gloster (842-2477); and **Bogart's** in the Ramada Inn at 854 North Gloster (844-5371), which has a unique glassed-in lounge where you can sit down and hear yourselves talk.

Useful Tips

Check conditions along the Natchez Trace Parkway by calling the visitor center in Tupelo, (601) 680-4025. **The Cottage Bookshop**, 214 North Madison in Tupelo, 844-1553, is one of Dixie's best. Browse among some 10,000 used, rare and first edition books with an emphasis on classics and Southern writers; open noon to 5 p.m. except Sundays, "other hours by chance or appointment."

Linger Longer: The Mississippi Delta

From Vicksburg north to Memphis, Tennessee, US 61 spans the Mississippi Delta — the low cotton-crop land that gave birth to the blues. **Greenville** was the spawning ground of a whole school of literary greats (Walker Percy, Hodding Carter, Shelby Foote). At **Clarksdale**, 162 miles north of Vicksburg, stop at the **Delta Blues Museum**, (601) 624-4461, free.

Turn east on MS 6, cross the Tallahatchie River, and pass through **Oxford**, home of "Ole Miss" (the University of Mississippi) and William Faulkner, who immortalized the town in his novels. Half a mile south of the town square you will find **Rowan Oak**, where Faulkner lived and wrote. Scribbled on its walls is the plot outline for his book, *A Fable*. Rowan Oak, (601) 234-3284, is open Tuesday through Saturday from 10 a.m. to noon and 2 p.m. to 4 p.m., free. On the Ole Miss campus you'll find exhibits in the **Center for the Study of Southern Culture** and the **Blues Archive**. Keep heading east on MS 6 to rejoin the main route of the Magnolia Trail at Tupelo.

If you've taken US 61 north all the way to **Memphis**, perhaps lured by the unexplainable magnetism of Graceland, you may want to visit Beale Street and Mud Island as well. Although **Beale Street** isn't quite what it used to be, you'll still find the blues played here. **Mud Island** on the Mississippi River has been transformed into an amazing park, capped by a 32-story tall glass pyramid that contains a statue of Ramses the Great. Also on Mud Island is the River Walk, a five-block long scale model of the lower Mississippi River, and a museum of river history that includes the Theater of River Disasters. Call (901) 576-7241 for hours and admission prices to the park and museum. Elvis Presley's **Graceland** mansion is unquestionably the greatest attraction in the Delta City. You can tour both the mansion and Elvis memorabilia exhibits (including two Lear jets and sundry cars) across the street. Mansion tour: adults $7.95, children 4-11 $4.75; complete tour: $15.95 and $10.95; (800) 238-2000. Memphis' most whimsical tradition remains the twice-daily parade of ducks through the lobby of the **Peabody Hotel**, (901) 529-4000.

From Memphis, it's an easy two-hour drive on US 78 to Tupelo via Holly Springs, Mississippi. Rich in Deep South history and culture, **Holly Springs** was home to ten Confederate generals as well as Mrs. U.S. Grant during the Union occupation. Rust College, in the heart of town, is one of the oldest black colleges in the South. Take time to drive the "Green Line Tour" past a few of Holly Springs' 64 antebellum houses, many of which you can visit during the April pilgrimage, (601) 252-2943. Stay in Holly Springs at **Hamilton Place**, (601) 252-4368, a fine bed and breakfast in a home built in 1838.

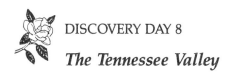 DISCOVERY DAY 8

The Tennessee Valley

YOUR THIRD DAY on the Natchez Trace Parkway will take you into Alabama and on through the limestone hills of Middle Tennessee. Detour to the Alabama Shoals communities along the Tennessee River Valley to stop at the homes of inspiring Helen Keller and W.C. Handy, "the Father of the Blues." Toward evening, you will arrive in Nashville, America's legend-filled, magnetic Music City, for an evening of pleasurable dining and entertainment.

Timetable Suggestion

8:30 a.m.	Breakfast and depart Tupelo.
9:00 a.m.	See Trace exhibits at Tupelo Park Center.
9:30 a.m.	Drive Natchez Trace Parkway to Colbert Ferry.
11:00 a.m.	Visit Ivy Green, Helen Keller's birthplace.
Noon	Lunch at the Right Track in Sheffield.
1:00 p.m.	See the home of blues genius W.C. Handy.
2:30 p.m.	Continue north on the Trace into Tennessee, inspect the ultramodern Saturn car factory.
6:00 p.m.	Arrive in Nashville, settle into your lodgings.
7:00 p.m.	Dinner and music in the heart of Nashville.

Magnolia Trail: Tupelo to Nashville (250 miles)

From Gloster Street in Tupelo, take McCullough Boulevard (Old US 78) west and after a mile look for the brown Natchez Trace Parkway signs to get back on the Trace north toward Nashville. Make your first stop of the morning three miles north at Natchez Trace Park Headquarters. Twenty-five miles up the Trace you'll be on a bridge over the **Tennessee-Tombigbee Waterway**, a Corps of Engineers project completed in 1985 that links the Tennessee River to the Gulf of Mexico. You can see one of the giant locks to your left. Turn left just after the bridge to get a closer view of the canal and learn details about this ambitious project. Just past Cave Spring you cross into Alabama, and forests give way to red-earth farmland. The Trace crosses the broad Tennessee River at historic **Colbert Ferry**. Retrace your route south six miles to the US 72 (Lee Highway) intersection and turn east toward the **Alabama Shoals** communities of Tuscumbia, Sheffield, Muscle Shoals, and Florence. Keep left on Old Lee Highway into Tuscumbia and follow the signs on Main

Street to Ivy Green, Helen Keller's birthplace and home on West Commons Street. Continue north on Main Street to Avalon Avenue. Turn right, then left on Woodward Avenue which takes you to the **Tennessee Valley Authority (TVA) Reservation** at Muscle Shoals. Take a right at the TVA Reservation sign and you'll be on a lush, landscaped parkway. This lovely area is actually a huge government project that produces a third of the world's chemical fertilizers. Cross the Tennessee River at **Wilson Dam and Lock** (highest single-lift lock in the world). Built in 1918, the Wilson project became a cornerstone of Franklin Roosevelt's river-taming, people-employing TVA projects of the 1930s.

Across Wilson Dam, turn left on Union Avenue and follow Spring Street into downtown Florence. Turn left at Court Street and then left onto West College Street to reach the W.C. Handy Home and Library. To return to the Natchez Trace Parkway, take Court Street toward the river, turn right at McFarland Drive, and follow AL 20/Savannah Highway approximately 18 miles to the Trace intersection. Ten miles north, you'll cross into south central Tennessee, a sweet land of limestone hills, hollows, and wholesome country living.

At Milepost 375, take the **Old Trace Drive** route for 2.5 miles to feel what travel was really like on the original road. Eleven miles north you come to Meriwether Lewis's gravesite, the last major point of interest on the Natchez Trace Parkway. Turn right on TN 20 toward **Summertown**, then take US 43 north into **Columbia**. From downtown Columbia, take US 31 and US 412 to Interstate 65 (or stay on US 31 to see the Saturn plant).

Tune your radio to WSM (AM 650) to pick up the toe-tapping, heart-rending, good-timing sounds of **Nashville**, tonight's destination. You'll be on I-65 straight into the heart of Music City. If you plan to stay at one of the Trinity Lane motels (see *Places to Stay*), keep on I-65 across the **Cumberland River** to Exit 87. The view across the Cumberland to downtown Nashville is stunning, night or day.

The TVA and Tennessee

When America was in the depths of the Great Depression, nowhere were things more depressed than in the Tennessee River Valley. But President Franklin Delano Roosevelt was a man with a plan. In 1933 the federal government created the Tennessee Valley Authority and began a massive series of public works projects here, the likes of which the world had never seen before or since. Nine dams were constructed for flood control and power generation, locks were built for navigation, and thousands of people in seven Southern states found jobs and relief from poverty. The task outlasted the Depression, and TVA today contines to build and create jobs and is still a major economic force in the Tennessee River region — as you'll see today in

THE TENNESSEE VALLEY

Alabama, and even more in *Discovery Days 10* and *11* in the Chattanooga area.

The great loop of the Tennessee River divides the Volunteer State into three distinct regions, each represented by a star on the Tennessee state flag. To the west lies the low, fertile cotton country of the Mississippi Delta and Memphis. Middle Tennessee encompasses the farms and hills of the Cumberland Plateau that surrounds the Nashville Basin. The ridges of the Appalachian Mountains rise in the east around Knoxville.

It's called the Volunteer State because of the readiness of Tennesseeans to sign up for the War of 1812 and the Mexican War.

The Best to See and Do

❀ *Along the Trace* — **Tupelo Visitor Center** (milepost 266) is park headquarters for the Natchez Trace Parkway; an amusing 12-minute film and exhibits that include a Kaintuck's outfit and gear make for a good start to the third and last day of your drive along the Trace. An impressive Native American site on the route is **Pharr Mounds** (milepost 287), constructed around A.D. 100. **Cave Spring** (milepost 308) is a pretty little grotto. At **Colbert Ferry** (milepost

327), Chickasaw George Colbert ferried Trace travelers across the Tennessee River from 1800 to 1819 — for a fee (Andrew Jackson is said to have paid George $75,000 to get his army across). Watch the broad Tennessee roll by from the pleasant picnic area. The **Old Trace Drive** at milepost 376 gives you a chance to experience what it was like to travel this road in the early 1800s. You slow down to 25 mph on the paved, but otherwise narrow and thickly-wooded country lane for a little more than two miles roughly parallel to the parkway.

Pause at **Meriwether Lewis** gravesite (milepost 386) to ponder the strange, melancholy fate of young Captain Lewis, who opened the Oregon Trail on the 8,000-mile Lewis and Clark expedition of 1803-1806. A national hero and Governor of Louisiana, Lewis was on his way to Washington D.C. when he stopped here for the night. Just what happened to him during those few, tormented hours? It's your guess.

❀ **Tenn-Tom Waterway** — French Governor Bienville wrote King Louis XIV in the mid-1700s that it might be a swell idea to dig a navigation canal between the Tennessee and Tombigbee rivers, to open commerce between the Tennessee Valley and the Gulf of Mexico. But no one got around to it until 1972 when the U.S. Army Corps of Engineers shoveled the first spadeful of the 459-mile-long ditch. Learn how it works at the Corps' Tenn-Tom Visitor Center on Bay Springs Lake, just north of Trace milepost 293. ("Tom Bigbee" is a purely fictional fellow — the spelling comes from the sound of the original Indian name for the river.)

❀❀ **Ivy Green: Helen Keller Birthplace** — At this unpretentious estate in Tuscumbia, a tragedy and a miracle took place that still moves those who come here. Helen was just 19 months old in 1882 when a severe fever left her blind, deaf and mute. Yet with the special help of Anne Sullivan, she went on to achieve academic honors and became a remarkable lecturer and writer. See the cottage room, with her cradle and toys, where she fought her fever, and in the yard put your hand on the water pump where Anne first discovered how to communicate words to Helen through the touch of water. Open 8:30 a.m. to 4 p.m. Monday through Saturday, and from 1 p.m. on Sundays; adults $3, children $1.   *The Miracle Worker,* a play about Anne and Helen, is performed here evenings in June and July. Call (205) 383-4066 for ticket information. Inquire about directions to the **Right Track** for lunch.

❀❀❀ **W.C. Handy Home, Museum and Library** — Here you'll find the piano on which Handy composed *The St. Louis Blues* and other standards. Fortunately for us, "The Father of the Blues" was aware of his place in music history; his wealth of memorabilia gives unique insights into the composer's life and American black culture as well. Far-sighted Florence city fathers acquired the hewn-log house from Handy in 1949 and rebuilt it on this site in 1968. The cabin is furnished with things you'd find in an Alabama black home near the turn of the century, and a friendly, informed guide will explain everything. Open Tuesday through Saturday 9 a.m. to 4 p.m., but often closed for lunch; adults $1 donation, children 25 cents.

❀ **Key Underwood Coon Dog Graveyard** — You read that right! It's an unusual tribute to beloved hunting dogs, with more than 100 interments and informative headstones. From US 72 seven miles west of Tuscumbia take Highway 247 twelve miles south; free.

❀❀ **Saturn Factory** — Built to blend in with the environment near Spring Hill, Tennessee, General Motors' new Saturn automobile plant is one of the most innovative in the world. Drive north from Columbia on US 31 about 13 miles (or take the Saturn Boulevard exit from I-65). Call (615) 486-5078 for the current tour schedule, free.

❀ **The Farm** — If you were a flower child, you'll be glad to learn that Stephen and Ina May Gaskin's community is still here. "Politically and religiously, we're hippies," asserts Stephen with happy conviction. About 300 people now live in individual homes, each adult paying a share toward community services. From TN 20, turn left onto Drake's Lane just west of Summertown and bear right until you reach the gate. To let them know you're coming and inquire about overnight stays, call John and Rosa Livingston, (615) 964-2397, or the gatekeeper, 964-3574.

Places to Stay

Convenient motel accommodations abound in Nashville, with handy clusters along West End Avenue, downtown on Union Street, to the north where I-65 crosses Trinity Lane, and near the Opryland Complex where Music Valley Drive parallels Briley Parkway. I find room rates on Trinity Lane generally easy to live with and access to Nashville's attractions from there is convenient. **Cumberland Inn, Econolodge** and **Thrifty Inn** on Trinity have rates below $30 in the spring; **Brick Church Inn, Drury Inn, Day's Inn**, and **Howard Johnson's** start above $40.

At Nashville's first-rate Tourist Info Center, just off I-65 at exit 85 on the east side of the Cumberland River, you'll find tempting discount cards for several motels. **Continental Inns** and **Interstate Inn**, both on Interstate Drive near the visitor center, offer spring specials below $30. Rates in the summer can be up to one-third higher than in spring. You probably won't need reservations except during Fan Fair, a week in June when country music fans flock to town to rub shoulders with the stars. A special treat downtown is the restored **Hermitage Hotel**, 231 Sixth Avenue North, (800) 251-1908, doubles from $100. For a room in a private home, call **B&B Host Homes** (615) 331-5244, or **B&B of Middle Tennessee**, 297-0883.

Places to Camp

Choose one of the commercial campgrounds on Music Valley Drive near the Opryland complex. Take I-40 east, then Briley Parkway north to McGavock Pike (exit 12B) to reach Music Valley Drive's campgrounds: **Two Rivers Campground** (615/883-8559), **Fiddler's Inn North** (885-1440), and **Holiday Nashville** (889-4225) offer full hookups for under $20.

If you can't handle the acres of asphalt, the Corps of Engineers provides several nice campgrounds on J. Percy Priest Lake, a few miles east of Nashville, and Old Hickory Lake, northeast near Hendersonville. Most are open April through October. **Cages Bend** on Old Hickory Lake is reached by taking Gallatin Pike through Hendersonville; call (615) 824-4989. **Cedar Creek** and **Shutes Branch** campgrounds, 882-4846, are on the south side of Old Hickory Lake. Drive east on Lebanon Pike (US 70) and look for signs after you pass The Hermitage. **Seven Points**, 889-5198, is on Percy Priest Lake. Go east on I-40 and turn south on Old Hickory Boulevard at exit 221, then left on Bell Road and follow the signs. Corps sites range from $7 to $14; you'll find showers at most of them. Seven Points and Shutes Branch are closest to The Hermitage, your first stop on *Discovery Day 10*.

Places to Dine and Hear the Music

Focus your activities this evening in Nashville's compact, convenient downtown dining and entertainment areas along Second Avenue and in Printers Alley. Quality entertainment is everywhere in Nashville, where it seems half the people you meet are musicians or aspiring songwriters. In Tennessee, places that serve liquor must also be set up to feed you. The **Old Spaghetti Factory**, 160 Second Avenue (615/254-9010) has tasty Italian pastas starting at under $10. Try the salads while you listen to piano, guitar and song at **Mere Bulles**, at 152 Second Avenue (256-1946). Stroll over to Printers Alley between Union and Commerce streets, and let your ears and eyes guide you. My favorite spot here is **The Captain's Table**, 313 Church Street at Printers Alley (256-3353), an intimate, clean, personable dinner club where you'll find seafood dishes for around $12 and equally satisfying music shows at 7:30, 9 and 10:30 p.m. (if you're lucky, you'll catch Diana Murrell and the Rhythm City Band before she's famous); then stay after midnight for the "dance and jam" session. Meet sax man **Boots Randolph** (cover $8) at his own club at 209 Printers Alley, or enjoy classical piano or guitar with a fine dinner ($12-$35) at **The Brass Rail** (254-1218). See other suggestions in *Discovery Day 9*.

Today's Shortcut

Running late? Take the bridge over the Tennessee River when you reach Colbert Ferry and just keep going north up the Natchez Trace Parkway. It's about five hours from Tupelo to Nashville.

Linger Longer: Shiloh

An easy detour to Shiloh National Military Park brings you to the scene of a truly tragic Civil War battle. Here on April 6 and 7, 1862, General Albert S. Johnston's Confederates attempted to defend the rail link to Memphis and the West against General U.S. Grant's Union Army. As so often happened, early Confederate skirmish victories were followed by eventual defeat by better-supplied Union forces. Of 100,000 young men who fought here, almost 24,000 were wounded or killed, including General Johnston. Turn left off the Natchez Trace towards Tishomingo on MS 25, which changes to TN 57 when you enter Tennessee near Pickwick Lake. From the Trace it takes about an hour to reach Shiloh; open daily except Christmas.

DISCOVERY DAY 9

Nashville

THIS MORNING YOU WAKE UP in Tennessee's friendly capital, the town known around the world as Music City. A happy blend of homespun and urban, Nashville has overtaken New Orleans as the largest city on the Magnolia Trail.

Spend the morning on Music Row, where you can trace country music to its roots and enjoy a hands-on music-making thrill in a truly historic recording studio. There's a new lady in Nashville — towering Athena. You'll find her at home in the graceful Parthenon replica. This evening, be in the audience when the *Grand Ole Opry* or *Nashville Now* hits the airwaves. Tonight, Nashville's nightspots will put you up close with the country, bluegrass, blues, and rock stars of tomorrow. You're bound to leave good-natured, warmhearted Nashville with a smile on your face and a song in your heart.

Timetable Suggestion

9:00 a.m.	Visit Country Music Hall of Fame and RCA Studio B on Music Row.
11:00 a.m.	Pay homage to Athena at the Parthenon.
Noon	Lunch at a Cracker Barrel or the Cooker.
1:00 p.m.	Visit single-star museums near Music Row and attend a *Crook and Chase* TV taping, or spend the afternoon at Opryland USA.
7:00 p.m.	Be a part of the *Nashville Now* television audience (weekdays), or attend *Grand Ole Opry* live radio broadcast at the Opry House (Friday and Saturday).
9:00 p.m.	Dinner and nightspot music on West End Avenue or at the Bluebird Cafe.
Midnight	If it's Saturday, take in the free *WSM Midnight Jam* radio broadcast from Ernest Tubb's Record Shop.

Getting to know Music City

Tennessee's lively capital on the Cumberland River has long been a publishing, banking and insurance center, but what makes it magic for millions is music. Perhaps the most vibrant music center in the world, the city is dotted with music shops, booking agencies, and over 100 recording studios.

NASHVILLE

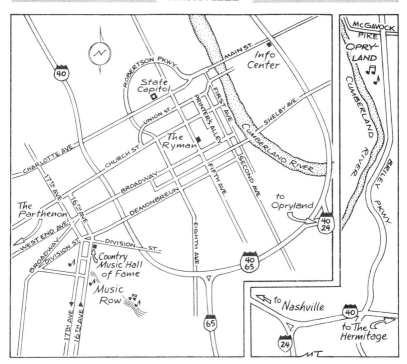

Sixty-five years after the *Grand Ole Opry* first hit the airwaves, guitar pickers, girl singers and songwriters still bring their dreams to Nashville. Chances are your young waiter or waitress is one of them — just ask!

Downtown Nashville is on the west bank of the Cumberland River, encircled by a freeway loop formed by Interstates 65, 40 and 265. If you stayed last night on Trinity Lane, make a quick stop at the **Tourist Info Center**, well-marked as exit 85 on I-65 right across the Cumberland River from Nashville's skyline. Then enter downtown on the Woodland Street Bridge. Downtown and Music Row are fairly compact and easy to navigate on foot or by car. Restored historic brick buildings line First Avenue along the river and Second Avenue, a popular restaurant area where it's safe to take your family even late at night. The **State Capitol** anchors the north end of downtown above Charlotte Avenue. Fabled **Ryman Auditorium**, the Mother Church of Country Music, stands on Fifth Avenue half a block north of Broadway. (Broadway near the Ryman is sleazy yet truly historic — probably more country music classics were first performed at decaying Tootsie's Orchid Lounge than anywhere else on earth.

Across the street is Ernest Tubb's original record shop.) The **Nashville Trolley** (242-4433) is a motorized shuttle that runs around downtown and out to Music Row for 50 cents.

Music Row, less than a mile southeast of downtown, is the home of most recording studios as well as a cluster of fan attractions. It's in an old residential neighborhood and even today is a mix of comfortable old houses converted into studios alongside modern entertainment industry buildings. Take Broadway west across I-40 and turn left on 17th Avenue. Make your way through a somewhat confusing intersection at Division Street and turn right down 17th Avenue South (here also called Music Square West). You'll pass RCA, United Artists, and other studios. Turn left at South Street or Grand Avenue, then left again onto one-way 16th Avenue (Music Square East). When you reach Division Street again, you'll be near the front door of the **Country Music Hall of Fame**. Nearby are a whole clutch of glitzy fan attractions such as Barbara Mandrell Country and the Hank Williams Jr. Museum.

Briley Parkway off either I-40 or I-65 takes you to the **Opryland USA** entertainment complex and a cluster of newish fan museums, restaurants and dancin' places about nine miles northeast of downtown. Another lively area is along **West End Avenue**, which branches off of Broadway and runs past Vanderbilt University. Venture out Gallatin Pike to Hendersonville to see where many of the most successful music stars live or to take some quiet time at Old Hickory Lake.

Country Music 101

It started in the Southern Appalachians probably, with simple, often plaintive and personal songs sung in a hypnotic falsetto and played on fiddle and dulcimer, but early radio quickly became an important "instrument" of country music. When "Judge" George Hay put a mountain fiddler named Uncle Jimmy Thompson on the air on Nashville's WSM one Saturday in 1925, the response from listeners was terrific. A little later, following a long grand opera broadcast, Hay ad-libbed, "From now on we will present the *Grand OLE Opry!*" The name stuck, WSM went to 50,000 watts, and folks all over the South and Southwest tuned in. Pretty soon, Jimmie Rodgers was on the air singing train songs and Tennessee guitar pickers donned cowboy outfits to emulate Gene Autry. Working people loved it all, and could not have cared less what music highbrows thought.

Country music has gone through a couple of revolutions but each time emerged with more fans than before. Master guitarist Chet Atkins worked with dozens of talented musicians at the RCA recording studio in Nashville in the 1960s developing the Nashville Sound; it adopted some of pop music's refinements, and suddenly the middle class discovered country. But wait! Just as country was drifting toward larger but older audiences and sounding less countrified, out of the honkytonks of Texas and Oklahoma rode Willie Nelson, Waylon Jennings and Merle Haggard, wearing Levis and scruffy hair and asserting country's earthy roots. The post-Beatles generation loved it; rednecks and hippies now flocked to the same concerts. This music was honest — from the heart, from the belly, from experience and simple dreams, from a self-effacing humor that makes life's loads a little lighter. Pretty soon, performers like Linda Ronstadt, Bob Dylan and Julio Iglesias came to Nashville to learn and record. Just everyone seems to love Patsy Cline, Dolly Parton, Roy Orbison, the Judds, and Alabama. Country may be "white soul music," but like jazz and the classics, it's also everybody's music.

It is hard to describe the bond between country music stars and their hard-core fans. The appreciation both ways is real and it is deep. Neither lets the other forget where they came from and how far they might go. In June, Music City's motel rooms fill up for **Fan Fair**, the annual face-to-face, fried chicken and autographs reunion of country music stars and fans. Y'all come!

The Best to See and Do

❀❀❀ **Country Music Hall of Fame** — Billed as "America's Number One Music Museum," the Country Music Hall of Fame and Museum is ideal for understanding country music and a fascinating slice of twentieth century American culture. You will see instruments, photos, spangly costumes, and broadcast recordings that trace the first 65 years of the *Grand Ole Opry*, as well as original hand-pencilled manuscripts of famous songs. Bluegrass, Western swing, honkytonk, Cajun, and rockabilly each have a corner, and you can enjoy clips of *Strawberry Roan* (Gene Autry), *The Road to Nashville* (Marty Robbins), and other films that featured country music. One clever section ("A Song Is Born") demonstrates the role of each instrument and simulates a typical studio "head session," in which arrangements are created.

When you're done at the Hall of Fame, take your ticket across 16th Avenue and through Roy Acuff Place to legendary **RCA Studio B** and one of Nashville's neatest treats. Here during the 1960s and 70s, the best studio musicians and sound technicians worked with top stars like Jim Reeves, Dolly Parton and Eddy Arnold to create hundreds of Nashville Sound classics. The control booth and studio are left just as they were, complete with Chet Atkins' 16-track recording console, once the finest in the world. You will be invited to sit at the controls yourself and mix sound from pre-taped tracks. Then stroll into the studio and tinkle a piano played by Jerry Lee Lewis, try a few notes on a steel guitar and other studio instruments held by famous hands, and step up to the microphone stand where Elvis Presley recorded over 100 songs, including *Are You Lonesome Tonight?*

The Country Music Hall of Fame, (615) 255-5333, is on Division Street at 16th Avenue in Music Row. The Hall of Fame and RCA Studio B are open daily 8 a.m. to 8 p.m. June through August, 9 a.m. to 5 p.m. the rest of the year; adults $6.50, kids 6-11 $1.75.

❀❀ **Ryman Auditorium** — The holiest shrine of country music, where Minnie Pearl declared, *"How-DEEE! I'm so proud to be here!"* at least a thousand times, is an imposing old brick building in the heart of Nashville. From countless southern country towns, working people would pack their families in the car and drive hundreds of miles to come here — to see and hear, on a steamy Saturday night, live and in person: Hank Snow, Maybelle Carter, Porter Wagoner, Jim Reeves, the Sons of the Pioneers, Ernest Tubb, Lefty Frizzell, Ray Price, Grandpa Jones, and Kitty Wells — the spangled superheroes of the airwaves. Its stage was where every country boy with a guitar and a song dreamed of singin' and pickin' some day. The Ryman was the home of the *Grand Ole Opry* for 31 years, and from WSM's Saturday night broadcasts here the world learned to love country music. The place never had air conditioning and performers were probably glad when the radio show moved to the spiffy new Opry House in 1974, but no one seriously considered tearing down the Ryman. (If the Pope moved across town, would they tear down St. Peters?)

The Ryman is on Fifth Avenue downtown, across from the Convention Center and half a block north of Broadway. Open every day 8:30 a.m. to 4:30 p.m., (615) 254-1445, adults $2.50, children 6-12 $1.

❀❀ **The Parthenon** — Cloned in full-scale detail from the original on the Acropolis in Athens, Nashville's Parthenon in lovely **Centennial Park** was conceived in 1897 as a temporary centerpiece for the Tennessee Centennial. It became so well-loved that a permanent, concrete version took its place in 1931. Inside stands Al Lequire's new 42-foot statue of *Athena,* **Goddess of Wisdom** — the second largest indoor statue in the world. It's an art museum too, including the fine James Cowan collection of American impressionist works. Centennial Park is on West End Avenue just past Vanderbilt University; turn right into the park when you see the Parthenon standing stately off in the distance.

The Parthenon's steps and columns attract young romantics; it's an interesting place to linger if you delight in public displays of affection. The Parthenon is open from 9 a.m. to 4:30 p.m. Tuesday through Saturday; adults $2.50, children and seniors $1.25. Call (615) 862-8431 for updates.

❀ **Fort Nashborough** — Visionary pioneer James Robertson came by land and here met John Donelson's thousand-mile river flotilla in 1780; together their parties built a new community on the American frontier. This log fort between First Avenue North and the Cumberland River is a replica of part of the original Fort Nashborough, where settlers signed the Cumberland Compact and fought Indians in the Battle of the Bluffs. See the inside free from 9 a.m. to 4 p.m. Tuesday through Saturday.

❀ **Tennessee State Capitol** — On the hill above Charlotte Avenue at the north end of downtown Nashville, the capitol is a pleasing Greek Revival masterpiece by famous architect William Strickland. U.S. President James K. Polk is buried here. A free tour will show you its features; open daily from 9 a.m. to 4 p.m.

❀ **Tennessee State Museum** — Davy Crockett's rifle, Sam Houston's guitar, Andrew Jackson's inaugural hat, an operating grist mill, and a good Civil War exhibit are what you'll see here. It's downtown on Deaderick Street in the James K. Polk Cultural Center; open Monday-Saturday 10 a.m. to 5 p.m. and Sundays from 1 p.m., free. Call 741-2692 to learn what else is there.

❀❀❀ **The** *Grand Ole Opry* — The *Opry* is the longest-running live radio show in history and it's still going strong. It went on the air in 1925 and has not missed a Saturday night live broadcast on WSM in the 66 years since. Hundreds of *Opry* "regulars" — talented cloggers, yodelers, comedians, guitar pickers, singers, and Texas swingers — have come and gone from its stage, many becoming entertainment legends. Today the broadcast originates from the spiffy **Grand Ole Opry House**, a 4,424-seat theater within the Opryland complex off Briley Parkway.

Opry radio performances are every Friday and Saturday night of the year, plus Tuesday, Thursday, Saturday, and Sunday 3 p.m. matinees from April through October. Friday and Saturday night times are 6:30 and 9:30 p.m. during the peak season, with Friday dropping to one 7:30 p.m. show November through April. Call (615) 889-3060 well in advance to confirm ticket availability. Reserved seat tickets are ordered in advance by mail (a good idea during the summer); indicate date and time when you write Opry Tickets, 2804 Opryland Drive, Nashville TN 37214. Evening show seats are $14.55 on the main floor and first balcony, $12.39 in the upper balcony. Main floor matinee seats are $12.39. *Special note:* Regardless of demand, a few hundred tickets for each two-and-a-half-hour show are held back for sale at the box office at the Opryland parking lot entrance on the Tuesday preceding the broadcast.

❀❀ **Opryland USA** — Opryland isn't so much an amusement park as it is a live music entertainment park. Pick from bluegrass, gospel, Broadway, Dixieland, rock, Western swing — whatever your musical bent — at a dozen "venues" here; few big names, but some pretty good young talent. Most Opryland entertainment is yours to enjoy as part of the price of admission, except for the daily $9.95 stage show that features a well-known headliner, and shows aboard the three-deck *General Jackson* showboat which departs the Opryland dock for three or four daily entertainment and dining cruises on the Cumberland River (morning cruise $13.95; evening dinner cruise $41.06; buffet $8.89). **Minnie Pearl's Museum**, a well-stocked record shop adjacent to the WSM studio, about 40 boutiques, and a wild indoor roller coaster called **Chaos** are other Opryland features. Since the Opry House itself is inside near the park entrance, you can combine an Opryland visit with a date for the broadcast show.

Like so many Nashville attractions, Opryland dates and times are quite seasonal. It's open every day in midsummer, weekends and Fridays in late spring and early fall, weekends only in early spring and late fall, and shuts down except for admission to the broadcasts during the winter; opening and closing hours are even more variable. Call (615) 889-6600 to get the schedule and avoid the disappointment of a locked gate. Everyone plunks down $23.65 for the single-ticket admission to all Opryland rides and venues; only children under four slip in free. You can come back to Opryland for a second or third day for $4. Add $3 to park your car.

❀ ❀ ❀ **Television Show Tapings** — Every day in Nashville a television show or special is in production, and you can be in the audience. There's little or no charge, but you must make arrangements with the studio in advance. Nearly all are produced by The Nashville Network (TNN), the cable TV arm of Opryland USA Incorporated. Call TNN's viewer services at (615) 883-7000 for times, seating, and talent lineups. When a superstar like Ricky Van Shelton or Reba McEntire is on, you'll want to make plans a week or more in advance.

Here's what you may see: *Nashville Now* is a 90-minute weeknight entertainment series hosted by Ralph Emery and aired live at 8 p.m. (be there before 7:30) from TNN's Opryland studio; usually one or more headliners are Ralph's guests. *Crook and Chase* is a daily interview and entertainment show taped at the Jim Owens Studio in the Music Row area. TNN also produces a weekly game show, country music television specials, and segments of the syndicated *Hee Haw* comedy and music show.

❀ **Star Museums** — Several country music stars have their own museums of memorabilia including their gold records, show costumes, personal movies, career awards, cars, and well-stocked gift shops so their fans can take something home. The more popular ones are open all year, others just from Memorial Day through Labor Day. Times and dates change, so call ahead to avoid disappointments; admission to each is from $2 to $6. Most are in two clusters — one along Demonbreun and Division streets on the fringe of Music Row, another in Music Valley off Briley Parkway in the Opryland area.

Music Row: **Hank Williams Jr. Museum** (242-8313) includes his dad's mementos and the hauntingly famous '52 Cadillac. At **Barbara Mandrell Country** (242-7800) you can record a song yourself. They make it easy by providing pre-recorded 24-track backgrounds and a headset with a sing-along voice if you need it; you get time to practice before you make your final cut. Your studio session costs $9.95 plus tape. **Country Music Wax Museum** (256-2490) includes a playable jukebox collection, a western wear store, and

Willie Nelson's gift shop. Webb Pierce's silver dollar glitzmobile, an Elvis Cadillac, and about 50 other interesting vehicles are in the **Car Collectors Hall of Fame** (255-6804).

Music Valley and elsewhere: **Boxcar Willie's Railroad Museum** (885-7400), the **Nashville Toy Museum** (883-8870), and yet another wax museum and car collection are on the McGavock Pike strip. Mary Reeves may greet you at the **Jim Reeves Museum** (226-2065) in lovely old (circa 1794) Evergreen Manor near Gallatin Road and Briley Parkway. **House of Cash** (824-5110) includes Johnny's amusing *I Got It One Piece at a Time* Cadillac and mementos of the famous singing Carter Family he married into. It's on Gallatin Pike in Hendersonville, across the road from Twitty City.

❀❀ **Twitty City** — What makes this single-star attraction special? Recording star Conway Twitty actually *lives* smack in the middle of it. His mansion is the centerpiece, but you can also stroll the grounds around the homes of his four children and his mother, visit a high-tech showcase of Conway's musical achievements, and perhaps even get a handshake and an autograph as he comes in from the road on the *Twitty Bird* show bus. Open 9 a.m. to 4:30 p.m. all year except December, (615) 822-6650. From Nashville, drive Gallatin Pike (US 31E) through Hendersonville; adults $8, children $4.50 and $2.50. At Christmas, Conway puts up 450,000 lights and keeps the grounds open from 5 p.m. to 10 p.m.

❀ **Opryland Hotel** — From the outside the huge Opryland Hotel resembles the Kremlin in Southern drag; inside is a delightful garden fantasy worth a visit even if you're not a guest (it's expensive — rooms start at $149). Come through the Magnolia Lobby into the Cascades, a lively water wonderland of fountains, waterfalls, a lake, and exotic plants such as ginger and jasmine, all under a six-story glass roof. (The Cascades' evening laser fountain show is a favorite of Nashvillians.) Step up on the promenade for bird'seye views, then venture further into the Conservatory, a two-acre tropical environment where trails, bridges and catwalks meander among 10,000 plants, including palms and banana trees that tower toward the palatial 110-foot high skylight. Call (615) 889-1000 if you'd like to stay.

Places to Dine

The cuisine of Nashville is Southern country cookin' — appetite satisfying portions fried chicken, country (salt cured) ham, biscuits and gravy, corn on the cob, fresh vegetables, and heaps of mashed potatoes. Some of the best and least expensive is at **The Cracker Barrel**, a popular home-grown chain of restaurants with country atmosphere — right down to real rockers on the porch and pressed metal soft drink signs on the walls. There's one on McGavock Pike near the Opryland complex. Breakfasts of grits, eggs, buttermilk biscuits with sawmill gravy, fried apples or hashbrown casserole start at $2.59. Complete Country Dinners for just $5. The **Loveless Motel Cafe** (take West End Avenue to Highway 100 and keep going), is cherished locally for its country cooking; call (615) 646-9700 to make reservations. **Melrose House**, 2600 Bransford Avenue, also features homestyle Southern cooking in a cafeteria and country music atmosphere. For a more upscale Southern menu try **Calhoun's**, at 96 White Bridge Road (356-0855) and 2001 North Gallatin Road (859-1050).

Many of Nashville's best restaurants are in the West End Avenue/Elliston Place area near Vanderbilt University. Broadway becomes West End Avenue west of I-40; Elliston Place is a block north of West End Avenue near Centennial Park. The informal West End **Cooker**, 2609 West End Avenue, serves up plentiful portions of lasagna, fish, fried chicken, and great salads at reasonable prices. American favorites start from around $11 at popular **Chef Sigi's**, 3212 West End (269-9999). **The Stock Yard** at 901 Second Avenue (255-6464) is a good bet for steak and seafood. **Julian's Restaurant Francaise**, 2412 West End (327-2412), has a fine French menu starting at about $18.

The dinner and music cruise on the Cumberland River aboard the *Belle Carole* leaves from Riverfront Park at the end of Broadway downtown at 7 p.m. nightly during the summer (weekends only in spring and fall). It's $31.25, and you should call (800) 342-2355 in advance to book passage. Check *Discovery Day 8* for downtown suggestions and take a look also under *Evening Fun*, since just about every place with entertainment also serves food.

Evening Fun

Live music talent abounds in Nashville's nightspots, as you'd expect, and your chances of hearing a performer whose name will someday become a household word (or finding yourself sitting next to a Music City luminary) are very good. **The Bluebird Cafe**, 4104 Hillsboro Road, (615) 383-1461, has become a real steppingstone to stardom; Mondays there are reserved for blues. **Douglas Corner**, 2106 Eighth Street (298-1688), sometimes showcases new country and pop recording acts. **Exit/In**, 2208 Elliston Place (321-4400), may treat you to rock, country, reggae or blues. **Bull Pen Lounge**, downstairs at the Stock Yard Restaurant (255-6464), features pickin' and singin' often with Nashville headliners. The **Station Inn**, downtown at 402 12th Avenue South (255-3307), and **Mere Bulles**, 152 Second Avenue North (256-1946), put their emphasis on bluegrass and jazz.

Bluegrass fans should also check out beer-and-chips **Bluegrass Inn** at 1914 Broadway (329-1112) and certainly **Monroe's Bluegrass Country** (885-0777) on Music Valley Drive near Opryland — especially on Tuesday nights. **Windows on the Cumberland**, 112 Second Avenue Street (244-7944), has a little of everything — acoustic music, jazz, improv comedy, poetry, and dramatic readings. Funky but legendary **Tootsie's Orchid Lounge** on Broadway around the corner from the Ryman is but an echo of its colorful past as the unofficial "green room" of the *Grand Ole Opry.* Two-steppers will enjoy the great dance floors at **Nashville Palace** (885-1540) on Music Valley Drive and **Wrangler's** (361-4440) at 1204 Murfreesboro Road. See *Discovery Day 8* for Printers Alley nightspots.

If you're in Nashville on a Saturday night, by all means be at **Ernest Tubb's Record Shop** (there are three — this one is on Music Valley Drive, 889-2474) for the *WSM Midnight Jam* broadcast. It's free and you'll see and hear several regular *Grand Ole Opry* acts, probably including *Opry* legend Ernest Tubb himself.

Places to Stay and Camp

See *Discovery Day 8.*

Useful Tips

The Tennessean has full entertainment listings in its Friday and Sunday editions; the *Nashville Banner* includes an entertainment guide on Thursdays. Nashville's **Tourist Info Center** is a convenient stop off I-65 at exit 85 just east of downtown, (615) 259-4700. Dominant cab companies are Yellow, 256-0101, and Checker, 254-5031. Care to leave your sightseeing driving to somebody else? **Grand Ole Opry Tours,** 889-9490, or **Country & Western Tours,** 883-5555, will be happy to show you around for about $15. Watch NASCAR drivers bend fenders on Saturday nights at the State Fairgrounds, 242-4343.

Grand Old Opry stars often turn up for interviews at the WSM-AM radio booth next to the Opryland record shop early on Friday and Saturday evenings before the *Opry* broadcast.

Linger Longer

You can easily spend two pleasurable, interesting days right in Nashville. If the television taping you want to see doesn't happen until tomorrow, stick around. Vary your second day by visiting *Belle Meade Mansion, Cheekwood Botanical Gardens* or *Travellers' Rest,* historic estates on the western and southern outskirts of the city.

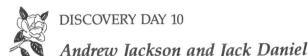

DISCOVERY DAY 10

Andrew Jackson and Jack Daniel

BEGIN TODAY with a visit to The Hermitage, the "frontier aristocrat" home of President Andrew Jackson, a towering figure who embodied that uncomplicated, by-the-bootstraps ruggedness so essential in bigger-than-life American heroes. In the afternoon make a leisurely drive south through Tennessee's hills and hollows to learn how quality whisky is made — the old-fashioned way — at Jack Daniel's, the nation's oldest registered distillery.

Cross south into Alabama to stay tonight in pleasant, prosperous Huntsville, where America's Space Age future thrives in remarkable harmony alongside a gracious Deep South past.

Timetable Suggestion

9:00 a.m.	Country breakfast at a Cracker Barrel restaurant.
10:00 a.m.	Visit Andrew Jackson's Hermitage.
Noon	Lunch, then head for Lynchburg.
2:00 p.m.	Whisky-makin' at Jack Daniel Distillery.
5:00 p.m.	Arrive in Huntsville, see Twickenham District.
6:00 p.m.	Check into a motel or Monte Sano State Park.

Magnolia Trail: Nashville to Huntsville, Alabama (115 miles)

After your visit to The Hermitage this morning, return toward Nashville on I-40 west and follow the signs to I-24 south. At **Murfreesboro**, 30 miles down the pike, leave I-24 at exit 81A, taking US 231 to **Shelbyville** (where curiosities include a still-functioning Studebaker garage). Proceed toward the courthouse square and keep an eye out for the signs directing you to Junction 82 south. Along Highway 82, a Tennessee Scenic Parkway, you begin to drive through the soft, sleepy, wooded hills and hollows that nurtured south-central Tennessee's legendary whisky-makin' tradition. Turn right at TN 55, 'round a bend or two, and pull in at the Jack Daniel Distillery, on your left just before entering **Lynchburg**. After your Lynchburg visit, continue southwest 15 miles on TN 55 toward Fayetteville, then take US 231 south across the Alabama state line and into **Huntsville**.

Tour the **Twickenham District** (see *Discovery Day 11*) before settling in if you have a little time this evening. (Turn left onto University Drive/Pratt Avenue, then right on Church Street through Big Spring Park in downtown Huntsville, then left onto Williams Avenue.) If you plan to camp at Monte Sano State Park, take the Governor's Drive exit (US 431), dip through the underpass, and go east on Governor's Drive toward the mountain. If Huntsville's very up-to-date motel strip is your choice, take the University Drive exit (US 72) west directly into franchise heaven.

The Best to See and Do

❀❀❀ **The Hermitage** — Make Old Hickory's impressive frontier estate your final stop in the Nashville area. Ambitious, brave, decisive, intensely (some say narrowly) patriotic, there's something quintessentially American about Andrew Jackson. The seventh President of the United States was, like Eisenhower, a true war hero, having routed the British in 1815 at the Battle of New Orleans. Like Harry Truman, he called 'em as he saw 'em. Like Ronald Reagan, he was no intellectual but charismatic and wildly popular during eight tumultuous years in office (1829-1837). On the dark side, he drove thousands of Native Americans from their southeastern homelands on the "Trail of Tears."

Like the rugged man himself, there's nothing particularly humble about The Hermitage. Built of site-made bricks in 1819, then rebuilt after an 1834 fire, the stately Greek Revival mansion contains the Jacksons' original furnishings and fixtures and nearly all of their personal possessions. Here, too, is the chapel and garden of Jackson's beloved and beautiful wife Rachel, who did not live to enjoy her husband's White House years. Both are buried here in Rachel's garden. A well-designed new visitor center and convenient cafeteria-style restaurant now accommodate The Hermitage's crowds of pilgrims (try to arrive early).

From downtown Nashville take I-40 east approximately ten miles to the Old Hickory Boulevard/Hermitage exit, then follow the signs north on Old Hickory Boulevard. The Hermitage is open 9 a.m. to 5 p.m. daily except Christmas and Thanksgiving; adults $7, seniors $6.50, youngsters $3.50, (615) 889-2941. Admission includes nearby **Tulip Grove** home, built for Jackson's nephew.

❀ **Stones River National Battlefield** — Bloody (23,000 casualties in two days) and costly to the Confederacy, this New Years 1863 battle pitted Braxton Bragg against the Union's General Rosecrans. A five-mile driving tour of sites includes the oldest Civil War memorial in the country. Take exit 78 at Murfreesboro and follow signs to US 41/70 south. Open daily 8 a.m. to 5 p.m., $1, nice picnic area.

❀ **Oaklands Mansion** — This italianate antebellum mansion in Murfreesboro features a monumental circular staircase and formal parlor filled with Victorian Rococo Revival furnishings. Jefferson Davis slept here (like George Washington, he got around). Oaklands Medical Museum is also on the site, at 900

North Maney Avenue near downtown Murfreesboro. Open Tuesday-Sunday; adults $3, children 6-16 $1.50).

❀ ❀ ❀ **Jack Daniel Distillery, Lynchburg, Tennessee** — Come see how country boys make good whisky at the nation's oldest registered distillery. Jack Daniel ads depict relaxed Lynchburg ("pop. 361") folks in denim overalls using time-honored, rustic techniques to concoct what comes almost naturally in these south Tennessee woods. Surprisingly, the image is fairly accurate.

A barrel house serves as the entrance for visitors. As you await your tour (you'll get a poker chip and listen for your color to be called), stroll the creaky plank floors and check out the hoop drivers, marking hammers, and other distillery tools on the wall. You'll climb lots of stairs as your good ol' boy guide takes you through the whole process, relating amazin' facts and amusin' anecdotes. They filter the 140-proof stuff with charcoal (for smoothness) made from local sugar maple cut up at their own sawmill and burned in ricks on the site. The original cabin-like office closed in 1952, but you can go inside and pore through old account books, and see the safe Jack kicked in a fit of temper that led to his early demise. After your tour, you'll be offered coffee or as fine a glass of lemonade as you'll find anywhere in the South. Free whisky samples? Nope — Moore County went "dry" in 1909! Allow an hour and a half for the free hour-long tour and refreshments. Jack Daniel Distillery, (615) 759-4421, is open 8 a.m. to 4 p.m. every day except New Year's Day, Thanksgiving and Christmas, but try to arrive well before 3 p.m. so you can see the bottling plant operation (it shuts down promptly at 4 p.m.).

Take time to visit Lynchburg's courthouse square, to your left a few hundred yards past the distillery. Herb Fanning's **Lynchburg Hardware and General Store** has old-time implements and turn of the century toys as well as distillery souvenirs. If there's no room at the table at Miss Bobo's Boarding House, try the White Rabbit Saloon for lunch and iced tea.

'Bama Bound

Today you return to Alabama for the second of three visits on your Magnolia Trail trip — each one showing a different face of a state that rightly claims to be the Heart of Dixie. Indeed, Montgomery was the first capital of the Confederacy, and its battle flag still flies proudly above the state capitol. What impresses me most are the unusual accomplishments made in Alabama by a number of remarkable people. There's Helen Keller, of course, and black scientist George Washington Carver who discovered all those things people could make with peanuts, Rosa Parks who sparked the Civil Rights revolution, and feisty populist (and segregationist) Gov. George Corley Wallace who dominated Alabama politics for a generation and campaigned strongly for the Presidency until crippled by an assassin's bullet in 1972. Wallace was later elected to his final term as governor mainly due to strong black support, which amazed his Northern critics. Explained a black campaign worker, "We Alabamians are the most forgiving people in the world."

Places to Stay

There are no enchanted mansion B&Bs in Huntsville that I know of, so give in to the lure of twentieth century amenities. Thanks to Huntsville's aerospace boom, you'll find a very complete array of up-to-the-minute chain motels and motor inns along University Drive (just east of downtown) which will give you easy access to the Space and Rocket Center tomorrow morning. Typical rates range from about $30 for two at **Knight's Inn** (205) 533-0610, to over $60 at the pricier of the two **Holiday Inns**. Or, if the sky's the limit ($100 and up for two), stay right next door to the Space Center at the **Huntsville Marriott** on Governor's Drive, (205) 830-2222 or (800) 228-9290.

Places to Camp

Monte Sano State Park, high on the mountain just east of Huntsville, has 89 pleasant forest campsites, cabins, grocery store, dump station and a playground, and it's open all year. It's also a wonderful example of Civilian Conservation Corps work done in the late 1930s. Take Governor's Drive east to Monte Sano Boulevard and turn left, then wind up the mountain to Nolen Drive and the park entrance. Hookup sites $9.50; call 1-800-ALA-PARK or (205) 534-3757 in Huntsville. If you arrive late, park at the security gate and follow signs to the first campsite on the left where a caretaker will let you in. The **Space and Rocket Center RV Campground**, next to the Marriott Hotel at the Center's entrance, is convenient; $10 hookups, (205) 830-4987.

Places to Dine

Unless you've been invited home by a friendly Nashvillian, have a great country breakfast at one of Nashville's **Cracker Barrel** restaurants (see *Discovery Day 9*). Three convenient choices for lunch, depending on when the hungries strike: The new lunch room at The Hermitage, picnic at Stones River Battlefield, or friendly sit-down feast at **Miss Bobo's Boarding House** in Lynchburg. She serves from 1 p.m. Monday-Saturday, advance reservations necessary: (615) 759-7394.

For dinner tonight in Huntsville, my choice is **Twickenham Station**, a railroad era restoration at 509 Williams Avenue across from the Von Braun Civic Center. Try their spinach salad with your prime rib or seafood. Call (502) 539-3797 to make reservations. Other possibilities: **Ol' Heidelberg** at 3807 University Drive for German cuisine, **Gibson's Barbecue** at 3319 S. Memorial Parkway, or **The Mill Bakery & Eatery** at 311 Jordan Lane near University Drive for homemade soups and breads.

Useful Tip

Pick up a guide to Twickenham and the Space and Rocket Center at Huntsville's Tourist Information Center in the Von Braun Civic Center, 700 Monroe Street, (205) 533-5723.

Today's Shortcut

If you've lingered in Nashville to see every star's museum or find somebody to play your song, you can forego the Magnolia Trail route through Huntsville. Take Interstate 24 from Nashville to Chattanooga *(Discovery Day 12)*, a two and one-half hour, 134-mile trip.

DISCOVERY DAY 11

Huntsville's Space and Rocket Center

LET YOUR IMAGINATION and sense of wonder soar at the Space and Rocket Center, the largest and best museum of its kind in the world. Walk through an unlaunched Skylab and peer into real Mercury, Gemini, Apollo, even Russian Soyuz space capsules. Gaze at the enormity of a complete Saturn V moon launcher, climb aboard the Lunar Excursion Module, ride a real centrifuge, and see what's in store for spaceflight in the twenty-first century. The day includes a tour of NASA's Marshall Space Flight Center.

After leaving Huntsville in the afternoon, drive along Lake Guntersville back into Tennessee, and gaze down on historic Chattanooga from Lookout Mountain. Retire tonight in a romantic parlor car "sleeper" at the restored Southern Railroad depot.

Timetable Suggestion

8:00 a.m.	Breakfast at Eunice's Country Kitchen.
9:00 a.m.	Arrive at U.S. Space and Rocket Center.
11:15 a.m.	Quick lunch at the "Lunch Pad."
Noon	See the fascinating *Blue Planet* film at the Spacedome Omnimax Theater.
1:00 p.m.	Tour NASA's Marshall Space Flight Center.
3:00 p.m.	Visit Twickenham or Harrison's Hardware.
3:45 p.m.	Head east towards Chattanooga.
5:30 p.m.	Enjoy the view from Lookout Mountain.
6:30 p.m.	Check in, dinner in Chattanooga.
8:30 p.m.	Nightlife at the Chattanooga Choo-Choo.

Getting to know Huntsville

In Huntsville, the very new exists alongside the very old in harmony and prosperity. Alabama's earliest English settlement (the state joined the Union here in 1819), Huntsville was born again in 1950 when Dr. Wernher Von Braun and 118 German rocket scientists came to town. Working in a facility the Americans set up just for him, the genius of the World War II Nazi rocket bomb program became the brilliant architect of America's space program. Von Braun's legacy goes on here today with development of satellite-based telescopes, permanent manned stations in space, and other wonders of tomorrow.

Downtown Huntsville is compact and interesting but can be confusing because of the one-ways. Here's a quick navigation: Come in from the north on Church Street and turn right on Monroe Street. Pass the **Von Braun Civic Center** on your right and turn left on Williams Avenue. You'll see the fanciful fountains of **Big Spring Park**. Turn left on Franklin Street and go two blocks to the courthouse square. Swing around the square where you'll spot **Harrison's Hardware**; the Schiffman Building on Eustis Street at the southeast corner is where actress Tallulah Bankhead was born. Stay on Eustis and you'll be in antebellum **Twickenham**. When it's time to leave, go west again back to Monroe Street and take Clinton Avenue to Memorial Parkway (US 231).

U.S. Space and Rocket Center

Take at least four hours to enjoy the world's largest space science museum. Huntsville's hands-on homage to our "final frontier" is more fun than even the jazziest amusement park. You can't help leaving with a feeling of pride and awe — and appreciation for what people can accomplish and what our future may hold. There's a lot worthwhile to see and experience here, so allow plenty of time for the adventure. Operated by the State of Alabama in cooperation with NASA, the Space Center is on Bob Wallace Avenue about five miles west of downtown Huntsville. If you stayed at a University Drive motel last night, take Sparkman Drive south to Bob Wallace and turn right.

When you buy your ticket you'll be given a map of the Center's inside and outside venues: The Space Center Museum, Spacedome Theater, Training Center (where Space Camp kids and Space Academy young people learn real spaceflight mission skills and design their own space stations), and the three rocket and space vehicle exhibit parks.

Ready? *Full ahead Warp-Factor Nine, Mr. Sulu!*

❀ ❀ ❀ **Space Center Museum** — Here's the *Skylab* you can walk through, plus several actual capsules from America's pioneering age of spaceflight, replete with reentry burns on their heatshields. There's a real atomic rocket engine (it never flew), the *Apollo 16* command module that carried three astronauts to the moon and back, and the "quarantine trailer" Neil Armstrong and Buzz Aldrin lived in temporarily after they returned from the moon. Sixty hands-on experiments invite you to find out how much you weigh on Mars, practice a lunar landing, and experiment with lasers and holograms. There's a full room of *Space Shuttle* exhibits and another of proposed living environments in space.

❀ ❀ ❀ **Spacedome Theater** — Look down on our dynamic, turbulent, beautiful Earth from more than 200 miles in space as you experience *Blue Planet*, a stunning cinema spectacular filmed by astronauts in space. Storms, landforms, city lights, vast seas pass far below in this remarkable sharing of our world. An Omimax projector and 67-foot domed screen open your eyes to

HUNTSVILLE, ALABAMA

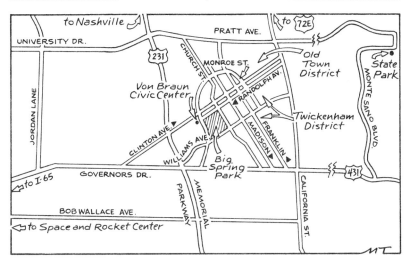

the depth and grandeur of the universe. Pick one of the frequent showtimes, and try to be in line before the one you want is announced over the public address system.

❀❀❀ **Rocket Parks and Shuttle Park** — Step outside into a field of giant and very real rockets that tell the story of American (and German) ambitions. Check out a *Nazi V1* and *V2*, used against the British in World War II and then "adopted," along with Dr. Von Braun, by the Americans after the war. There's a 66-foot-high Jupiter-C Redstone — the kind that launched the first U.S. satellite — as well as a Mercury-Atlas, a Titan, and finally the monstrous, 363-foot multi-stage *Saturn V* that put humans on the moon. A once super-secret *SR-71 Blackbird* spy plane is there too.   Adjacent Shuttle Park has a lofty full-scale Shuttle mockup complete with million-gallon fuel tank and twin solid fuel boosters. Beyond it is the futuristic-looking Habitat, a dormitory for Space Camp kids. Also outside you can experience "G's" in the real (if somewhat tame) centrifuge.

U.S. Space Camp and Space Academy — Young people from fourth-graders through high school come here to learn real space science skills. On five- or ten-day schedules they experience semi-weightlessness, build and launch small rockets, do physics experiments, and take on astronaut roles on a simulated Shuttle mission using real NASA equipment. You'll see them at the Training Center and scooting around the museum in NASA-style light blue jumpsuits, looking just like the astronauts many hope to be. Space

Camp has been so popular that there's now a weekend Aviation Challenge program so adults can try their wings, too.

❀❀ **Marshall Space Flight Center** — Climb aboard a bus at the Space Center's front door for a narrated hour-and-45-minute tour of the sprawling Army Redstone and NASA facilities. You'll stop at rocket test pads and an astronaut training center, and visit cavernous hangars housing a walk-through mockup of a proposed space station, a unique new craft for moving satellites from one orbit to another, and other wonders.

As you end your day in space, leave a banana on the memorial to Miss Baker, the long-lived first primate to fly in space — it's a Space Center tradition.

The Space and Rocket Center is open every day 8 a.m. to 7 p.m. from Memorial Day though Labor Day, and 9 a.m. to 6 p.m. the rest of the year. Ticket price (adults $11.95, children 3-12 $6.95) covers everything except lunch and trinkets. If you have time for just one part (the museum, Spacedome Theater, or the Marshall Space Flight Center) admission to each is $6.95. Call (800) 633-7280 for latest updates and applications for the Space Academy.

Other Things to Do and See:

❀❀ **Twickenham Historic District** — Ideal for either leisurely walking or a pleasant slow drive, Twickenham and adjacent Old Town are virtual living museums of nineteenth-century American architecture. Antebellum Twickenham is the area just west and south of the courthouse square, stretching from Franklin Street to California Street, and from Randolph Avenue on the north down to Lowe Avenue. Mostly Victorian **Old Town**, north of Randolph Avenue, is still undergoing a lively restoration. Pick up a walking tour booklet at the visitors bureau (see *Discovery Day 10's Useful Tip*) or hop on the motorized Huntsville Streetcar (50 cents) at the visitors bureau or Harrison Brothers Store and take the half hour downtown loop route that includes Twickenham. The Streetcar runs Tuesday-Sunday, but only until from 10 a.m. until 3 p.m.; call (205) 539-1860 for schedules.

❀❀ **Harrison General Store** — Choose your washboard or horsecollar in Alabama's oldest (1897) continuously functioning hardware store. It's open for business Monday through Friday from 9 a.m. to 5 p.m. at 124 South Side Square in the center of Huntsville.

❀ **Constitution Hall Museum Village** — Costumed guides explain Old South customs as they escort you through 16 reconstructed antebellum buildings adjacent to the hall where Alabama first entered the Union in 1819. Start the one-hour tour Monday through Saturday from 9 a.m. to 3 p.m. at Constitution Hall at the corner of Franklin and Gates streets in downtown Huntsville, (205) 532-7551; adults $3.50, seniors and children $1.50.

❀ **Burritt Museum** — This local history and archaeology museum is in an unusual, straw-insulated mansion that overlooks Huntsville not far from Monte Sano Park. Open noon to 5 p.m. Tuesday-Sunday, 535-2882, free.

❀ ❀ **Russell Cave National Monument** — Prehistoric people of several cultures liked this cave — they were here continuously for 8,000 years. The park's interpretive staff demonstrates how paleolitic tools and weapons were made. From US 72 at Bridgeport, just south of the Tennessee state line, turn left drive eight miles on county roads 91 and 74. Russell Cave is open from 8 a.m. to 5 p.m. every day and there's no admission charge.

Magnolia Trail: Huntsville to Chattanooga (110 miles)

Get on US 72 east (Lee Highway) just north of downtown Huntsville, and head east on this four-lane road through a pretty, wooded landscape dotted with tidy little farms. Near **Scottsboro,** 40 miles out of Huntsville, you begin to cross a series of bridges over inlets of **Guntersville Lake**, another TVA reclamation project along the Tennessee River. If it's springtime, you may see prolific redbuds in bloom. You'll also see the cooling towers of a TVA nuclear power plant to your right. The road narrows as you cross back into Tennessee near South Pittsburg, then just outside of town you'll get on Interstate 24 east. *Set your watch ahead one hour as you cross into the Eastern Time Zone.* Throughout this otherwise soft and inviting landscape, you're met with billboard suggestions to "See Rock City," plus Looking Glass Caverns, Ruby Falls, and other private attractions that hope to snare a few of your travel dollars. Fireworks concessions at the state line reflect differing state pyrotechnics laws. Here also you begin to see tempting invitations to factory outlet stores and malls. This marketing trend seems to have started in earnest in Boaz, Alabama, and has spread around the southeast (bargains can be found, if you're prudent — see *Linger Longer*).

After spanning **Nickajack Lake**, I-24 makes a curious jog into and out of the state of Georgia. Stop at the Tennessee Welcome Center (before 5 p.m.) to get the latest on Chattanooga's many attractions. Then take Exit 174 (Tiftonia) to put you on Cummings Highway (US 41), which leads to this evening's destinations at Raccoon Mountain, Lookout Mountain, and downtown Chattanooga.

Places to Dine

Breakfast at **Eunice's Country Kitchen** is a Huntsville tradition you shouldn't miss. Good ole boys, Kiwanis clubbers and rocket scientists mix easily here. Someone will point out that if you want coffee, you fetch it yourself — but tradition at Eunice's requires that you carry the pot and offer refills to everyone in the house before returning to your table. Tell a whopper and Eunice herself may invite you to sit at the "Liar's Table," an honored place for "bizness folks and preachers." Order the country ham and biscuits. Eunice's is at 1004 Andrew Jackson Way, just north of downtown. If you miss breakfast, try to be there for lunch. Otherwise, the obvious stop for lunch today is the **Lunch Pad**, the cafeteria at the Space and Rocket Center, but lines can be long at noon.

Mt. Vernon Restaurant, 3509 Broad Street, is my first choice for dinner tonight in Chattanooga. Pick one of the refined, relaxing rooms and enjoy friendly, attentive service as you choose from a very complete and imaginative menu (most entrees under $10). The broccoli casserole and Amaretto pie are heavenly. Mt. Vernon is on your left after Cummings Highway becomes Broad Street. A call ahead for reservations, (615) 266-6591, will assure you a table on busy Friday and Saturday nights (closed Sundays). The lively **Station House** at the Choo-Choo Complex features stage entertainment by the waiters and one of the most abundant salad bars in Dixie. Also at the Choo-Choo you can climb aboard the **Dinner in the Diner** for a romantic evening repast or order a pizza at **The Silver Diner**. Call (615) 266-5000 for information and reservations at Choo-Choo Complex restaurants. The *Southern Belle* leaves Ross's Landing at the end of Broad Street at 7 p.m. (6:30 p.m. on weekends) for dinner and entertainment cruises on the Tennessee River. Thursday through Sunday Dixieland dinner/music cruises run two-plus hours and cost $25-$30; Wednesday's Lockmaster Cruise runs an hour longer. Book your dinner passage by calling (615) 266-4488.

Places to Stay

Sleep tonight in a brass bed aboard one of the 24 romantic parlor cars stationed at the **Chattanooga Choo-Choo** depot, 1400 Market Street (you can't miss the big neon sign on top of the station). For Friday and Saturday stays, it's best to call (800) TRACK-29 a month in advance for your reservation. The fare is $105 for two. On Lookout Mountain you'll find several inviting inns: Bargain-priced **Mountain Air Resort Motel**, 1206 Lula Lake Road, (404) 820-2012 serves you both continental breakfast and an afternoon snack. Family room rates are just $30 in spring and fall and $35 in summer months. Antique furnishings inside old mountain-stone buildings and a lovely garden with a stone arch are features of **Chanticleer Inn**, 1300 Mockingbird Lane, (404) 820-2015, one block from Rock City. Rates for two start at about $40. **Alford House**, 2501 Lookout Mountain Parkway, (615) 821-7625, is a traditional B&B with rooms for two at $45 and $55. Just off I-24 at Exit 174 you will find convenient **Scottish Inns**, **Super 8** and other newish motels in the $30-$45 range.

Places to Camp

Raccoon Mountain Campground west of town is my favorite place to park the van for the night. It's a "happening" (see *Discovery Day 12*) as well as a scenic hideaway nestled in the valley of Black Creek. Nearby you can go trail riding, prowl through the limestone cave, splash down a waterslide, or strap on a hangglider (gulp!) and plunge off the mountainside. The only problem may be convincing the kids to leave tomorrow. Rates from $10 to $15, hookups, laundry, store, (615) 821-9403. From the Tiftonia exit, take U.S. 41 one mile north to the entrance.

Evening Fun

Amuse yourself tonight at the Chattanooga Choo-Choo Complex, where you can window shop, enjoy music at the **Station House**, or dance at the **Penn Station** lounge. Looking for something livelier? Try a club in the Brainerd Road area east of Missionary Ridge: **Backstage Dinner Playhouse** (629-1565), **Comedy Catch** (622-2233), **The Playmate** (to find a dancing partner), or the **Germantown Pub** at the corner of Brainerd and Germantown Road.

Useful Tips

Telephone area code for all of Alabama is (205). Chattanooga's is (615), but some Lookout Mountain phones are in Georgia (404). The Chattanooga Visitors Bureau is at 1001 Market Street, call (615) 756-TOUR.

Linger Longer: Ave Maria Grotto

If you get your fill of space technology by lunchtime, consider an easy one-hour drive south from Huntsville to see the religious wonders of the world in miniature at Ave Maria Grotto in **Cullman**. From the Space and Rocket Center, take US Alt 72 (Governor's Drive) 20 miles west to Decatur. Then drive 28 miles south on I-65 to Cullman and take exit 308 (US 278 east) one mile to St. Bernard Abbey. A Benedictine monk here devoted 40 years to creating a walk-through garden of 150 miniatures of revered shrines and churches. Ave Maria Grotto is open every day until sunset, adults $3.50, seniors $3, children over 6 $2, (205) 734-4110.

Clarkson Covered Bridge, a double 250-foot span over Crooked Creek, is on County Road 11 north of US 278 about nine miles west of Cullman. Continue east on US 278, then take AL 75 and AL 168 into **Boaz**, the original factory-outlet shopper's paradise. Return to the main route on US 431 north to Guntersville Lake and AL 79 to Scottsboro.

DISCOVERY DAY 12
Chattanooga

GAZING ACROSS this serenely delicate landscape of ridges, wooded plateaus and a meandering river valley below, it's at first hard to imagine that the greatest armies of the North and South clashed here in a bloody, desperate tug-of-war that probably sealed the fate of the Confederacy. Follow the footsteps of Generals Rosecrans, Grant, Sherman, Thomas, Longstreet, and Bragg, and more than 150,000 young, brave combatants at Chickamauga Battlefield, Lookout Mountain and Missionary Ridge — which together comprise America's largest and oldest National Military Park.

Chattanooga is one of America's original tourist towns. You can still pick from an enchanting buffet of natural and manmade diversions: ride a real steam train, soar in a cable-guided hangglider, explore several caves, and return to an innocent child's world of another time (before video games and cartoon violence) at Rock City Gardens.

Timetable Suggestion

8:00 a.m.	Breakfast, drive up Lookout Mountain.
9:00 a.m.	Scan the city and battlefields from Point Park.
10:00 a.m.	See Rock City and Reflection Riding, or Raccoon Mountain attractions and TVA Pump Station.
Noon	Lunch in Chattanooga (or picnic at Chickamauga).
1:00 p.m.	Chickamauga Battlefield and Missionary Ridge.
3:00 p.m.	Ride Tennessee Valley Railroad steam locomotive.
5:00 p.m.	Depart for Great Smoky Mountains National Park.
7:30 p.m.	Arrive in Townsend, Tennessee. Dine with the mountain folks, settle in for the night.

Getting to know Chattanooga

In 1863, Chattanooga was the key railhead and gateway to much of the South — vital to the Confederacy and a major prize to the Union. General Rosecrans' Union force met stunning defeat at the hands of Braxton Bragg's Confederate army in the dense woods around Chickamauga Creek in a two-day battle that left 24,000 casualties. But Grant and Sherman came a'callin' a few weeks later, and after hand-to-hand combat on Lookout Mountain and Missionary Ridge, the Union secured Chattanooga for good. The city's final

CHATTANOOGA

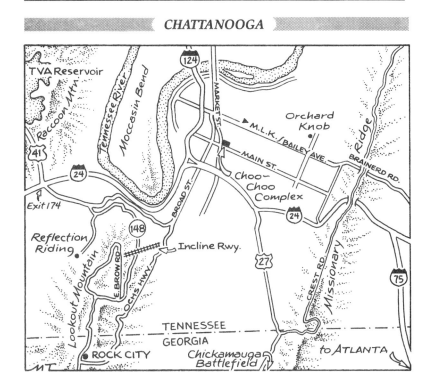

ignominy came when General Sherman used it to launch his scorched-earth march through Georgia.

Orient yourself to Chattanooga's complex geography from Park Point at the tip of **Lookout Mountain**, above the western entrance to the city. Looking north, **Moccasin Bend** on the Tennessee River is directly in front of you, with downtown Chattanooga to the right. Interstate 24 skirts the southern edge of downtown and cuts through **Missionary Ridge** off to your right (east). **Raccoon Mountain** is to the west of Moccasin Bend. The Georgia state line is at your back, just two miles away. To your right and south into Georgia on the plain below is **Chickamauga Battlefield**. After you've seen the Raccoon Mountain and Lookout Mountain attractions, take Broad Street into downtown for lunch, then Rossville Boulevard (US 27) nine miles south into Chickamauga Battlefield. Return to the city on South Crest Road, which runs along the top of Missionary Ridge. One of the nicest things about Chattanooga is that many of its best attractions are free.

The Best to See and Do

❀ ❀ ❀ **Lookout Mountain's Park Point** — Confederate forces held this commanding overlook until routed in a mist-shrouded October attack often called the "Battle Above the Clouds." From US 41, take TN 148 and East Brow Road to the top of the mountain. Pick up a free guide to Chickamauga-Chattanooga at the Park Service visitor center across the street from Park Point. Note the handshake between Confederate and Union soldiers atop the **New York Peace Memorial**, then take the short, steep trail down to the **Ochs Museum** and overlook for your scan of the city. (If you're feeling adventurous, step out on the Bluff Trail and hike a steep mile and a half down to the **Cravens House**, the Confederate bastion.) There is no admission charge to any unit of Chickamauga-Chattanooga National Military Park.

❦ ❦ **Rock City Gardens** — Opened in 1932, this mountainside collection of flowers and rocks and fairyland scenes is probably America's oldest, best known, and best-loved tourist trap. Unlike the slick, dazzling, modern "parks," low-tech Rock City has a sweetly naive quality that reflects a more innocent era and brings back little kids (like me) year after year. Along the trail you'll pass tiny ponds and waterfalls, spot elves, fairies and storybook people, and take in lofty views from Swing-along Bridge and the Sky Bridge. Squint hard and you really can see seven states. Over 400 plant varieties grow amid ten acres of rock formations with names like Needle's Eye, Mushroom Rock, and Fat Man's Squeeze. To get there from anywhere on Lookout Mountain, follow the omnipresent signs through a gracious area of older resort homes and across the state line into Georgia. Rock City is open from 8:30 a.m. until sundown every day but Christmas; admission is $3.75 for kids 6-12, $7.25 for adult kids; (404) 820-2531.

❦ **Incline Railway, Ruby Falls, Confederama** — If commercial attractions are your cup of tea, pick one of these Lookout Mountain lures. The Incline Railway, one of the world's steepest rail ascents, runs up and down Lookout Mountain (adults $5 round trip, kids $3), from a depot almost across from Confederama at the bottom to a gift shop and observation deck at the top not far from Park Point. Ruby Falls wants $7.25 ($3.25 if you're 6 to 12) to take you on an elevator deep into the mountain's caverns to see a lighted 145-foot subterranean waterfall. Some 5,000 toy soldiers and lots of lights attempt to recreate the Battle of Chattanooga on the "world's largest miniature battlefield" at Confederama (adults $4, children $2).

❦ ❦ **Reflection Riding** — Drive through this serene, English-style nature preserve nestled between Lookout Creek and the mountain, then stroll the elevated wetland walkway at adjacent **Chattanooga Nature Center** where a wildlife rehabilitation laboratory cares for injured and orphaned animals. Take Cummings Highway (US 41) to Old Wauhatchie Pike at the foot of Lookout Mountain and turn left on Garden Road. Admission to everything is $1.50 ($1 for children and seniors); open 9 a.m. to 5 p.m. every day except Sunday mornings and holidays.

❀❀❀ **Chickamauga Battlefield** — Here's where you'll begin to get a sense of the enormity of the struggle for Chattanooga. Yet the beauty and stillness of these fields and woods, studded with countless leftover cannon and hundreds of monuments, still belie the mayhem that went on here for two bloody days in September 1863. Stop at the new Centennial Center and check out the **Fuller Collection** of 355 period shoulder and side arms, then drive the seven-mile loop of significant sites. Some of the best are right alongside US 27, which runs through the heart of the battlefield. **Wilder Tower**, an 85-foot Union monument that looks like a giant chess rook, affords climbers to the top a terrific view of the whole battlefield. Chickamauga is a favorite of Civil War reenactment buffs; call (404) 866-9241 to find out when the next battle will take place. You may have to run a gauntlet of traffic and junky development on US 27 through Fort Oglethorpe to get there, but Chickamauga is worth the hassle.

❀❀ **Missionary Ridge Drive** — The climax of the Siege of Chattanooga took place along this ridge. After the arrival of Grant and the opening of a fresh supply line to the Union army holed up in town, Gen. George Thomas's Army of the Cumberland took nearby **Orchard Knob** on November 24. The next day Thomas moved against Bragg's huge Confederate force on Missionary Ridge and reached its heights in one of the great charges of the War Between the States. Bragg's line collapsed and he retreated into Georgia. The South never recovered from the rout. From US 27 north of Chickamauga, turn right onto **South Crest Road** to drive the length of this spectacular, often flower-mantled ridge, now a neighborhood of very fashionable garden homes interspersed with monuments and memorials.

❀❀❀ **Chattanooga Choo-Choo Complex** — The restored and imaginatively enhanced Southern Railway station has become the lively heart of downtown Chattanooga. Gaze up at the Grand Dome in the terminal, stroll the formal gardens between the old canopied tracks, dine or sleep aboard brocade-decorated passenger cars, check out a dozen retail boutiques, and discover the brightly painted antique Choo-Choo itself, famous symbol of Chattanooga's railroading past. **General Longstreet's Gallery**, devoted entirely to authentic Civil War relics, memorabilia and art, is one of the best shops of its kind in the South. Own a genuine dragoon sword for around $300, or fondle it for free. A recently discovered cache of Confederate currency is for sale here, bill by bill. The Choo-Choo Complex is at 1400 Market Street, just east of Broad Street and north of Interstate 24.

❀❀ **Tennessee Valley Railroad Museum** — Ride behind a real steam locomotive on a 45-minute round-trip over bridges and through a tunnel. Climb aboard at the Grand Junction Station on Cromwell Road (take the Jersey Pike exit off TN 153) or the other end of the line on North Chamberlain Avenue, where you can explore the shops and a turntable. The train runs daily June through Labor Day, but only on the weekends in spring and fall; the fare is $6.50 for adults, $3 for children 6 to 12. Call 894-8028 for schedule updates.

❀ **Raccoon Mountain Attractions** — Satisfy your death wish by jumping off a cliff in a cable-guided hangglider ($5, ages five months to 86 years), or soar above it all in an open-air ultralight airplane ($15 to $35, depending on how long you stay up), at **Raccoon Mountain Flight Park**. Your flight instructor is a wild-eyed fellow in a coonskin cap. Cheery gallows humor signs inform you that "NO ONE HAS EVER GOTTEN HURT — YOU WILL BE THE FIRST," and "THE CABLE BROKE ONLY ONCE LAST WEEK."

Up the hill, **Raccoon Mountain Caverns** features a tame half-mile limestone cave walk ($5.50, $4 for kids), and more ambitious four-hour wild cave tour. To keep you on the mountain all day, there's also a riding stable, waterslide, 2,350-foot bobsled ride, go-carts, and a very complete campground. Take the Tiftonia exit off I-24, and drive north one mile on US 41. Call (615) 821-9403 for times and details.

❀❀ **Raccoon Mountain TVA Pumped Storage Plant** — Want to see some clever engineering? At this newish project (completed in 1980), huge pumps inside the mountain use excess nighttime TVA power to pump Tennessee River water up to a mountaintop reservoir; they let it fall when the demand for electricity increases, and the pumps then become massive generators. All the pipes and turbines are painted bright primary colors. An elevator takes you 1,100 feet down to view the works on a fascinating and free 30-minute tour. To get there, take US 41 past the Raccoon Mountain Caverns entrance and go another six miles up the mountain.

The Tennessee Aquarium — Re-creating the freshwater habitats found from the Appalachians to the Gulf of Mexico, this modern new aquarium rises at the end of Broad Street at Ross Landing on the Tennessee River in downtown Chattanooga. It's the keystone of revitalization along the city's riverfront that includes converting the old Walnut Street Bridge to a pleasant pedestrian parkway. Call (615) 756-8687 for aquarium hours and admission.

Magnolia Trail: Chattanooga to Townsend (125 miles)

Depart Chattanooga on Interstate 75 north, which you can reach from downtown by going about five miles east on I-24. Sail along the Interstate through soft hills and pine groves for 60 miles until you approach **Sweetwater** (exit 60). Here you face a choice. If nightfall is approaching, continue on I-75 another 24 miles and take exit 81 at Lenoir City to reach US 321, which goes through **Maryville** and directly into Townsend, tonight's destination.

If you still have two or three daylight hours left when you reach the Sweet-water exit, you can turn here onto TN 68, the "Lost Sea Pike." (Not a sea, but

CHATTANOOGA TO THE BLUE RIDGE

a four-acre underground lake navigated by glass-bottomed boats, **Lost Sea** is six miles from I-75 just off TN 68 near Sweetwater; open daily until dusk, adults $7, children $3.50.) Then at **Madisonville**, take US 411 north and east across Tellico Lake into Maryville, where you'll turn east into the foothills on US 321 and drive 20 very scenic miles along the Little River into **Townsend**, a growing but still peaceful village on the edge of Great Smoky Mountains National Park. High waterfalls and onyx formations make **Tuckaleechee Caverns** one of the better local cave attractions. These caverns are three miles off US 321 near Townsend (open April through November, call 615/448-2274 for times, adults $6, children $3).

Places to Dine

Gather provisions for a picnic on the grass at Chickamauga Battlefield.

Rock City Gardens has a pleasant, very inexpensive family restaurant, kids' menu under $2.75. (See *Discovery Day 11* for other places to eat and places to stay in Chattanooga.)

This evening in Townsend, enjoy the mountain version of country cookin' at Sue Handley's **River View Restaurant**, smack dab on the Little River. Butter fried chicken is the specialty, the biscuits are heavenly, and an all-you-can-eat buffet is just $5.95, but it's out only until 8 p.m. **Hearth and Kettle**, **Smoky Mountain Restaurant** and **Smoky Junction** are other Townsend favorites. Many of Townsend's restaurants are seasonal operations, coming to life sometime in April. Few stay open past 9 p.m.

Places to Stay

Room rates are very seasonal in Townsend, downright cheap late fall through mid-May, but $10 to $20 more for the same room in the late spring and summer months. **Highland Manor,** (800) 321-0286; **Cades Cove Lodge,** (615) 448-6967; and **Valley View Lodge,** (800) 528-1234, on US 321 start at about $36, $40 and $50 respectively during the summer season. Closer to the park and the river on Scenic Route 73 are **Laughing Horse Motor Inn,** (615) 448-6316; **Scenic Motel,** 448-2294; and **Riverstone Lodge,** 448-6677. For a truly rustic low-budget adventure, check out the **Hillbilly Hilton**'s eclectic array of hillside cottages and log lodges, (615) 448-6463. The "camper cabins" were $30 when I was there last, but non-summer rates for everything are negotiable between you and the proprietor, David Hmielewski.

Places to Camp

Campers have a choice of staying at one of Townsend's well-equipped commercial campgrounds along the Little River or going into Great Smoky Mountains National Park to **Cades Cove** or **Elkmont.** Cades Cove campground, ten miles into the park on Laurel Creek Road, has a store and bicycle and horse rentals, but no showers; $11 per night. You should make reservations two to four weeks in advance if you plan to arrive between May 15 and October 31. It's a bit of a nuisance, because you must make them in person at the park (436-5615 for information only) or by writing Mystix, 9450 Carroll Park Drive, San Diego, CA 92121 — or call Mystix at (619) 452-0150 if you're charging with Visa or Mastercard. Cades Cove and Elkmont are also the departure points to several of the nearly 100 free backcountry campsites in the park. In Townsend along Scenic 73 very close to the park entrance you'll find **Little River Village Campground,** (615) 448-2241, **Lazy Daze Campground,** 448-6061, and **Tremont Campground,** 448-6363, with sites from $10 to $17.

Linger Longer

The **Ocoee River,** just 35 miles east of Chattanooga on US 64, has some of the nation's best whitewater runs. These rafting outfitters can get you on the water: Cripple Creek Expeditions, (800) 338-RAFT; Cherokee Rafting, (615) 338-5124); and Ocoee Outdoors, (615) 338-2438.

It's a two hour (119-mile) drive on I-75 from Chattanooga to **Atlanta.** Atlanta's downtown is glass-and-steel U.S.A., but there's a share of the Old South here too. Take in the music clubs in **Kenny's Alley,** visit the **Carter Presidential Center,** Martin Luther King Jr. sites, and the laser light show on **Stone Mountain.** Stay at the **Woodruff Inn,** once Atlanta's finest sportin' house, at 223 Ponce de Leon Avenue, (800) 473-9449. Across the street is **Mary Mac's,** probably the most authentic Southern restaurant anywhere (serving everything from pot likker to hoppinjohn), and cheap too! Return to the Magnolia Trail through Georgia's mountain empire: take GA 400 to Dahlonega or I-985 through Gainesville, explore the backroads around Cleveland and alpine Helen, maybe drive the Russell Scenic Highway to Brasstown Bald. Enter North Carolina near Franklin and Highlands.

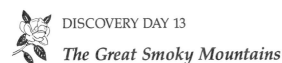

DISCOVERY DAY 13

The Great Smoky Mountains

THESE ANCIENT, MIST-MANTLED mountains are the breathtaking climax of the Appalachian chain, the eastern spine of the United States. Even the Native Americans called them "smoky" for the tendrils and billows of blue mist that slip through the troughs and tumble across the ridges of these 300-million-year old mountains.

Great Smoky Mountains National Park, straddling the border between Tennessee and North Carolina, is an astonishingly beautiful ecosphere, supporting in its temperate, moist wilderness deep hardwood and evergreen forests, more than 1,500 kinds of flowering plants, and enough of everything wild and wonderful to satisfy ten million human visitors every year. It is by far America's most popular national park. The pleasures of the Smokies are both spectacular and subtle. Don't just drive through — get out of the car and take to foot. These quiet, stable, yet dramatic mountains help you ignore time and feel in your soul a renewal and a deep peace not possible in any city. Surrender, and accept the blessing!

Timetable Suggestion

8:00 a.m.	Country breakfast, pack a lunch and head into Great Smoky Mountains National Park.
9:15 a.m.	Motor through Cades Cove.
Noon	Tranquil picnic along Newfound Gap Road.
Afternoon	Stop at inviting sites, walk a few miles along the Appalachian Trail, gaze out from Clingmans Dome.
4:30 p.m.	Visit Oconaluftee Village, Museum of the Cherokee.
7:00 p.m.	Dinner in Maggie Valley or Asheville.
9:30 p.m.	Retire at a cozy Asheville bed & breakfast inn, or camp at Smokemont.

Mountain Folks

The accent changes in the Southern Highlands *("Hey, son . . .")*. People you'll meet in these mountains have as much, maybe more, in common with their Appalachian neighbors up the Blue Ridge as they do with lowland Southerners. These ranges are older than the Alps or the Andes, and the mountain way of life, from Scottish and English roots, also reflects antiquity and tradition — with homespun values, old-time religion, and music out of another time.

The sounds of fiddle and dulcimer and the staccato dance of cloggers (kids learn clogging not long after they learn to how stand) ring out at dozens of small mountain festivals. Traditional Appalachian crafts include woodcarving, furniture-making, broom-making, white oak basketry, stoneware pottery, caning, and quilting. Be sure to try cornbread and beans, redeye gravy, and fresh cobbler at a homey cafe in an out-of-the way mountain town.

Great Smoky Mountains National Park (Townsend to Cherokee: 80 miles)

Entering Great Smoky Mountains National Park is free, and so is access to everything but overnight stays at the ten developed campgrounds. Except in the worst weather, the roads you'll be taking through the park are open all year.

From Townsend, Scenic 73 takes you immediately into the park. Turn left when you come to **Laurel Creek Road**, which winds seven miles to the **Cades Cove Loop Road**. After your Cades Cove visit, backtrack along Laurel Creek and continue on **Little River Road** through the gorge and deciduous forest until you reach the park headquarters and visitors center at **Sugarlands** (named for the sugar maples that once grew here). Here's the place to gather more information about the park or have an early picnic lunch. (If you plan to have lunch in Gatlinburg, turn north here on US 441 and brace yourself for how suddenly this busy town appears in front of you.) From Sugarlands, get on **Newfound Gap Road/US 441** and begin the dramatic 3,000-foot climb into spruce-fir forests and cooler temperatures. At the Newfound Gap summit you cross into North Carolina. **Clingmans Dome Road** takes off to the right along the ridge. Stop at the Spruce/Fir Quiet Walkway to learn more about this alpine environment, dominated by red spruce and Fraser fir. Continue south off the ridge on Newfound Gap Road, past Smokemont Campground and the **Oconaluftee** visitors center. The southern terminus of the **Blue Ridge Parkway** appears on your right just before you leave the park and enter the **Qualla Cherokee Reservation**. Two miles later you're in **Cherokee**.

Vast bouquets of wildflowers grace the slopes, coves and alpine balds of the Smokies in spring and summer. The park's renowned wildflower display (and the parade of tourists) begins in April with redbud and dogwood blossoms, then azaleas and mountain laurel, and finally the purple and white rhododendrons in June and July. Crowds return in October for the fall display of turning leaves. Cooler weather brings hoar frosts and occasional snows, turning the park into a crystalline fantasyland. The National Park Service (NPS) people here do a first-rate job both to protect what is natural and provide for the interests of everyone, from car-window visitors to back-country

GREAT SMOKY MOUNTAINS NATIONAL PARK

adventurers. They make your choices easy, with well-marked roads and trails, and clear, interesting little folders right where you need them.

The Best of Great Smoky Mountains National Park

❀❀❀ **Cades Cove** — Hewn-log houses, a mill, cantilevered barns, simple frame churches, and pasture lands are preserved by the National Park Service in secluded Cades Cove as reminders of a pioneer and mountain way of life that persisted here and elsewhere in the Smokies for a hundred years. Although many buildings are right where their owners left them when the park was created in the 1930s, others were moved and reconstructed in the **Cable Mill** area. Stroll the trail from the visitor center to see the mill race and dam. Peer into the smokehouse, Becky Cable's house, and the corn crib and barn with their clever counter-weighted overhanging beams. During summer months, watch a blacksmith at work at this outdoor museum of mountain life. Because of the open meadows and fields in Cades Cove, it's one of the best areas in the park for spotting deer, wild turkey, birds, and groundhogs. All this makes Cades Cove very popular. Even with an early start, traffic crawls along the 11-mile one-way Cades Cove Loop Road.

❀ **The Chimneys** — You'll see these stony pinnacles first from an overlook on Newfound Gap Road (good spot for a picnic). If you're tempted to take a closer look, two miles up the road is the Chimney Tops trailhead. It's an often steep two-mile trail in — allow two to three hours round-trip for the hike.

❀❀❀ **The Appalachian Trail** — This wilderness footpath wanders 2,015 miles along the backbone of eastern America from Georgia to Maine, and

70 miles across the length of Great Smoky Mountains National Park. Leave your car in the lot where the trail crosses Newfound Gap Road and strike out for at least a mile or two on this famous crest trail — even if you don't think of yourself as a hiker. Bear in mind you're in thinner air at 5,000-foot altitudes, and people from lowland areas may tire more quickly than usual. If you go more than a mile or two, don't neglect to bring along something to protect you from sudden drops in temperature and the possibility of rain.

If you're a walker and have enough daylight for a three or four hour hike, consider heading east 4.4 miles to **Charlie's Bunion**. You will probably meet a number of backpackers along the way, each with his or her own story of what's ahead to be seen and enjoyed.

❀❀ **Clingmans Dome** — A short, paved trail from the parking lot takes you to a dramatic tower on top of the highest point in Tennessee (and the park). Don't be intimidated by the sweeping, free-standing concrete spiral that launches you through the sky to the top of the tower; it's an easy ascent, even for wheelchairs. (The crowds may be daunting, however.) The 360-degree eagle's-eye views are terrific from 6,642 feet high. Yet imagine how it must have been before urban air pollution cut visibility here in the Smokies by as much as 30 percent.

❀❀❀ **Quiet Walkways** — Don't fail to take at least one of these short (about a half-mile each) walkouts from the highway into nature's realm. Each has a different theme, explained in the handy pamphlet guide you pick up at the start. At one, you'll learn about the odd "stilted" birch trees — their seeds germinate on top of a fallen log and send roots down; after the log decays away, the tops of the roots are left high and dry several inches above the ground!

Getting to know the Cherokee Indians

Most Cherokees were exiled west in the 1830s on the infamous Trail of Tears, but a small band holed up in these North Carolina mountains. Here they stayed, and finally their right to this land was affirmed in Washington. Today this area lying south of the national park is the Qualla Cherokee Indian Reservation.

The Cherokee were the most sophisticated of the so-called civilized Southern tribes, with a written language, log-built homes, and a knack for adopting European ways. But Georgia's politicians refused to honor the solemn treaties — white settlers wanted the land — and that was that. Hundreds died in the forced exodus of most of the nation. Yet here the strong Cherokee character and culture live on. If you can, take time to appreciate more of their story by seeing the Oconaluftee Village and *Unto These Hills* drama.

❀❀ **Oconaluftee Indian Village** — Here is how a Cherokee village looked two centuries ago. At this "living exhibit" community, Cherokee people demonstrate the making of baskets, pottery, weapons, and dugout canoes. The council house and other log structures show more evidence of their high civilization during colonial times. Open daily 9 a.m. to 5:30 p.m. only from May 15 to October 25; adults $7, children $3. (Because of the earlier closing time, come here before you visit the museum.)

❀ **Museum of the Cherokee Indian** — Strangely modern exhibit space explains the history of the Cherokee people and displays their traditional clothing and crafts. Combine a 20-minute stop here with a visit to the equally interesting (and free) **Qualla Arts and Crafts Mutual** store across the street. Check out the feather and beadwork pieces, clever toys, and pottery by Amanda Swimmer. The museum is open Monday through Saturday to 8 p.m. and Sundays to 5:30 in the summer, but only until 5 p.m. the rest of the year; adults $3.50, children $1.75.

❀❀ *Unto These Hills* **(drama of the Cherokee)** — From the arrival of DeSoto in 1540 through the shameful Trail of Tears exodus, this excellent two-hour outdoor summer theatrical, starring Cherokee actors, brings alive the remarkable story of these Native Americans. Daily except Sunday from mid-June though August with pre-show entertainment beginning at 8 p.m. Call (704) 497-2111 to get $9.50 reserved seats. General admission: adults $7.50, children $5.

It's convenient to stay overnight in Cherokee after the performance; choose from several motels along US 441 and US 19. Close-in **Craig's Motel**, 497-3821, and **Drama Motel**, 497-3271, are typical ($40 during the summer drama and October foliage seasons, $10 less the rest of the year).

Magnolia Trail: Cherokee to Asheville (55 miles)

Backtrack three miles on US 441 and get on the **Blue Ridge Parkway** at its southern terminus just inside the entrance to the park. Exit 14 miles later at US 19, and drive east through **Maggie Valley** (yes, there really was a Maggie — you'll find countless depictions of her in a yellow bonnet and apron on signs and souvenirs here). About 13 miles east of Maggie Valley, connect with Interstate 40 for the final 23 miles to **Asheville**. As you approach the mountain city, exit onto the I-240 west loop, then get off at the Montford Avenue exit and swing back under I-240 to get to a recommended bed and breakfast in the Montford District.

Places to Eat

Open your picnic basket at Elkmont Campground or an overlook on Newfound Gap Road — wherever you are when the hungries strike. For lunch at a restaurant, duck into busy Gatlinburg, just two miles north of the Sugarlands visitors center. The **Pancake Pantry** serves breakfast all day and gourmet sandwiches, soups and salads for lunch. **Ogle's Buffet** is a long-time Gatlinburg favorite where you're invited to go back for seconds. **J. Arthur's** is a pleasant country restaurant on US 19 in Maggie Valley.

Tonight in Asheville enjoy the good times at **Smoky Mountain Barbecue and Bluegrass** (formerly Bill Stanley's) at 20 Spruce Street, (704) 253-4871. There's usually fiddlin' and cloggin' and the food is hearty and very inexpensive. **23 Page**, now in the Heywood Park Hotel, (704) 252-3685, serves European and American entrees from about $10 in a quiet, candlelit atmosphere. Retreat to 1950s ambiance and traditional specials at **Westside Grill** on Patton Avenue (252-0956). On Tunnel Road try **The Windmill European Grill** (253-5285) for German and Italian, and **China Palace** (298-7898) for excellent oriental choices. An insider's favorite for family meals is the come-as-you-are **Mountain View Restaurant** on Brevard Road (667-8877).

Places to Stay

Asheville is blessed with several very comfortable bed and breakfasts, particularly in the lovely Victorian Montford District. **AppleWood Manor** is tucked away in a wooded garden setting at 62 Cumberland Circle. Fresh flowers in your room and fresh-baked breads with homemade preserves and orange pecan waffles or brie omelette at breakfast will make for a dreamy stay. Rooms from $75 to $100; call (704) 254-2244 for reservations. Also in Montford are **The Lion and the Rose**, 255-ROSE, Tudor-style **Cornerstone Inn**, 253-5644, **Flint Street Inns**, 253-6723 — two turn-of-the-century homes that share a charming English garden — and **Carolina Bed & Breakfast**, 254-3608.

In the Biltmore Estate area you'll find the **Cedar Crest Victorian Inn**, (504) 252-1389, prices from $45 to $60. Homemade afghans keep you cozy at **Aberdeen**, 254-9336. A tower overlooks Biltmore Village at the rustic **Reed House**, 274-1604. Breakfast is served on the wraparound porch where you can enjoy the view from a rocker or porch swing. There's an outdoor hot tub at **Corner Oak Manor**, 253-3525. (If there's no room at the inns, you'll find older motels along Patton Avenue and newer ones on Tunnel Road.)

The legendary **Grove Park Inn**, once the paragon of American mountain resorts, is described in *Discovery Day 14*.

Places to Camp

First choice is **Smokemont**, three miles north of the Oconaluftee visitors center and six miles north of Cherokee, in Great Smoky Mountains National Park. Although Smokemont is open all year, reservations are necessary from May through October — only through Mystix, 9450 Carroll Park Drive, San Diego, CA 92121; (619) 452-0150.

Cherokee has two dozen full-hookup campgrounds, including **Happy Holiday**, (704) 497-7250, **Adventure Trail**, 497-3651, and relaxing **Fort Wilderness**,

497-9331. *Special Note:* The inns in Asheville are so nice and so convenient that campers should consider moving indoors tonight.

Useful Tips

For information updates from Great Smoky Mountains National Park call (615) 436-1200 or (704) 497-9146. For more about Cherokee, (800) 438-1601; Gatlinburg, (800) 822-1998; Pigeon Forge, (800) 221-9858. To get an interesting one-hour auto Tape Tour of the Smokies to narrate your drive, send $11.95 to CC Inc, P.O. Box 385, Scarsdale NY 10583.

Linger Longer

Here are three very different ways to linger in the Smokies:

Trip #1: Waterfalls Wonderland — Tucked away in the Nantahala and Pisgah National Forests south of Cherokee are a series of waterfalls and small mountain resort villages that make for a lovely day or half-day adventure. Take US 441 south from Cherokee about 30 miles toward Franklin, North Carolina. Turn east on US 64 and drive along the **Cullasaja River Gorge**, viewing Dry Falls and Bridal Veil Falls on your way to into **Highlands**. Near **Cashiers** (pronounced *CASH-ers*), lovely Toxaway Falls cascades 125 feet below the highway. If you can't tear yourself away from the beauty of it all, stay at **Victorian Old Edwards Inn** in Highlands, (704) 526-5036. Continue east on US 64 to Brevard, then turn left at US 276 which offers more wonderful waterfalls and brings you back to the Blue Ridge Parkway about 25 miles from Asheville. This loop from Cherokee to Asheville is about 140 miles.

Trip #2: Gatlinburg and Pigeon Forge — Gatlinburg, a sort of mountain Las Vegas without the slot machines, huddles up to the park about two miles north of the Sugarlands visitors center. Farther north along US 441's intense strip of tourist tee-shirt shops, wax museums, wedding chapels, and an Elvis Hall of Fame, is burgeoning Pigeon Forge.

Dolly Parton's **Dollywood** is a surprisingly tasteful and engaging country theme park across the Little Pigeon River from the highway hubbub. There's an emphasis on mountain folklore and, of course, country music, but the biggest attraction is the eagles. Through a unique arrangement with the National Foundation to Protect American Eagles (NFPAE), Dollywood has become both hospital and home for injured and ill bald and golden eagles and other birds of prey. After rehabilitation, many are returned to the wild, but those deemed "unreleaseable" become permanent residents of the **Wild Birds of Prey** aviary and star in a dramatic and instructive 30-minute show that puts you up close with the big birds. Dollywood is open daily from May through October; adults $19.99, children 4-11 $13.99 (tickets bought after 3 p.m. will get you in free the next day). Call (615) 428-9488 for Dollywood's exact times, which change with the seasons.

Yankees sit on one side of the arena and Rebs on the other at **Dixie Stampede** in Pigeon Forge, an action-packed, two hour "dinner attraction" wild-west drama, with Brahma bull riding for dessert; shows at 6 and 8:30 p.m., adults $21.95, kids $13.95, (615) 453-4400. Watch mountain craftspeople at their work in some 40 studios and shops along an eight-mile loop at **Great Smoky Arts and Crafts Community**, three miles east of Gatlinburg on US 321. Get a bird's eye view of the mountains from the Aerial Tramway that sails regularly from downtown Gatlinburg to the **Ober Gatlinburg** ski complex; adults $5, kids $2. A dozen miles further on US 321 will take you to Cosby, Tennessee, and the **St. Francis House of Peace**, an interesting cross-shaped hewn-log building with no locks — you're welcome to pray or meditate there night or day.

Staying the night? Both Gatlinburg and Pigeon Forge are packed with resort inns, motor lodges, condominiums, and guest houses in all price ranges; call **Smoky Mountain Accomodations**, (800) 231-2230. Several close-in hostelries such as the **Brookside Resort**, (615) 236-5611, have rooms with balconies overlooking a rocky stream. The rustic **Wonderland Hotel** (1912) is actually inside the park near Elkmont Campground; take life easy in one of the many rockers on the veranda. The Wonderland serves three meals a day; rooms $39-$70, (615) 436-5490. You have to hike in to remote but popular **LeConte Lodge**, (615) 436-4473.

Trip #3: Great Smokies Backcountry — Park and lock your car, slip on your pack, and walk into the wilderness for a day and a night. The park is laced with more than 900 miles of hiking trails and 96 hike-in backcountry camp-sites. Pick up the very complete *Great Smokies Trail Map* and *Walks and Hikes* guide to the most popular trails at any ranger station. Then write your own very simple backcountry permit. There's no charge for your permit, but call (615) 436-1231 if you want to stay over at one of the rationed shelter camp-sites. Also ask to see the Park Service's detailed *Trail and Campsite Notebooks*, to help you decide which backcountry trail and destination is for you. Many trails connect with the roads you'll be driving through the park.

DISCOVERY DAY 14

Asheville and the Blue Ridge Parkway

NESTLED BETWEEN THE SMOKIES and the Blue Ridge, homey, gracious Asheville was synonymous with "mountain resort" for the movers and shapers of twentieth century America. Thomas Edison, Henry Ford, the Rockefellers, and a bevy of Presidents came up here to get away from it all. You'll see what unlimited money and good taste can accomplish as you lose yourself in the Biltmore Estate's 250-room French Renaissance chateau, one of the most lavish private homes ever built.

This afternoon, take a dramatic crestline drive along the Blue Ridge Parkway to Mount Mitchell, highest point this side of the Mississippi River. Pause at a refreshing waterfall overlook above Linville Gorge, then return through the heartland of Appalachia to Asheville.

Timetable Suggestion

8:00 a.m.	Breakfast at your Montford District B&B.
9:00 a.m.	Literary sleuthing at Thomas Wolfe's home.
10:00 a.m.	Explore the fabulous Biltmore Estate.
Noon	Lunch at one of Biltmore's restaurants, then visit the formal gardens or the winery.
2:15 p.m.	Head up the Blue Ridge Parkway.
3:30 p.m.	Environmental lesson at Mt. Mitchell.
4:30 p.m.	Walk the trail to Linville Falls overlooks, or —
5:00 p.m.	Gaze across the Southern Highlands from Grandfather Mountain.
6:30 p.m.	Head back to Asheville through Spruce Pine.
8:00 p.m.	Dinner and music at Bill Stanley's Barbecue & Bluegrass.

Getting to know Asheville

This pleasant city of 60,000, the metropolis of the North Carolina highlands, made its mark as a summer resort for the well-to-do — but more important to you (and most who live in the region) is its location in the midst of a mountain domain of Appalachian culture and marvelous expressions of nature. Here merge the French Broad and Swannanoa rivers. The **Blue Ridge Parkway** skirts around Asheville just to the south and east. Asheville's street

ASHEVILLE, NORTH CAROLINA

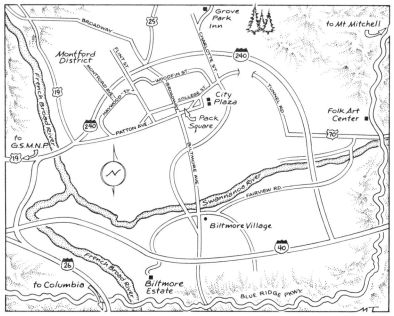

patterns can be confusing, with several main routes that unexpectedly change names and directions, so take a moment with the map to orient yourself. **Interstate 40** runs west-to-east just south of Asheville; I-240 takes off from I-40 to the west of the city and loops over just north of downtown. **US 25** runs north to south through the city as Merrimon Avenue, Broadway and Lexington avenues, Biltmore Avenue, and Henderson Road. Patton Avenue runs west to east, merging into College Street just beyond **Pack Square** in heart of town. You'll know when you're at Pack Square because of the giant obelisk in honor of Civil War governor Zebulon Vance. Keep going east on College and you'll be on Tunnel Road (US 70) heading east toward the Blue Ridge Parkway. (You can also reach the Parkway by heading south on Biltmore Avenue/US 25.)

Downtown Asheville today faces an architectural identity crisis; fascinating older buildings in a variety of fanciful styles compete with some awkward attempts at blocky glass-and-steel conformity. At **City/County Plaza**, just east of Pack Square, the weird and wonderful (some say just weird) pink granite art deco city building stands in contrast to the stately (some say stuffy) Greek Revival county building. Asheville's newish civic center complex is on **Haywood Street** — about where it can't decide whether it's Flint Street running north, or still Haywood Street making a gradual 180-degree swing to the west and south. Inside the loop thus formed by Haywood and Patton streets are Wall Street, Battery Park and Page avenues, which have interesting small shops and restaurants.

The rediscovered **Montford District**, now undergoing a gradual and well-deserved renovation, is on rolling hills just across I-240 northwest of downtown; get there by taking Flint Street or Montford Avenue across I-240. Keep the map handy to avoid disorientation.

The Best to See and Do

❀ ❀ **Thomas Wolfe Memorial** — "You can't go home again," wrote Thomas Wolfe — but you can go to the boyhood home of this tormented and brilliant novelist, and explore it almost exactly as it was when his mother ran a boarding house here. Detail for detail, this rambling, porch-skirted white frame Victorian at 48 Spruce Street is the Dixieland Boardinghouse of Wolfe's autobiographical first novel, *Look Homeward, Angel*. Ring the doorbell and a guide will appear; open 9 a.m. to 5 p.m. except Sunday mornings (adults $1, students 50 cents). Wolfe and short story master O. Henry are both buried in Asheville's Riverside Cemetery.

❀ ❀ ❀ **Biltmore Estate** — Zillionaire George W. Vanderbilt, heir to a railroad baron's bundle that makes today's fortunes seem like small change, thought it would be nice to have a tasteful house in the country. So a thousand men started to work in 1890, and by Christmas Eve, 1895, the Vanderbilts and their guests could relax by the fire in grand splendor within the 250-room centerpiece of the most lavish estate ever built on this continent. High-ceilinged halls, galleries, and room after opulent room are decorated with rare art and sculpture from throughout the world: gaze at the chess set Napoleon took with him on exile to St. Helena, priceless Ming Dynasty china, and portraits by Sargent and other masters. Vanderbilt was a man of innovation as well as taste — the place includes the first indoor bowling alley and early-day automatic clothes washers and dryers to make things easier for the help.

Stroll the English walled formal garden, Italian garden, and vast rose garden — all designed by Frederick Law Olmsted, the same fellow who planned New York's Central Park. Beyond lie 7,000 acres of private forest lands, pasture and vineyards — roaming room fit for any king. Red wines, whites, rosés, and sparkling wines are made at the **Biltmore Estate Winery**, where you may tour and taste.

Biltmore is south of downtown Asheville. Reach the entrance gate by taking Broadway/Biltmore Avenue (US 25) south and turning right just after you cross the Swannanoa River. If you're coming in from the west on Interstate 40, take exit 50 onto US 25 and go three blocks north to the gate. The house and grounds are open daily from 9 a.m. to 7 p.m., but the ticket office closes at 5 p.m.; admission is $18.95 for adults, students $14, kids under 12 free. Call (704) 255-1700 to find out about seasonal events.

❀❀ **Grove Park Inn** — E. Wiley Grove made a pile of cash selling Bromo-Quinine health tonic but took his own chronic bronchitis to the mountain air for a cure. Here at Asheville's Sunset Mountain he decided to build "the finest resort hotel in the world . . . full of rest and comfort and wholesomeness," and hired his untrained son-in-law to design and build it. Opened in 1913 (complete with a William Jennings Bryan speech), the place remains a classy monument of rustic architecture. Huge granite boulders were hoisted into place for the walls; the 120-foot-long Great Hall features two massive rock fireplaces that are fueled by tree trunks; furniture, carpets and copper fixtures were all handmade by an army of craftspeople. Nearly everyone who was rich and famous in the first half of the century slept here. Even if you don't, Grove Park Inn is worth a visit.

The basic room rate is $165 April-November, slightly less in winter; (800) 438-5800. For the full experience be sure your room is in the original Main Inn (F. Scott Fitzgerald's was room #441), not the two modern wings recently tacked on. Viewing the sunset from the terrace is an Asheville tradition. Take Charlotte Street north of I-240 to Macon Street to enter this splendid world.

❀ **Biltmore Industries Homespun Shops** — Mrs. George Vanderbilt founded Biltmore Industries in 1901 so that the children of Biltmore's many servants could turn mountain yarnmaking and wool-weaving traditions into income-producing trades. Adjacent to the Grove Park Inn, the buildings today are a free museum and gallery of traditional Appalachian crafts. Open Monday-Saturday 9 a.m. to 5:30 p.m. and Sundays 1 p.m. to 6 p.m. April through October; Monday-Saturday to 4:30 p.m. the rest of the year.

Blue Ridge Parkway (Travel Loop: 130 to 160 miles)

You'll feel like you're on top of the world as you drive the spectacular Blue Ridge Parkway, a winding and often windblown parkland highway that follows the highest ridges of the Appalachians from Great Smoky Mountains National Park to Shenandoah National Park in Virginia. Started in 1935 to provide Depression-era employment as well as to connect the two parks, the Blue Ridge Parkway was finally completed in 1987 — a 470-mile two-lane ribbon in the sky. Sometimes in spring, dark mist cascades in great rolls overhead across the highway — the Blue Ridge Parkway is a place of dramatic as well as tender moods. Like the Natchez Trace, it is part of the National Parks system, but because of the terrain the going is slower (speed limit: 45 mph). It has many tunnels and tight turns, and portions of it may be closed in winter or during bad weather. Parkway headquarters, (704) 259-0701, will give you travel conditions on the route.

Today you'll drive 66 miles on the Parkway (79 miles if you go as far as

Grandfather Mountain), then return to Asheville on another mountain highway through highlands towns in Yancey County.

From the Biltmore Estate, take Interstate 40 west to the US 74 exit and get on the Blue Ridge Parkway just south of the interchange. If you're in downtown Asheville, Tunnel Road (US 70 east) will also take you directly to the Parkway. You'll drive through the **Black Mountains**, which include Mount Mitchell, then along a stretch of the **Blue Ridge** itself. When you reach Linville Falls at Milepost 316, decide whether time and weather conditions will let you go as far as **Grandfather Mountain**, a 26-mile round trip from this point. Turn north on US 221, then go west four miles on Road 194 to Ingalls. Here you meet US 19E, and follow it through the mountain towns of **Spruce Pine**, Micaville, Burnsville, and Mars Hill back to Asheville. A few miles south of Micaville is **Celo**, a Quaker community founded on the principles of social theorist Arthur Morgan. South of Mars Hill, US 19 becomes a freeway, quickening your last 18 miles back to Asheville.

Along the Blue Ridge Parkway

❀❀ **Folk Art Center** — Housed in a surprisingly harmonious modern building beside the Blue Ridge Parkway, the Folk Art Center is operated by the Southern Highland Handicraft Guild as a museum of mountain handwork skills, a gallery of the best work of today's craftspeople, and a shop where you can choose from guild members' ironwork, dolls, brooms, stitchery, puppets, furniture, "whimmy diddle" toys, and other fine and clever creations. Learn from the artisans themselves as they throw a pot, stitch a coverlet from hand-dyed yarns, dance a reel, or pluck on a dulcimer (call 298-7928 to find out what will be going on when you arrive). The Folk Art Center is at Milepost 382, about half a mile north of where Tunnel Road (US 70) meets the Parkway. Open 9 a.m. to 5 p.m. every day (except major holidays), and often longer in summer and fall; free, but donations are encouraged.

❀ **Craggy Gardens** — Rhododendrons bloom in fiery profusion here in mid-June. Trails lead to the rhododendron balds and picnic areas from the visitor center at Milepost 365.

❀❀ **Mount Mitchell** — At 6,684 feet, this is the highest point in the U.S. east of the Mississippi. Turn off at Milepost 355 to Mount Mitchell State Park, stop near the summit, and take a short walk up to the observation tower. The dead and dying evergreen trees you see here are evidence of an ecological calamity — acid rain.

❀ **North Carolina Minerals Museum** — Make this stop near Milepost 331 if you're fascinated by mining and gemstones. It's open daily until 5 p.m. May through October (to 6 p.m. between Memorial Day and Labor Day); adults $3.50, seniors $3, students $2.50. For a little more, you can poke around in an emerald mine and visit the **Company Store** and **Antique Music Museum** at **Emerald Village**, near the town of Little Switzerland just off the Parkway.

❀❀ **Linville Gorge and Falls** — Stop at Milepost 316 and take the path that cuts through the rhododendron to get a close look at the bi-level waterfall cascading toward steep-walled Linville Gorge. The overlooks into the chasm may tempt hikers to explore the trails leading down to the rugged **Linville Gorge Wilderness** and surrounding **Pisgah National Forest**; check at the visitor center about trails and campsites.

❀❀ **Grandfather Mountain** — The panorama around you is breathtaking and vast from Grandfather Mountain, at 5,964 feet the highest point in the Blue Ridge range. The mountain, a suspension footbridge, and a native wildlife "environmental habitat area" along the road to the summit are part of a privately-owned preserve that's also one of North Carolina's most popular commercial attractions. Watch hangglider pilots soar off the mountain at 10:30 a.m. and 1, 3, and 4:30 p.m. daily, if the weather's okay.

Continue 13 miles past Linville Falls on the Blue Ridge Parkway to the US 221 intersection near the town of Linville. The road up the mountain is open daily 9 a.m. to dusk from April through mid-November, but only to 5 p.m. weekends in winter (weather permitting), (704) 733-4337; adults $7.50, children 4-12 $4. At this point you have the choice to go on (see *Linger Longer*) or return via either the Parkway or US 221 through Linville, Pineola and Crossnore, to get to the US 19 route back to Asheville.

Places to Dine

Pause for lunch right inside the Biltmore Estate at **Deerpark Restaurant** (274-1776), or the more casual **Stable Cafe**. **Stone Soup** at 50 Broadway and **The Bread Board** at 1000 Merrimon Avenue in Asheville feature healthy soups and salads. If you plan to be on the road, have a picnic made to order by Stone Soup or **The Movable Feast** (252-2837). At the **Grove Park Inn**, you have a choice of several restaurants including the outdoor Sunset Terrace, super-elegant Horizons, and the less formal Carolina Cafe (252-2711 for reservations at all three). **The Marketplace** on Wall Street (252-4162 — try the duck-stuffed ravioli!), and **Gatsby's** at 13 Walnut Street (254-4248), are very good downtown choices. **Turkish Ike's** on Merrimon Avenue is a lively Asheville favorite. (See also *Discovery Day 13*.)

Places to Camp

Lake Julian District Park, south of Asheville, is a good choice for tonight. Take Biltmore Avenue/Hendersonville Road (US 25) to just south of the Blue Ridge Parkway and turn right at State Road 280. Open all year, call 684-0376 before dark.

Useful Tips

Biltmore Village, adjacent to the entrance gate to the Biltmore Estate, was dreamed up by the Vanderbilts as a model village social experiment. Today these English-style buildings are shops and boutiques, some selling regional items. More little shops and galleries to prowl are in Asheville's **Wall Street** area downtown. **Malaprop's** at 61 Haywood Street is one of the South's most interesting bookshops; sip exotic coffees downstairs and have a sandwich there too.

Area code is (704) for all telephones in western North Carolina. For more about Asheville and the Southern Highlands call (800) 257-1300, or 258-3916 locally.

Linger Longer

Here are two tantalizing highlands excursions off the Blue Ridge Parkway:

Trip #1: Black Mountain — Take US 221 south at Linville Falls, drive about 20 miles through Pisgah National Forest, then turn right at US 70 just north of Marion. US 70 joins Interstate 40 at Old Fort; drive eight miles east and get off at Black Mountain. Check out the antique shops on Cherry Street, then stop for a drink at smokeless **McDibb's Bar**, a friendly hangout where you'll hear classical or sometimes live local music.

Trip #2: Mountain Towns — Leave the Blue Ridge Parkway at US 321. A turn south takes you to the **Blowing Rock**, where updrafts produce curious phenomena (open daily to 8 p.m. May through October, adults $3, kids $1). Two miles north of the parkway on US 321 is the terminal for the cutesy **Tweetsie Railroad**, a narrow-gauge coal-fired steam train that runs through a contrived western town complete with Indian raids and a shootout. Continue north about five miles to **Boone** (named after Daniel, who had a cabin here in the 1760s), a mountain music center. Go another six miles to Vilas and turn left on NC 194. Visit the **Mast General Store** in Valle Crucis, then keep going through Banner Elk, Cranberry, Minneapolis, and Plumtree. You'll now be on US 19 which takes you through Spruce Pine and Yancey County and back to Asheville.

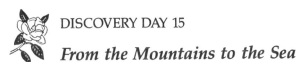

DISCOVERY DAY 15

From the Mountains to the Sea

TODAY YOU'LL SAIL DOWN from the mountains on Interstate 26 through the lush forests of South Carolina to the Carolina Low Country, then dine and sleep tonight in eighteenth-century Charleston, a city that lives and breathes her illustrious, revolutionary past.

On the way down, pause in the serenity of Connemara, the mountainside farm of poet/biographer Carl Sandburg, or wander the trails through Congaree Swamp's untouched stand of giant pines, cypresses and hardwoods.

Timetable Suggestion

8:00 a.m.	Breakfast.
9:15 a.m.	Depart Asheville.
10:00 a.m.	Walk Carl Sandburg's Connemara and muse, as he did, on Little Glassy Mountain. Pet the goats.
12:15 p.m.	Lunch in Greenville (or wait until Columbia).
2:30 p.m.	Cruise through Columbia, South Carolina's well-planned capital city.
6:00 p.m.	Check into your inn or B&B in Charleston.
7:00 p.m.	Dinner and nighttime fun in City Market area; stroll Waterfront Park along the Cooper River.

Magnolia Trail: Asheville to Charleston (300 miles)

From Asheville, take Interstate 40 or loop freeway I-240 west to where they merge. **Interstate 26** begins at this point, and you'll follow the I-26 signs towards Spartanburg, Columbia and Charleston. Soon you begin your descent from the mountains, crossing the Eastern Continental Divide. Leave I-26 at exit 23 (23 miles from Asheville) and follow the signs to **Flat Rock** and the Carl Sandburg Home; from US 25, turn left onto Little River Road at the Flat Rock Playhouse. The visitor center at Sandburg's Connemara is just to the left of the playhouse. After your visit, turn right and return to US 25.

Here you can choose to proceed south via either Spartanburg or Greenville, South Carolina. Both routes are scenic and about the same distance, with the Greenville route a little more leisurely. For the **Greenville** option, stay on US 25 past Tuxedo, across the state line, and down through wooded hills on a divided four-lane into Greenville. The four-lane becomes Business

ASHEVILLE TO CHARLESTON

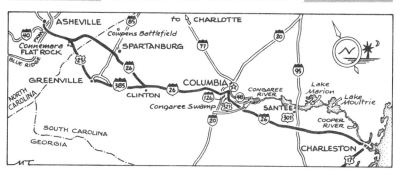

25/SC 276 as you enter the city. You'll pass the lovely fountains and gardens of the Furman University campus. Follow the SC 276 or Bypass 276 signs to the entrance to Interstate 385. This freeway whisks you out of Greenville toward a rendezvous with Interstate 26 at **Clinton**, 40 miles south. (If you want to make tracks after Connemara, retrace your route back to exit 23 on I-26, and head toward **Spartanburg**, a textile and peach-packing center. There's a South Carolina visitor center just beyond the state line. You'll pass Walnut Grove Plantation on your way toward Clinton and Columbia.)

One hour (55 miles) south of Clinton, I-26 skirts by **Columbia**, South Carolina's capital. Take Interstate 126 across the Congaree River and straight into Columbia's compact downtown. Turn right at Huger Street, and look on your right for the South Carolina State Museum and visitor information center. Depart Columbia by turning right on Blossom Street (US 176/321), cross the Congaree and follow the signs to rejoin Interstate 26 south.

South of Columbia the land flattens out: you're now in the South Carolina **Low Country**, forested with crepe myrtle and loblolly pines (forests cover 70 percent of the state). Drive 120 miles on Interstate 26 from Columbia to Charleston, where the freeway ends. Take the King Street or Meeting Street exit straight into the heart of enchanting **Charleston**.

Getting to know South Carolina

A palmetto tree in the middle of the state flag stands for South Carolinians' admirable and cussed resistance to outside authority: in 1776, British cannon-balls bounced harmlessly off a palmetto-log fortress on Sullivan's Island in the first decisive American victory of the Revolutionary War. Francis "Swamp Fox" Marion harassed the British from his watery hideaways, and Gen. Thomas "Gamecock" Sumter finally drove the British out of the state. It didn't end there. In 1860, South Carolina was the first state to secede from the Union, and the War Between the States began here when a rebel shell exploded over Fort Sumter in Charleston harbor. Most South Carolinians I've met have both a sense of pride and a wonderful sense of humor in regard to their illustrious past.

Your eighth-grade teacher may have explained how mountains, piedmont and coastal plain make up the geography of the Southeastern states, but South Carolinians recognize just two regions — Upcountry and Low Country. Tidy Columbia is smack dab on the Fall Line between Upcountry and Low Country. Columbia's neat grid of streets on the east bank of the Congaree River makes it easy to appreciate on a short visit. Occupying an historic old textile mill, the visitor center and State Museum are on Huger Street where it crosses Gervais Street. Turn left onto Gervais, go to Assembly Street, and you'll be at the State House, a hardy survivor of Sherman's deprivations.

The Best to See and Do

❀❀❀ **Carl Sandburg Home National Historic Site** — The Pulitzer Prize-winning historian and poet needed a quiet place to study, write and play his guitar; his wife Paula needed a place to raise goats. They found it in the bucolic mountains and pastures of Flat Rock, North Carolina. Here they lived and worked for 22 years, and you can see and touch the things that filled their busy lives. While Sandburg read and labored at his typewriter into the wee hours in his crowded upstairs study, then sang and played folk songs in the afternoon, Paula and their daughters managed the farm and tended the grandchildren. Paula Sandburg was known worldwide for her prizewinning chikaming, nubian and toggenburg goat herds, the descendants of which still live at Connemara.

The farmhouse remains just as the Sandburgs lived in it, with stacks of magazines and papers and simple but useful furnishings. The walls are lined with thousands of well-thumbed-through books, and cardboard boxes filled with correspondence, clippings and notes fill the basement. Pause a moment in Sandburg's cluttered study; his typewriter sits atop an orange crate with his green eyeshade nearby. He could have walked out of the room a moment ago. Downstairs, Paula's desk reveals the accolades she received for her goat breeding program. Let yourself be charmed by the "goat nursery" in the basement, and be sure to see the brief video of Edward R. Murrow interviewing Sandburg at Connemara.

Walk the short distance up to **Little Glassy**, a broad rock a hundred yards or so up from the farmhouse, or, if there's time, take the Spring Trail 1.3 miles up to **Big Glassy Mountain**, where you can enjoy, as Sandburg did, an unobstructed view of the Blue Ridge. Then walk down to the main goat barn to pet the lovely goats. Connemara opens at 9 a.m., the first farmhouse tour begins at 10 a.m. Open every day except Christmas, admission $1. Allow at least an hour and a half for your visit.

❦ **Cowpens National Battlefield** — Here's an important Revolutionary War site where the clever strategy of Daniel Morgan routed much larger forces under the command of British Col. Banastre Tarleton in January 1781. *Daybreak at the Cowpens* slideshow explains the battle (adults $1, children 50 cents). Take I-85 from Greenville through Spartanburg, then US 221 north for 10 miles.

❦ **South Carolina State House** — Sherman's cannons shelled the almost-new capitol in 1865, and bronze stars mark the places where cannonballs struck. It's in the heart of Columbia on Gervais Street, seven blocks east of Huger Street. Free tours go every half hour, Monday through Friday.

❦ **McKissick Museum** — This free museum on the University of South Carolina campus in downtown Columbia includes a priceless collection of 20th Century Fox "Movietone News" newsreels preserving haunting images of pre-television filmed history, as well as an impressive Art Nouveau collection. The McKissick is open every day except holidays and it's free.

❦ **Riverbanks Zoo** — Most of the 1,500 animals, including sea lions, penguins and a rare Siberian tiger, live in almost-like-home environments (no cages, except for the birds) at one of the Southeast's best zoos. It's just off I-126 as you come into Columbia. Adults $3.75, seniors $2.50, children $.75; open 9 a.m. to 4 p.m. daily.

❦ ❦ **Congaree Swamp National Monument** — Here is the last significant stand of virgin riverbottom hardwood forest in the United States, as well as towering old cypresses and loblolly pines. Such rich swamp environments once stretched from Maryland to Texas, but nearly all were decimated by loggers beginning in the 1880s. Frequent flooding is this swamp's "secret" — continually enriching the ground beneath and perpetually creating an environmentalist's paradise. Stroll the boardwalk to Weston Lake, take one of the loop trails, and escape into the wilderness that protected Francis Marion, the legendary Swamp Fox, and his band of American revolutionaries. You'll feel as the Swamp Fox did: "I look at the venerable trees around me and know that I must not dishonor them."

To get to Congaree Swamp, take Assembly Street south from downtown Columbia and veer right onto Bluff Road/SC 48 at the State Fairgrounds. The park entrance is just off SC 48, 20 miles southeast of Columbia. Open 8:30 a.m. to 5 p.m. every day; canoeing is a delight here, but you have to bring your own or rent one in Columbia. After your visit, take a country drive shortcut by turning right on SC 48. Turn right again on US 601 and drive 23 miles to Interstate 26 south.

Places to Dine
After today's long drive, choose one of the several tempting restaurants

you'll find along both sides of Charleston's night-lively City Market. Prices are generally reasonable, and you'll enjoy the best array of fresh seafood since you left Louisiana — including Charleston's own she-crab soup. **Cafe 99** at 99 South Market Street, (803) 577-4499, features casual indoor and patio dining until midnight, with musical performers both inside and outside (weather permitting) until 2 a.m. Choose from over 40 entrees, including seafood platters from $10 to $13. Right next door, **Mistral Restaurant** (722-5708) serves country French and seafood cuisine at moderate ($10-$15) prices. Try the dreamy shrimp pecarte (jumbo shrimp stuffed with crab meat in a bed of pasta) at **Port City Cafe**, 36 North Market Street (577-5000). In the old Seaman's Chapel at the corner of East Bay and Market streets are **Cafe 32** and the **L.A. Grill** (723-3614), which has a wide-ranging international menu. **Appleby's Neighborhood Grill** at 24 North Market Street (723-3531) serves an eclectic menu including seafood, steaks and marinated chicken from $5 to about $10. **Tommy Condon's Irish Tavern** on Church Street will give you a warm welcome. Reservations are advised for Mistral, L.A. Grill, and Port City Cafe. (See *Discovery Day 16* for more Charleston restaurants.)

As you come into Greenville, **Gene's Restaurant** on Business 25 makes a convenient lunch stop; **Braden's** at 1818 Augusta Street (242-5998) has historic South Carolina atmosphere and an award-winning menu. Lunchtime in Columbia? Try the **Seaboard Diner** at the Amtrak station just off Gervais Street, **S&S Cafeteria** at 1411 Gervais, or the vegetarian **Basil Pot** on Rosewood Drive.

Places to Stay

Convenient lodging in Charleston can be expensive. Call well ahead of time for reservations if you plan to be here on a springtime weekend, or you may find yourself roomless. Call several months ahead if your arrival corresponds with the Spoleto Festival (May-June). On the plus side, once you're here you can walk everywhere.

Elegant inns and B&Bs abound in charming Charleston. Ask about off-street parking when you call for reservations. **Cannonboro Inn**, 184 Ashley Avenue, has six Victorian rooms with fireplaces, private baths, and off-street parking; rates from about $70, (803) 723-8572. You get a gourmet breakfast and have free use of 10-speed bicycles for touring. **Two Meeting Street Inn** (723-7322) is a Queen Anne mansion right on the Charleston's Battery (book well in advance). Enjoy gourmet breakfast in the formal dining room at **1837 Tearoom/Bed and Breakfast**, 126 Wentworth Street (723-7166). **Rutledge Victorian Guest House**, 114 Rutledge Avenue (722-7551), offers comfortable B&B values starting at $45 with continental breakfast. **The Hayne House** is one block from the Battery at 30 King Street (577-2633). Pricier ($80 and up) inns in the heart of Charleston include **133 Broad Street B&B** (577-0392),

Kings Courtyard Inn, 198 King Street (800/845-6119), and **Maison DuPre**, 317 East Bay (723-8691), where you're invited to "Low Country Tea."

Many Charlestonians offer hospitality in their own homes. For information and reservations call **Charleston Society Bed and Breakfast**, (803) 723-4948, or Charlotte Fairey at **Historic Charleston Bed and Breakfast**, 722-6606. Bear in mind that lodging rates in Charleston are often seasonal, with highest tariffs in the spring and best bargains in late winter. Downtown Charleston is often completely booked on spring weekends and during Spoleto Festival. As a last resort, try the franchise hotel cluster on Spring and Cannon streets near the entrance to the Ashley River Bridge, or the group of chain motels up I-26 at Montague Avenue (exit 213) in North Charleston.

Places to Camp

There's now a very nice, full-service RV campground close to Charleston, thank goodness. **The Campground at James Island County Park**, (803) 795-9884, is about 12 minutes from downtown, across the Ashley River off US 17 and the Folly Beach Road, on Riverland Drive. Leave your vehicle and take the convenient shuttle into town. Before hurricane *Hugo*, overnight van and RV camping was allowed in the back parking lot at **Patriots Point** near the *Yorktown*. It's quiet, safe, has a wonderful view of the harbor, great access to Charleston attractions, and was free. At this writing, the camping policy has been suspended. However, since long-range plans call for an eventual campground facility at Patriots Point, it may be worth your while to get an update: (301) 884-2727 or 881-4231.

Otherwise, try **Charleston KOA**, 15 miles northwest of the city on US 78 (797-1045); **Oaks Plantation Campground**, eight miles from town on US 17 south (766-5936); or **Lake Aire RV Park** in Rantowles (571-1271).

Evening Fun

Charlestonians feel safe and comfortable strolling their downtown at night, and so should you. Take in the music at or near where you dine tonight in the **City Market** district. Wander both sides of Market Street from King Street to the fountains of refreshing **Charleston Waterfront Park** along the Cooper River. Stop in where the sounds and the atmosphere appeal to you.

Linger Longer: Santee Cooper

Have an extra day for lolling around? Exit at US 301, 40 miles south of Columbia, and drive 16 miles east to Santee, **Lake Marion** and **Lake Moultrie**. Enjoy catfish and bass fishing, boating and golf. Camp at **Santee State Park** or stay overnight at one of dozens of lakefront fishing camps and inns in the Santee Cooper recreational region. Return via Interstate 95 to the main route to Charleston.

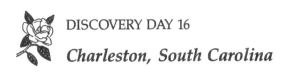

DISCOVERY DAY 16

Charleston, South Carolina

SOMEHOW, THE TWENTIETH CENTURY skipped almost the entire lower peninsula of Charleston, South Carolina.

This doesn't bother "livin' in the past" Charlestonians one bit.

Charleston is America's most intact colonial city — there are some 1,500 historic buildings south of Calhoun Street — yet it's a miracle everything's still here. In 300 years the city has endured recurrent floods, hurricanes, tornadoes, epidemics, five major fires, and a big earthquake in 1886. Charlestonians point with pride to the seemingly whimsical "earthquake bolts" that keep many old brick buildings in one piece.

More than just renowned architecture, Charleston is an entire gracious antebellum attitude and way of life preserved between the Ashley and the Cooper rivers (both wryly named after the same fellow: Ashley Cooper, the Third Earl of Shaftesbury, one of the city's eight blueblood founders). Charlestonians have a mirthful attitude about their preoccupation with the past. Pivotal in both the American Revolution and the birth of the Confederacy, Charleston is sometimes called the Holy City — not only for its many church steeples but, some say, because folks here fervently worship their ancestors.

Timetable Suggestion

8:15 a.m.	Leisurely B&B breakfast.
9:00 a.m.	Take Jack Thomson's Civil War Walking Tour (or my self-guided walking tour if it's his day off).
10:00 a.m.	See *Dear Charleston* at the Preservation Society, or enjoy "Livin' in the Past" van tour of the city.
11:00 a.m.	Explore the Aiken-Rhett mansion.
12:30 p.m.	Lunch in the past at Moultrie Tavern.
1:15 p.m.	Drive over the Cooper River to Patriot's Point, wander through aircraft carrier *Yorktown*, then explore Fort Moultrie.
Afternoon	Visit Magnolia Plantation on the Ashley River, or shop at City Market and along King Street.
7:30 p.m.	Dinner cruise around Charleston Harbor.
9:45 p.m.	Music at City Market, or say goodnight.

Getting to know Charleston

When the South rises again, it's likely to start in Charleston. Despite the city's tranquil elegance and easygoing contentment with the way things were, it's been a hotbed of rebellion. The first decisive victory of the American Revolution (at Fort Moultrie in 1776) and the first shots of the War Between the States (Fort Sumter, 1861) both happened here.

Plantations of rice and indigo and a prosperous merchant class made Charleston America's richest city before Civil War. In her narrow streets with names like King and Queen, cobblestone-paved alleys, dainty gardens, and formal buildings, Charleston still feels English — and would even more so if not for her delicate-looking subtropical *piazzas* (porches). The typical Charleston two-story single house has two front doors — a formal one at the street that opens to the long, open piazza, and a second door from the piazza into the house. It's the only city I know of where you can see what's behind the front door even when it's closed!

Both blacks and whites seem happy to live in another time. True to the city's tradition of rebellion, black citizens around Spring Street not long ago vetoed the city's plan to declare their historic neighborhood officially historic — thus slowing the advance of "white blight" gentrification into their stable community.

Charleston's downtown and historic district are one in the same, occupying virtually the entire area south of US 17, which crosses the peninsula and connects the main bridges over the Ashley and Cooper rivers. Main arteries north-south through downtown include **Rutledge Avenue**, and **King, Meeting** and **East Bay** streets. **Calhoun, Market/Beaufain, Broad** and **Tradd** streets run east to west across the peninsula. Having been laid out by the English, Charleston's narrow, cobblestone side streets zig and zag and meet at odd angles — in fact, there's one named Zig Zag Alley. The areas west and east of the rivers are logically referred to as West Ashley and East Cooper. **Sullivan's Island** and **Isle of Palms** are to the east across the Cooper River.

Plan well ahead of time if you want to visit Charleston in the springtime. The two-week **Spoleto Festival of Arts** (see *Fairs, Feasts and Festivals*), brought here by Gian-Carlo Menotti in 1977, fills every room in the city. Atlantic breezes in summer and very late, mild winters make Charleston pleasant just about anytime.

Walking Charleston

This is a wonderfully compact walking city with history and beauty around every corner. Most places of interest are between King Street and East Bay Street from Calhoun Street down to the Victorian mansions along Battery Park at the tip of the peninsula. Here's a quick walking route:

Beginning at the **City Market**, walk south on Church Street, turn right on

Cumberland, then left down Meeting Street. At Broad Street you'll encounter the **Four Corners of Law**, where local, state, federal and divine authority are neatly represented by City Hall, the County Courthouse, the post office, and St. Michael's Episcopal Church (patterned after London's St. Martin's-in-the-Field). Turn right on Tradd Street to see fine examples of Charleston single and double houses, replete with earthquake bolts and "Charleston green" shutters. Take pretty Legare Street down to South Battery Street and turn left. One block later you're at **Battery Park**. You may want to pause to enjoy the view and the breeze here, where (as many a Charleston child has been told) the Ashley and Cooper rivers merge to form the Atlantic Ocean.

At 16 Meeting Street just off Battery Park is the richly detailed Calhoun Mansion, still a private home but open for your ooh's and ah's. Note the rope design framing the doors and windows, a Charleston symbol for the home of a merchant. Continue around the Battery and take East Battery Street up to Water Street, turn left, then turn right up Church Street past the Heyward-Washington House and **Cabbage Row** of *Porgy and Bess* fame. A right turn at Elliott Street and a left onto East Bay will lead you the handsome corner at Broad Street where you'll see the **Old Exchange and Provost Dungeon**. Take Broad Street two blocks to Church Street and turn right. On Chambers Street, to your right, is the **Old Slave Mart**, now a museum of black history (usually open from 10 a.m. to 5 p.m., adults $3, kids 75 cents). Continue north on Church Street past the Huguenot Church and back to the City Market.

Tours abound in Charleston, but two stand out. Historian Jack Thomson's two-hour **Civil War Walking Tour** of Charleston starts at 9 a.m. Wednesday through Sunday from the courtyard of the Mills House Hotel, 115 Meeting Street. Call him at (803) 722-7033 for reservations; adults $10, kids under 12 free. **Livin' in the Past**, 871-0791, is my favorite van tour. It's fun, the guides are excellent, and three daily two-hour excursions include a lingering walk through the Edmondston-Alston House on the Battery. One-hour tours start every half hour beginning at 9:15 a.m.; the two-hour tours start at 10 a.m., noon, and 2 p.m. (adults $15, children $8). Call ahead and they'll stop for you at any downtown inn or site along the route.

The Best to See and Do

❀❀❀ **The Battery** — Lined along the north side by this old city's finest Victorian mansions, Battery Park (sometimes called White Point Gardens) is where Charleston opens up to meet the sea. Pause amid the palmettos, live oaks, war monuments, ghosts, and live Charlestonians, and gaze out across the water. It's easy to imagine the emotions felt here when that first shell exploded over Fort Sumter in 1861.

❀❀ *Dear Charleston* — Whimsical, insightful and intelligent, this wonder-

CHARLESTON, SOUTH CAROLINA

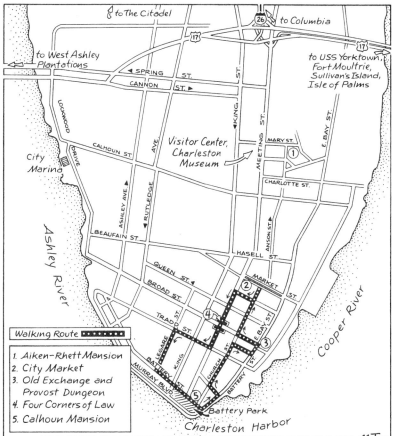

ful 42-minute show is the best film introduction to a city I've ever seen. You'll get a real insider's view of the character of Charleston and its people. *Dear Charleston* is presented at the Preservation Society Visitor Center at King and Queen Streets every day at 10 and 11 a.m., noon, and 2, 3, and 4 p.m.; adults $3, children $1.50, (803) 723-4381.

❀ **Old Exchange and Provost Dungeon** — In the upstairs Great Hall in 1774, South Carolina elected its delegates to the Continental Congress. Soon after, the British imprisoned three signers of the Declaration of Independence downstairs in the Provost Dungeon. Visit the brick catacombs of the dungeon for a scary look at eighteenth-century prison conditions: lifesize figures sit on straw in dank quarters with the roughest of provisions. Kids will be especially fascinated. The Old Exchange is at 122 East Bay Street at the end of Broad Street; open Monday through Saturday from 9:30 a.m. to 5 p.m., Sundays from 1 p.m.; adults $2.50, children $1, (803) 792-5020.

❀❀❀ **Aiken-Rhett Mansion** — You'll feel like you're in a newly-opened time capsule of Deep South history in this unrestored palace that was once the toast of Charleston. Although *Hugo's* winds forced the temporary closing of the second floor, I hope you'll find it open again by the time you arrive. If so, you'll step into a bedroom that stayed locked and untouched for 50 years (in mourning for the first Mrs. Rhett, who died there), until the Charleston Museum bought the place from the last Mrs. Rhett in 1972. At that time, her servants were still cooking over wood stoves in the courtyard.

Wonders keep turning up. There's a flushable chamber pot, mirrored petticoat table, and a pair of exquisite gilt vases bought 140 years ago in Paris and found in the attic still wrapped for the voyage across the Atlantic. General P.G.T. Beauregard headquartered on the third floor, and you'll see a letter from Jefferson Davis commenting on his stay here. This place is faded Southern glory at its absolute best! The Aiken-Rhett Mansion, 48 Elizabeth Street, is open from 10 a.m. to 5 p.m. daily (Sundays from 1 p.m.); adults $4, seniors $3.60, children $2, (803) 723-1159.

❀❀❀ **Charleston's Churches** — The tallest structures in downtown Charleston are its many soaring church steeples. **St. Michael's Episcopal** (1751), the French protestant **Huguenot Church** (1845), Catholic **St. Mary's** (1839), **Circular Congregational Church** (1681 and 1891) and **Beth Elohim** (1794 and 1840), the birthplace of the American Jewish Reform movement, are historic downtown houses of worship open weekday mornings on a regular basis so you can have a peek inside. You'll find most of them along my walking tour. Stop at the churchyard of **St. Philips Episcopal**, 146 Church Street, to see the graves of statesman John C. Calhoun, Declaration of Independence signer Edward Rutledge, U.S. Constitution signer Charles Pinckney, and *Porgy* author DuBose Heyward. The epitaphs are fascinating.

❀❀❀ **Patriot's Point/Carrier** *Yorktown* — This is the most complete hands-on maritime museum I've ever seen. In one stop you can wander around inside an old submarine, a destroyer that survived World War II kamikaze attacks, a Coast Guard cutter that sank a German U-boat, and the world's first nuclear merchant ship. Best of all, you have free range of the aircraft carrier *Yorktown*, the "Fighting Lady" of World War II and Vietnam. On both her hangar deck and flight deck are about 20 historic aircraft: an F-86 Sabre jet, a B-25 bomber, a restored gull-wing Corsair, and more. Painted stripes guide you on six different routes through this huge floating city. You can even take the helm in the pilot house and eat at the ship's cafeteria. From downtown, take the Cooper River Bridge and bear to your right on US 17 Business Route so you can make an immediate right turn into Patriot's Point. Open every day from 9 a.m. to 6 p.m. (to 5 p.m. November through March); see absolutely everything for $8, or $4 if you're a kid 6-11, (803) 722-1691.

❀❀❀ **Fort Moultrie** — Here you can see the whole history of American coastal defense, from 1776 through the fascinating technological changes of the Civil War and anti-submarine eras, until the fort went out of service in 1947. Two huge World War I era "disappearing" recoil rifles plus earlier and later big guns stand watch over the harbor. Perhaps the most fascinating part is the **World War II Command Post**, authentically maintained right down to the pinup calendars, *Collier's* magazines, tube radios, and Lucky Strike cigarettes. (It's easy to imagine General Ike walking in at any moment!)

After his courageous resistance in Florida, Seminole Chief Oceola was held at Fort Moultrie and was buried here.

If you pick just one historic fort to visit in the Charleston area, make it Fort Moultrie. Go east over the Cooper River and stay to the right on US 17 Business Route, then swing right on SC 703 to cross onto Sullivan's Island. Turn right at Middle Street and drive a mile and a half to the fort. Open from 9 a.m. to 5 p.m. (6 p.m. in summer), free, (803) 883-3123.

❀ **Fort Sumter** — Early one April morning in 1861, a Confederate mortar shell exploded directly above Fort Sumter — which sits on an island five miles out in Charleston Harbor — and the War Between the States was underway. (Independent South Carolinians just wanted the Federal presence to go away, but weren't very diplomatic about it.) The Yankees evacuated and Confederates moved in. For two years Confederate forces holding the fort weathered almost daily shelling that reduced the once impressive three-story bastion to a giant pile of bricks.

Despite Fort Sumter's place in history, there's not a lot of it left and it takes two and a half hours to get there and back. The lowest levels have been excavated and the National Park Service does a fine job interpreting what happened here and what remains. There's no charge once you're here, but there is for the boat ride. **Fort Sumter Tours**, (803) 722-1691, departs from both Patriot's Point (last boat at 4 p.m.) and the City Marina on the Ashley River (last trip usually 2:30 p.m.); adults $8, seniors $7, children $4.

❀❀ **City Market** — City Market's three pleasant blocks of open-air stalls is a great place to see Charleston's famous sweetgrass baskets being woven by the hands of black craftswomen and to shop for locally-made items from cotton dresses to cookies. Spend $1 to see Civil War curiosities such as the Palmetto Guard flag at the **Daughters of the Confederacy Museum** upstairs above the Market. Small antique stores, bookshops and galleries line King Street down from Market Street.

❀ **Harbor Tours** — Up the Cooper River is one of the world's largest naval bases, best seen on a boat tour that also includes a run past Fort Sumter and Patriot's Point in Charleston Harbor. The harbor tours of Fort Sumter Tours, Inc. (722-2628) and Gray Line (722-1112) run about two hours; adults $8, children $4. Both outfits also offer dinner cruises of the harbor.

❀❀ **Ashley River Plantations** — Pristine *Drayton Hall*, the first of three Low Country rice and indigo plantations along the Ashley River, is as original as a 1738 house can get. The oldest Palladian Georgian example in America and the Drayton's family home for seven generations, it's so original that it has *never* had electricity or inside water pipes. Fascinating are the intricate wood and molded plaster interior details. Cross the Ashley River and take SC 61/Ashley River Road for about nine miles. Hourly tours usually from 10 a.m. to 5 p.m., adults $6 (766-0188). Just a little farther up SC 61 are two old plantations renowned for their lush gardens and grounds, though their main houses are missing due to a fire and the Civil War. *Magnolia Plantation and Gardens*, still owned by the Drayton family after 300 years, gives you room to roam with canoe and nature trails, a horticultural maze, and the original estate garden with its 900 varieties of camellias. Open daily from 8 a.m. to 5 p.m. (Thursday through Saturday to 8 p.m. for moonlight strolls), adults $7 (571-1266). Henry Middleton and his son Arthur, who signed the Declaration of Independence, put some 100 slaves to work for ten years to create America's oldest landscaped gardens at *Middleton Place*. In the stableyards you may see a blacksmith, a candlemaker, a weaver, or a milkmaid, doing things once common at a self-sustaining Low Country planation in the years between the Revolution and the Civil War. Open daily from 9 a.m. to 5 p.m., adults $8 (556-6020).

❀ **Charles Towne Landing** — Here's where the English first settled in 1670, and though no original buildings still stand, you can climb aboard a replica of a seventeenth-century trading vessel. What makes this place special is the surrounding 663-acre forest park where animals native to the area in colonial times roam free. Take US 17 across the Ashley River, follow SC 171 to the right, and look for the entrance on Old Towne Road. Open daily to 5 p.m. (6 p.m. in the summer), great for picnics.

Places to Dine, Evening Fun

Step into **Moultrie Tavern** and you're back in 1862. It's a wonderfully underplayed re-creation, right down to the maids' costumes, the drinks, and much of the menu. For lunch, try the chicken or rabbit foragers pie (about $6), chicken and dumplings ($5), or an outrageously generous open-faced sandwich for just $4. If you're there for dinner, I suggest duck, rabbit or quail Confederate game pie ($14). Libations include English Bass ale on tap, a cider and bourbon toddy, or Madeira wine such as was favored by George

Washington. The past just doesn't get much better than this! Moultrie Tavern is at 18 Vendue Range, which takes off East Bay Street near the new Waterfront Park; open Monday through Saturday, 11:30 a.m. to 2:30 p.m. and from 6 p.m. for dinner, (803) 723-1876.

Why not take a romantic dinner cruise out in the harbor tonight? Call the *Spirit of Charleston*, (803) 722-2628, or Gray Line's *Charles Towne Princess*, 722-1112, before 1 p.m. for reservations. Both depart from the City Marina. Find Low Country specialties at **East Bay Trading Company** at the corner of East Bay and Queen streets, 722-0722, or **Poogan's Porch**, 72 Queen Street, 577-2337. (See *Discovery Day 15* for more Charleston restaurants.)

Places to Stay
See *Discovery Day 15*.

Useful Tips
Charleston's pleasant new **Visitor Reception and Transportation Center** (VRTC) is in a restored 1832 railroad warehouse on Meeting Street, between John and Ann Streets, across from the Charleston Museum. Here you can abandon your car and choose from an overwhelming array of van, carriage and walking tours (or just park and strike out on your own with this book in hand). The VRTC telephone number is (803) 722-8338. Reach the National Park Service (the forts and new Snee Farm unit) at 883-3123.

The Footlight Players perform at the **Dock Street Theatre** at Church and Queen streets, site of the oldest theatre in the Colonies. Call 723-5648 for information on productions and show times. Check the free *Omnibus* tabloid or the *Weekend* section of the *News-Courier* for entertainment updates.

Linger Longer
There's so much to see in Charleston, you may want to plan a second full day here. Care to take some time at the beach? Hurricane *Hugo* tore up man-made structures on **Isle of Palms**, but the beach is as beautiful as ever. **Ocean Inn** on Pavilion Drive happily survived the hurricane. Call Dena Wall, (803) 886-4687, for reservations (rates from $55). You'll be about 12 miles from downtown Charleston, across the Cooper River and out SC 703 through Sullivan's Island.

 DISCOVERY DAY 17

Savannah

SAVANNAH IS AS HISTORIC and intact as Charleston, yet its character is completely different. Shrouded under the arms of grand old oaks draped with long tendrils of Spanish moss, Savannah may be the quintessential Southern city. Twenty-two lush, quiet squares scattered throughout the nation's largest Historic Landmark District say to you, "relax and savor me."

Vary your stay with a visit to Fort Pulaski, a virtually original medieval-style moated fort, the last and best ever built.

Timetable Suggestion

8:00 a.m.	Breakfast, leave Charleston via US 17.
10:00 a.m.	Arrive at the Savannah visitor center.
11:00 a.m.	Stroll around Savannah's famous squares.
Noon	Lunch at Mrs. Wilkes' Boarding House.
2:30 p.m.	Drive to Fort Pulaski National Monument.
5:00 p.m.	Explore Factors Walk and River Street.
7:00 p.m.	Dinner at Garibaldi's or Elizabeth's.
9:00 p.m.	Music and good times on River Street.

Magnolia Trail: Charleston to Savannah (100 miles)

Cross the Ashley River and head west out of Charleston on US 17/Dixie Highway for about 50 miles. Turn left on US 21 at Garden's Corner and go 12 miles into pretty old **Beaufort** (pronounced *BYEW-furt*), boat-lined gateway to Fripp and St. Helena islands. For a short time after the Civil War these islands were granted to freed slaves; a few descendants hang on, some still speaking the unusual Gullah tongue.

Leave Beaufort on SC 170 across Port Royal Sound. Near the route is the big U.S. Marine Corps boot camp at **Parris Island**. Unless you're fascinated by the lifestyles of the terminally self-indulgent, forego the temptation to visit **Hilton Head Island**. Thickets of heavily landscaped, upscale condo developments (here dubbed "plantations") sport 300 private tennis courts and dozens of golf courses, all secured behind trendy guard booths. Cross the New River, bear left and take SC 170 Alternate and US 17 Alternate across the new Talmadge Bridge over the Savannah River into Georgia and downtown **Savannah**. Turn left at Oglethorpe Street, then right onto Martin Luther

CHARLESTON TO SAVANNAH

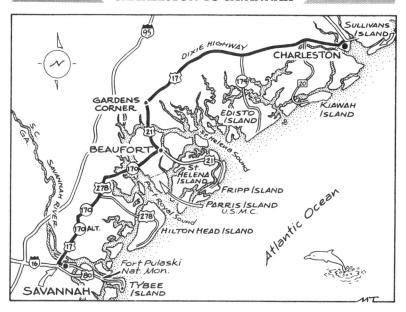

King, Jr. Boulevard. Stop one block later at the Savannah's excellent visitor center in the restored brick Central of Georgia Railroad Station. In the same building you will find the well-planned Savannah History Museum.

Georgia, largest state in the eastern U.S., is the home state of a number of very memorable folks, both real and mythical: Dr. Martin Luther King, Jr., Jimmy Carter, Scarlett O'Hara, Uncle Remus, and Pogo Possum.

Getting to know Savannah

General James Oglethorpe imagined his Georgia colony as a refuge for debtors and the oppressed. King George imagined Georgia as a handy buffer against the Spanish, and granted him a charter. Oglethorpe designed the 24 original garden-like squares himself, set up Savannah on a riverbank a dozen miles from the sea, and banned rum, slavery and lawyers. Utopia withered, but Savannah prospered for 100 years as the cotton trade center of the world.

Magnificent or modest, nearly all Savannah Historic District houses are built this unusual way: the street floor, vulnerable to floods, was reserved for servants and the kitchen; steps lead from street level up to the high and dry parlor floor, where the owner and his family lived. Today, street floor quarters are often rented as an apartment, as well as the carriage house

SAVANNAH, GEORGIA

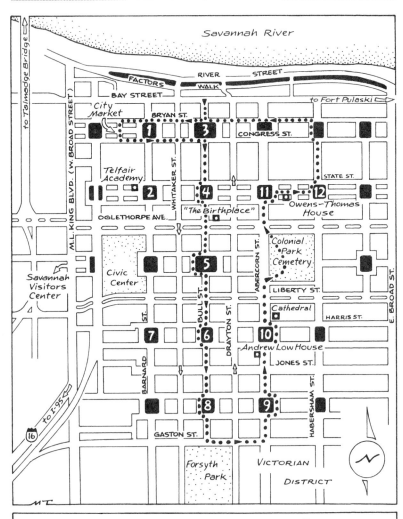

1. Ellis Square	5. Chippewa Square	9. Calhoun Square
2. Telfair Square	6. Madison Square	10. Lafayette Square
3. Johnson Square	7. Pulaski Square	11. Oglethorpe Square
4. Wright Square	8. Monterey Square	12. Columbia Square

Stroll the Squares Route: •••••►

around the back. An amazing number of Savannah's finest houses were designed by 20-year-old prodigy William Jay, who was to the city's architecture what Mozart was to music.

Twice Savannah's urban treasures have been saved from human catastrophe. In 1864, General William T. Sherman burned and pillaged a wide swath through Georgia on his way to Savannah, but left the city intact "as a Christmas present" for President Lincoln. But what Sherman spared was nearly lost in the 1950s when developers began to dismantle the city for parking lots and coveted "Savannah gray" bricks. After the City Market was leveled in 1954, Savannahians banded together to buy up and restore threatened buildings. Today, visitors and townspeople alike enjoy two and a half square miles of historic charm.

Exploring Savannah

The National Historic Landmark District, which includes all of downtown Savannah, is neatly framed by the **Savannah River** on the north, Gwinnett Street on the South, Martin Luther King Jr. Boulevard (formerly West Broad Street) on the west, and East Broad Street on the east. South of **Bay Street**, businesses, stately homes and churches intermingle around the 22 surviving squares. **Bull Street** bisects downtown, running from City Hall on Bay Street south to **Forsyth Park**. You can't be in a hurry crossing north to south, however, since most main arteries (Barnard, Bull, Abercorn, Habersham streets) are interrupted by four or five squares before you reach Gaston Street. South of Gwinnett Street is a vast, ethnically diverse **Victorian District**. North of Bay Street is **Factor's Walk**, a string of old cotton warehouses. Steep ramps and passageways lead down to **River Street**, where Savannah parties into the night.

Savannah is fun to explore on foot. Angela Williams' fine **Savannah Walking Tour** starts at Orleans Square across from the Civic Center and includes a stop to explore the Green-Meldrin Home, a domed Gothic Revival palace that became General Sherman's headquarters. Her two-hour walk is $12 for adults, $4 for children, by reservation only: (912) 232-3905. The Gray Line, in cooperation with the **Historic Savannah Foundation**, starts two-hour walking tours from several locations at frequent intervals every day; call 234-TOUR for reservations. A super treat from either outfit is the 8:30 a.m. Monday through Friday "Savannah Breakfast Stroll" that stops at Mrs. Wilkes' Boarding House (adults $17, including the breakfast!). Feet weary? Savannah's the Southern city most appropriate for a horse and carriage tour. **Carriage Tours of Savannah** departs on the hour daily (9 a.m. to 3 p.m.) from Madison Square and the Savannah visitor center; adults $10, children $4; call 236-6756 for details.

The Best to See and Do

❀❀❀ **Savannah's Squares** — Take my two-hour stroll through a dozen of Savannah's loveliest squares, Forsyth Park and fascinating Colonial Park Cemetery. The route goes past or near all the other Historic District highlights.

Oglethorpe's grand scheme reserved lots for churches and public buildings at opposite sides of every square, giving these shady "front yards" an enduring community function. Each square has statuary, a fountain, horticulture, or history that makes it different. Curiously, a square's name and the person honored there are rarely one in the same: Polish cavalry hero Casimir Pulaski's statue is in Monterey Square, not Pulaski Square two blocks west, as you might expect. Oglethorpe's statue is in Chippewa Square, and Revolutionary War hero Nathaniel Greene is buried not in Greene Square, but Johnson Square. Look for the whimsical dolphin downspouts on many homes, a signature unique to Savannah.

Begin at the **City Market** and walk east on West Congress Street past *Ellis Square* to *Johnson Square*. Turn right and go south on Bull Street through or around *Wright*, *Chippewa*, *Madison*, and *Monterey* squares, then two blocks farther toward the large fountain in azalea-filled **Forsyth Park** on the edge of the Victorian District. Walk east past Drayton Street one block to Abercorn Street and turn left. Stroll north on Abercorn through *Calhoun Square* and *Lafayette Square* (admire the stained glass from inside St. John the Baptist Cathedral) to **Colonial Park Cemetery**. Pause here to inspect the curious tombstones. Bored Union troops quartered here altered some of the dates, resulting in people whose lives appear to have spanned 300 years. Cross Oglethorpe Street and continue north two blocks to *Oglethorpe Square*. Turn right on President Street, meet *Columbia Square*, and go north on Habersham Street to *Warren Square*. Turn left on East Bryan Street, which will take you past *Reynolds Square* to *Johnson Square* and the City Market. Two short blocks north across Bay Street are Factors Walk and the Savannah River. You can also do this route by car, but you won't save much time.

❀❀ **Factors Walk and River Street** — North of Bay Street stands the old **Cotton Exchange** where cotton merchants (called "factors") once lorded over the world's cotton supply. Most of the warehouses are now shops and galleries. Steep, ballast-stone paved "ramps" and iron walkways lead down the bluff to River Street, where you can drink and dine late and watch the ever-changing scene on the Savannah River. Notice the statue of the **Waving Girl**, a real Savannahian named Florence Martus who for forty years greeted with a wave of her handkerchief every ship that entered the harbor.

❀❀ **Ships of the Sea Museum** — How do they get those handbuilt model ships into bottles? You'll see 75 ships-in-bottles, plus dozens of larger, wonderfully detailed models of seafaring vessels spanning 2,000 years of maritime history, a ship's carpentry shop, and collection of figureheads displayed in an old cotton warehouse with entrances at 503 East Bay Street and 503 River Street. Open daily from 10 a.m. to 5 p.m., adults $2, students 75 cents, (912) 232-1511.

❀❀ **Owens-Thomas House** — Designed by William Jay in 1816 and built on Oglethorpe Square, this tabby (seashell concrete) villa is regarded as America's finest example of Regency architecture. You'll see the original kitchen and furnishings of the first owners. Open Tuesday through Saturday from 10 a.m. to 5 p.m. and Sunday and Monday afternoons; adults $4, students $2, kids $1.

❀ **Juliette Gordon Low Shrines** — Colorfully eccentric Savannahian Juliette "Daisy" Low left her mark as the founder of the Girl Scouts of America. The Regency-style house at 142 Bull Street, where Miss Daisy was born and spent her childhood, is locally known as simply **"The Birthplace"** (appended by the sly remark, "and *you* thought it was in Bethlehem?"). Designed by William Jay in 1818, the house is maintained by the Girl Scouts. Open daily (but not on Wednesdays) from 10 a.m. to 4 p.m., Sundays from 12:30 p.m. to 4:30 p.m.; adults $3, students $2.25, (912) 233-4501.

Juliette Gordon married the son of wealthy cotton merchant Andrew Low and lived as an adult in his mansion at 329 Abercorn Street on Lafayette Square, where she started the first Girl Scout troop in 1912. The **Andrew Low House** is open daily (except Thursdays) from 10:30 a.m. to 4 p.m., Sundays from noon to 4 p.m.; adults $3.50, students $2, Girl Scouts $1, 233-6854.

❀ **Telfair Academy of Arts** — Savannah's cultural center and the oldest public art museum in the South, this 1818 mansion on Telfair Square was built on the site of the British colonial governor's residence. (The architect? William Jay, of course.) Telfair houses a fine collection of Impressionist paintings and works by Kahlil Gibran. Open Tuesday through Saturday from 10 a.m. to 5 p.m. and Sundays afternoons; adults $2.50, seniors and teens $1, 232-1177.

❀ **King-Tisdell Cottage** — Savannah's black heritage museum and art gallery is in an early Victorian house at 414 Huntingdon Street. Open weekdays 11 a.m. to 4 p.m., weekend afternoons from 1 p.m.; adults $1.50, students $1, 234-8000.

❀❀❀ **Fort Pulaski National Monument** — Marvelously medieval and perfectly preserved, Fort Pulaski gets my vote as the best old fort experience in Dixie. It's dramatic defeat in 1862 forever changed how forts are built. Guarding the entrance to the Savannah River on Cockspur Island, it was thought to be among the world's best bastions — but the Yankees had a fresh trick up their sleeve: rifled cannons. Replacing cannonballs, the new high-tech shells easily penetrated the 8-foot-thick brick walls. With Fort Pulaski's quick surrender, the millennium of masonry forts was finished.

Walk the drawbridge across the water-filled moat and pass through the sally port into the parade ground. Arched vaults built of 25 million bricks in the finest masonry surround you. Peer into the officers' mess (set up for dinner), enlisted men's quarters (replete with straw-mattress bunks), quartermaster's stores, and medical dispensary. In summer you'll see full-dress reenactments of Civil War era military life. From Savannah, take Bay Street and the President Street Extension east, then continue across the Wilmington River on US 80/Islands Expressway, and turn left where you see the Fort Pulaski sign. Open daily 8:30 a.m. to 6:45 p.m. from Memorial Day to Labor Day, and to 5:15 p.m. the rest of the year; (912) 786-5787. A $1 museum fee (for people ages 12 to 62) is charged only during summer months.

Coming back from Fort Pulaski, devoted fort-freaks might take a look at restored **Fort Jackson**, which dates to the War of 1812. It's on the Savannah River, about three miles east of the city. Open daily 9 a.m. to 5 p.m.; $2.

❀ **Tybee Island** — Tybee is Savannah's face to the Atlantic, 18 driving miles east of town. At the end of the road you'll find a relaxed, homey (kudzu on the palms), Southern beach resort community with the feel of the 1950s; convenient parking ($3 all day) and a decent recreational beach. To reach Tybee from Savannah, drive east on Bay Street, continue on the President Street Extension, then cross the Wilmington River and follow US 80/Islands Expressway to Tybee. On the way, turn in at **Fort Screven** and climb the 73 steps to the top of the old 1773 lighthouse for a grand view of the island and the outlet of the Savannah River into the ocean.

Places to Stay

Historic Savannah has many first-rate inns on or very near the squares. Among them are the **Gastonian**, (912) 232-2869, where you'll be treated to a full breakfast, cordials and pralines; **Ballastone Inn**, 236-1484; **Eliza Thompson House**, 236-3620, which has a lovely courtyard fountain; **Foley House**, 232-6622; and the **Jesse Mount House**, 236-1774, where your hostess is a concert harpist. Most have off-street parking and rates starting at about $90. Elegant **17 Hundred 90 Inn**, 236-7122, is more hotel-like but includes a fine restaurant downstairs. Modestly-priced **B&B Inn**, 238-0518, is in a great location and features a full breakfast (rooms with shared bath start at $38).

Overlooking Forsyth Park near the Victorian District are two relaxing inns from about $85. Enjoy piano music with wine in the parlor at **Forsyth Park Inn**, 102 West Hall Street, 233-6800; English antiques surround you at **Magnolia Place Inn**, (800) 238-7674. Everything booked? Call Alan Fort at (800) SAY-RSVP or (912) 232-RSVP, or **Savannah Historic Inns**, (800) 262-4667.

Places to Camp

Skidaway Island State Park, six miles southeast of Savannah off Diamond Causeway, has 100 wooded $8 sites with water and electricity; showers, laundry, pool, (912) 356-2523. **Bellaire Woods Campground** is two miles west of I-95 on GA 204, $10 to $16.50, 748-4000. **River's End Campground** is on Tybee Island, 786-5518.

Places to Dine

Chef Elizabeth Perry prepares wondrous "nouvelle Southern" specials at **Elizabeth on 37th** at the corner of Drayton Street. Call (912) 236-5547 for reservations; dinner only, closed Sundays. Inventive **Garibaldi's** in the old Germania Firehouse at 315 Congress Street, 232-7118, and the nearby **Savannah Bistro** are also top choices. Down on River Street, **Dockside Seafood**, 236-9253, is a pleasant and inexpensive place for lunch or dinner. Try the whole mackerel at the **River House**, 234-1900, which has a nice view of the harbor. Also on River Street: **Exchange Tavern** for sandwiches, the **Shrimp Factory**'s big salad, and **W. G. Shucker's** for oysters and a lively atmosphere.

Breakfast ($3.75) or lunch ($7) at **Mrs. Wilkes' Boarding House**, 107 West Jones Street, 232-5997, is a Monday through Friday Savannah experience that shouldn't be missed. There's no sign, "boarding house reach" is standard etiquette, and you bus your own dishes. Arrive for breakfast promptly at 8 a.m.; lunch is on the table from 11:30 a.m. to 3 p.m. Popular cafeteria-style **Express Cafe & Bakery** is at 39 Barnard Street in the City Market.

Evening Fun

In the City Market you'll find **Mikki's Jazz Club**, a friendly black music spot, and popular **Hard-Hearted Hannah's**. Along River Street and Factors Walk, just follow your ears and stop in where you hear what you like.

Useful Tips

The Georgia telephone area code is (912) for everywhere you'll be in *Discovery Days 17, 18* and *19*. After stopping at the visitor center, you can check out the adjacent **Savannah History Museum** (open daily, adults $2.75) and the old Georgia Southern roundhouse (Friday-Tuesday from 11 a.m., adults $2), all of which are parts of the most intact pre-Civil War railroad complex you'll see anywhere. Call (912) 944-0455 for Savannah updates.

Drop in at **E. Shaver Fine Books** on Madison Square (behind the DeSoto Hilton) for works by Eugenia Price *(Stranger in Savannah)* and Georgia field guides. There's a cluster of antique shops at Bull and Liberty streets.

Linger Longer

Tranquil Beaufort, South Carolina, on the Intracoastal Waterway is the picturesque jumping-off point for adventures (both natural and man-made) on St. Helena, Fripp, and Hunting islands. Call (803) 524-3163 to discover more.

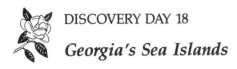

DISCOVERY DAY 18

Georgia's Sea Islands

How ample, the marsh and the sea and the sky!
... Somehow my soul seems suddenly free.

YOU CAN EXPECT TO FEEL as ecstatic as poet Sidney Lanier as you traverse the enchanted Marshes of Glynn on your way to St. Simons Island, Sea Island and Jekyll Island — three of the thirteen major barrier islands that form Georgia's intricate Atlantic coastline. Once the playlands of American aristocracy, each of these spellbinding sea islands reveals its own adventuresome blend of natural wonders, curious history, and timeless pleasures.

Timetable Suggestion

8:30 a.m.	Breakfast, depart Savannah.
10:00 a.m.	Explore St. Simons Island and Sea Island.
12:30 p.m.	Lunch on St. Simons or in Brunswick.
1:30 p.m.	Visit the "Millionaires Village" historic district, then bicycle the Jekyll Island loop.
3:30 p.m.	Loll in the sand and surf, golf, play tennis, or fish the rest of the day. Stay at the Jekyll Island Hotel, eat and sleep when you feel like it.

Magnolia Trail: Savannah to Brunswick (80 miles), plus a swing through the Golden Isles (approximately 40 miles)

Go south on Savannah's Martin Luther King, Jr. Boulevard, and take the ramp to **I-16**, which quickly whisks you out of town. Eight miles west, get on **I-95** south. For the next 60 miles you'll cross broad tidewater rivers, salt marsh habitat, pasture lands, and deep pine forests. You'll see lots of bird life here, including osprey, turkey vultures, and possibly a cattle egret perched on a cow's back. Further south, you cross cypress swamps and the broad Altamaha River. Turn off at Exit 9 and take **US 17/Dixie Highway** (or the Golden Isles Parkway at Exit 8) about ten miles towards Brunswick. You'll see the **Golden Isles Visitor Center** in an older Spanish-style building on your left as US 17 becomes Glynn Avenue. Pick up detailed maps and information here, then turn left and cross the Marshes of Glynn on the Torras Causeway (toll: 35 cents) to reach **St. Simons Island** and **Sea Island**.

Return to the Golden Isles visitor center and turn left to approach down-town Brunswick and Jekyll Island. Gloucester Street, to your right, will take you into old **Brunswick**, a town with English architectural treats, a shrimp and crab fleet, and an enchanting moss-mantled courthouse square. To get to **Jekyll Island**, stay on the four-lane US 17 (here called Ocean Highway), cross the wide Brunswick River, turn left at GA 50/Jekyll Island Road, and drive six miles to the island.

Georgia's Island Coast

A string of thirteen large, wooded barrier islands backed by marshes, rivers, and the Intracoastal Waterway guards Georgia's Atlantic coast from Savannah to Florida. Sea breezes in summer and the moderating influence of the longshore current in winter make for a pleasant year-round climate, salubrious for ghost crabs, loggerhead turtles, resurrection fern, osprey, and human beings. Many of these islands were once the private property of American titans of industry, who had the good sense to preserve and pro-tect much of their complex natural ecology — if mainly for sport hunting. Where plantations and summer estates once prevailed, vast wildlife refuges now dominate Wassaw, Ossabaw, Blackbeard (named for the pirate said to have had a hideout there), Sapelo, and Wolf islands. Most are reachable only by boat, including tranquil **Cumberland Island National Seashore** (see *Linger Longer*).

The Spanish called St. Simons, Sea Island and Jekyll Island the "Golden Isles of Guale" — not for imagined riches, but for the way light plays on the marsh grasses and tide-swept beaches. Linked by causeways, these islands can be explored and enjoyed in a day.

The Best of the Golden Isles

Here is what you'll encounter on these three very different islands in the order you should see them if you plan to stay tonight on Jekyll Island:

St. Simons Island — St. Simons is a happy balance of the natural, recrea-tional, historic, and residential. Unspoiled marshes and woods are still plen-tiful, yet the homes and visitor-oriented businesses sprinkled around the island seem to fit in quite comfortably. After you cross over the Intracoastal Waterway and Frederica River onto the island, keep right and drive Kings Way to the island's village center and recreation-oriented Neptune Park and pier. Next to the park is the **St. Simons Lighthouse**, which you can climb up for an aerial survey of the Golden Isles, and the **Museum of Coastal History** in the former lightkeeper's house. Both are open Tuesday through Saturday from 10 a.m. to 5 p.m. and Sundays from 1:30 p.m.; admission $1.50 for adults, $1 for children. To find the island's best beach, take Ocean Boulevard to Massengale Park and the U.S. Coast Guard station. A boardwalk through

THE GEORGIA SEA ISLANDS

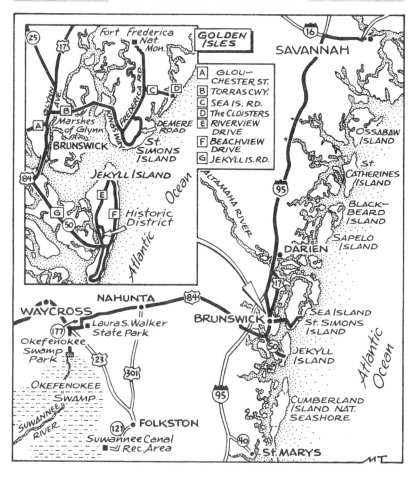

the dunes leads you to a very nice, broad gray-sand stretch of Atlantic beach, somehow still exempt from the discouraging shore erosion seen elsewhere.

Drive Frederica Road about five miles north through the middle of St. Simons to reach Gothic-style **Christ Church**, rich in literary history, and **Fort Frederica National Monument**. Here you'll see the tabby ruins of the British fort, part of its moat, an interpretive museum, and archaeological outlines of James Oglethorpe's Frederica village. Oglethorpe set up the fort and town on St. Simons in 1736 to keep the Spanish from pushing northward from Florida. Indeed, the Spanish advance into the British colony of Georgia was halted in 1742 at the **Battle of Bloody Marsh** (you'll see the historic marker on

Demere Road). The monument is open 8 a.m. to 6 p.m. daily in the summer and to 5 p.m. the rest of the year; adults $1, children and seniors free. Also on St. Simons are three major golf courses, public and private tennis courts, and bike trails paralleling all the island's main roads.

Sea Island — This family-owned island to the east of St. Simons is occupied by **The Cloister**, one of the most congenial and quietly relaxing grand resorts on earth. It's well worth a look even if you're not staying here. Auto magnate Howard Coffin made a fortune in Detroit building Hudson cars, but his heart was here. Teamed with his nephew Bill Jones, they opened a "friendly little hotel" on their island in 1928. Fortunately, they shared a magnificent sensitivity for tasteful creature comforts as well as concern for the environment. From stem to stern, Sea Island is beautifully landscaped for dreamy garden strolls. Fresh flowers are everywhere. Sailing, waterways fishing, golf, tennis, horseback riding on the beach, innovative programs for children, and two ballrooms with dancing to live bands every night are among the many diversions, but it's the way the place makes you feel that's special — an irresistible suggestion of absolute serenity and comfort. From St. Simons, take Sea Island Drive across the Black Banks River, cruise the quiet lanes and stop at the splendid Spanish-style Cloister itself. There's no charge to look. If you're tempted to spend your island day here, see *Places to Stay.*

Jekyll Island — For half a century the exclusive "winter Newport" and hunting preserve of the Rockefellers, Vanderbilts, Morgans, and Pulitzers, Jekyll Island was turned over to the State of Georgia in 1947, and now it's everybody's island. But the millionaire barons made some nice improvements. At immodestly-named **Millionaires Village** (now the Jekyll Island National Historic District) they built a cluster of handsome mansion-cottages in a variety of styles, a lovely chapel with Tiffany stained glass windows, a dock for their yachts, and the rambling, turreted Jekyll Island Clubhouse. There's something for everyone on Jekyll: ten miles of beautiful Atlantic beach, a 20-mile network of bicycle trails, four fabulous golf courses, a premier tennis facility with lighted clay courts, deep-sea fishing and dolphin-watching excursions from the Jekyll Island Club Wharf, **Summer Waves** water park with a wave pool and two scary water slides, the tabby ruins of Georgia's first brewery, trails through palmetto groves and along the marshes, and places to eat and stay — plus summer treats such as nightly professional theatre productions and a guided night hike to see loggerhead sea turtles.

Take US 17 across the Sydney Lanier Bridge and turn left onto the **Jekyll Island Causeway/GA 50**. A drawbridge over the Intracoastal Waterway brings you onto the island, where you stop to pay a $1 "parking fee" to bring your car onto the island. Turn left just beyond the toll station to visit the Historic District on Riverview Drive. A 90-minute guided tram tour through the millionaires' domain starts from the museum in the old Jekyll Island Club stables hourly from 10 a.m. to 3 p.m. (adults $7, children 6-18 $5). **Riverview Drive** and **Beachview Drive** circumnavigate the island, but because it's compact (just seven miles long) the best way to get to know Jekyll is on a bicycle. Stop at the miniature golf course and rent one for $4 an hour, $7 for four hours, or $10 for the whole day. Tandems, kiddie seats and three-wheel bikes can be rented there too. Bicycles are also available at most of the hotels along the beach. A handy shopping area with a drugstore, laundromat, gas station, and restaurants lines Ben Fortson Parkway between the toll station and Beachview Drive. Stop at the welcome center on Jekyll Island Causeway for a map and details about all the recreational offerings, or call the Jekyll Island Visitors Bureau at (800) 841-6586 (locally 635-3636).

Other Places

❀ **Sapelo Island** — Once a plantation and then the private domain of conservation-minded Howard Coffin and R.J. Reynolds (of cigarette fame), ecologically splendid Sapelo is now a wildlife refuge and home of the University of Georgia's Marine Institute. It's reachable only by a 25-minute ferry ride from Darien, just off I-95 north of the Altamaha River. A half-day $5 bus tour is the best way to enjoy the island. Call Darien's welcome center, (912) 437-6684, for schedule and reservations.

❀ **Brunswick** — You wouldn't know it from Glynn Avenue, but Brunswick (population 20,000) has a distinctly English touch and Victorian character. Streets are named for English towns, royalty and heros (Norwich, London, Albermarle, George), revealing the town's pro-British sympathies in the Revolutionary War. Protected from storms by the islands and St. Simon's sound, Brunswick's once strategic port along Bay Street is now lined with fishing boats and seafood packing plants. Turn right from Glynn Avenue/ US 17 onto Gloucester Street and you'll be in Old Town Brunswick. Norwich, Union and Newcastle streets will lead you past the town's gracious "places" (squares) and old homes. Particularly romantic is the Glynn County Courthouse Square. Gloucester Street ends at Brunswick's harbor along Bay Street.

❀ **Hofwyl-Broadfield Plantation** — How did large rice plantations once thrive in the coastal marshlands? You'll see the slave-built dikes and canals that made it possible at Hofwyl-Broadfield, on US 17 just south of the Altamaha River. Open 9 a.m. to 5 p.m. Tuesday-Saturday, and from 2 p.m. Sundays; adults $1.50, children 75 cents.

Places to Dine

St. Simons Island: **Mallery's** ("homestyle seafood"), **Brogen's** (popular for sandwiches), and **The Binnacle Lounge**, all clustered in the St. Simons village near Neptune Park, are handy for lunch. There's also the **Crab Trap** and **Crabdaddy's** on Ocean Boulevard. If you're on St. Simons this evening, pleasant dining can be found at **Blanche's Courtyard**, 440 Kings Way (638-3030), which gets high marks for seafood, and the **Delegal Room** in the King and Prince Hotel (638-3631).

Jekyll Island: You'll enjoy eating alongside the spirits of the millionaires in the columned, pink and white Grand Dining Room of the **Jekyll Island Club Hotel.** Try the blackened pork loin (about $15) or delicate chicken American. Call 635-3311 for reservations. Lunch is also served here ($5 to $10), or try the informal and sunny **Cafe Soltera** in the same building. On Beachview Drive try **Blackbeard's Restaurant** (635-3522) and **Zachry's Seafood House** (635-3128), or **The Wharf** restaurant at the marina (635-3800).

Places to Stay

Jekyll Island: Sleep in pampered turn-of-the-century splendor at **The Jekyll Island Club.** Once the clubhouse for the rich and famous who owned the island, this gracious, rambling centerpiece overlooking the quiet Jekyll River is now operated by Radisson Resorts. Room rates range from about $70 to $160 in winter and $80 to $200 in the peak April through August season, (912) 635-2600. If you'd like to stay on the beach side of the island, try apartment-style accommodations in the $50 to $100 range at **Villas by the Sea**, (912) 635-2521, or **Jekyll Estates Inn**, 635-2256. You can rent bicycles for touring the island at all three.

Brunswick: Victorian bric-a-brac mantles, tennis courts across the street, high tea at 4 p.m., and the palms and oaks of Halifax Square are parts of the ambience at **Brunswick Manor**, 265-6889, a bed and breakfast in a 100-year-old-mansion.

St. Simons Island: **Mary Gaubert's Bed and Breakfast**, 638-9424, has two locations within half a block of the beach, nice rooms for $72. **Country Hearth Inn**, 638-7805, is a motel in the middle of the island that serves breakfast, rates from $50.

Sea Island: Partisans claim **The Cloister** is the finest resort in the world, and it's hard to argue with them. Everything about this idyllic playground engenders bliss and comfort, earning it every imaginable travel award. Take a room in the older buildings (they're even nicer) along the quiet Black Banks. Rates range from just under $200 to over $350 per day for two, which includes all meals and just about everything else. Call (800) SEA ISLA for reservations.

Places to Camp

Jekyll Island Campground is the only place for campers and RV travelers on the island, but it's a delight. Nestled beneath the live oaks and pine woods on Beachview Drive at the island's north end are its 200 campsites, complete store, laundry, and showers. You're a short walk from an uncrowded Atlantic beach. Full hookups $14, tent sites $10, (912) 635-3021.

An alternative experience and a super bargain is the **Hostel in the Forest**, ten miles west of Brunswick off US 84. You sleep in a real treehouse or cozy geodesic dome for $6 per person; it has hiking and biking trails, fishing pond, and shuttle to and from Brunswick. Call Tom Dennard at (912) 264-9738 for reservations.

Linger Longer: Cumberland Island National Seashore

Immense solitude, tranquility and unspoiled beauty surround you in Cumberland Island's dunes, marshes and forests. It remains pristine because the only convenient way to get there is on the twice-daily National Park Service boat from **St. Marys**. Your companions will be aquatic birds, feral horses and sea turtles. Camp overnight beneath a moss-draped oak, then scan the horizon for bottlenose dolphins at sunrise.

From Brunswick, drive 30 miles south on I-95 to reach St. Marys in Georgia's southeastern corner. The ferry makes two daily round trips (except Tuesdays and Wednesdays in winter), departing St. Marys at 9 a.m. and 11:45 a.m. and the island at 10:15 a.m. and 4:45 p.m.; adults $7.95, seniors $6.63, children $4.08. Call (912) 882-4335 for reservations, since only 300 lucky souls are allowed on the island at a time.

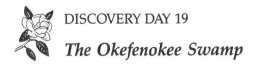

DISCOVERY DAY 19

The Okefenokee Swamp

TODAY'S ROUTE HEADS WEST through the pine timberlands of south Georgia. Venture into the silent Okefenokee Swamp, a primeval realm of dark mirror-like waters, moss-draped giant cypresses, floating islands, strange blooming plants, plentiful alligators, and quiet canoe trails, where slowly moving currents give birth to the lyrical Suwannee River.

Rest tonight in Thomasville, an elegant small town where health-seeking northerners found a pine-scented refuge in Victorian times.

Timetable Suggestion

8:30 a.m.	Breakfast at Bluebird Cafe in Brunswick.
10:30 a.m.	Arrive at Okefenokee Swamp Park, rent a canoe.
1:15 p.m.	Lunch in Waycross.
2:00 p.m.	Watch the trains move at Rice Switchyard.
4:30 p.m.	Enjoy quiet Thomasville's elegant streets.
6:30 p.m.	Dine at Mom & Dad's Italian Restaurant, then sleep in Southern comfort in a Thomasville home.

Magnolia Trail: Jekyll Island to Thomasville (182 miles)

After leaving Jekyll Island, turn left onto **US 84**, cross under I-95, and head west on the broad four-lane through the slash pine timberland of south Georgia toward Waycross. The soldier-like rows of pines, logging trucks, fire towers, and sawmills leave no doubt you're in the heart of Georgia's lumber and pulpwood country. Eight miles east of Waycross, turn south on **GA 177** through lovely **Laura S. Walker State Park**. Cross US 23 and drive five miles further south on the Vereen Bell Highway to reach **Okefenokee Swamp Park**. After your visit, a left turn onto US 23 will take you seven miles into **Waycross** (population 20,000), an important railroad crossing point (and thus its name). Waycross is also a mecca for fans of Pogo Possum, the Okefenokee's most famous critter.

Continue 100 miles west on US 84 through Homerville, Valdosta and Quitman — traditional south Georgia towns with nifty architectural touches, such as Quitman's elegant courthouse and fountain. Take US 84/Smith Avenue into the heart of rose-scented **Thomasville** (population 19,000).

WAYCROSS TO THE GULF OF MEXICO

Okefenokee National Wildlife Refuge

The Okefenokee Swamp, a 600-square-mile otherworld of aquatic wonders, is one of North America's largest and most ecologically complete swamp environments. Mysterious and silent yet teeming with life, virtually the entire swamp is a national wildlife refuge, open to visitors but closed to exploitation. Here stand ancient, towering bald cypress trees, survivors of the fires and logging that once ravaged this vast peat bog. Here also Chief Billy Bowlegs and his Seminole band held out against white encroachment for 20 years, then escaped to the Everglades of Florida. The swamp is the source of both the Suwannee and St. Marys rivers, which mark the northern limits of the entire Florida peninsula. Okefenokee means "trembling earth," a sensation you may experience as you trod the swamp's unstable, wildflower-trimmed islands. Swamp gasses lift great chunks of peat to the surface, then tree roots grow down to anchor these floating islands.

You can get into the Okefenokee from three main access points, each featuring a different aspect of the swamp. The best way to experience the swamp's magic is by canoe, and you can rent one (with paddles or a small motor) at all three entrances. **Okefenokee Swamp Park** at the northern end is easy to reach from today's route; you'll see lots of swamp life, but it's comparatively tame and nearly all the towering cypresses were logged out long ago. The **Suwannee Canal** on the east side affords excellent guided or do-it-yourself canoe excursions into the swamp's watery "prairies." **Stephen C. Foster State Park**, 47 miles off the travel route, provides the ultimate swamp adventure, best appreciated by experienced canoers who have time for a whole day amid the majestic 500-year old cypresses in the heart of the Okefenokee (see *Linger Longer*).

The Best to See and Do

❀❀❀ **Okefenokee Swamp Park** — Easy to get to, this private non-profit attraction gives a very thorough introduction to the swamp and many of its fascinating critters, although it's a bit overly managed. Find out what keeps the Okefenokee alive at Swamp Creation Center. Make your acquaintance with several alligators, learn about snakes in the serpentarium, and take the boardwalk out to a 90-foot tower for a spectacular aerial view of miles of deep swamp wilderness. Visit a nest of darling, playful otters.

Go on the 25-minute guided motorboat tour that's included in the price of admission, then rent a canoe at the same dock and strike out at your own pace for a closer look. You'll float on a glassy waterway through a lovely alien realm where bug-eating pitcher plants, giant dragonflies, water lilies, wild orchids, egrets, ibises, chameleons, and an occasional alligator or two are right at home. You'll see stumps and knees of the giant cypresses cut down before the swamp became a wildlife sanctuary. The canoe trail is set up so you can't get lost — even if you want to!

The park is open every day from 9 a.m. to 6:30 p.m. during Daylight Savings Time, and to 5:30 p.m. in late fall and winter. Admission is $7 for adults, $6 for seniors, $5 for children 6-12; (912) 283-0583. Canoes rent for $7 per day.

❀❀ **Suwannee Canal Recreation Area** — Deepen your Okefenokee experience with a self-guiding wilderness canoe trip through grassy swamp "prairies" alive with herons, sandhill cranes, bitterns, ibises, and other wading birds. There is a 3,400-foot boardwalk, hiking trails, and a restored island homestead. You'll see more large bald cypresses here than at Okefenokee Swamp Park.

To get there, turn south on US 301 at Nahunta and drive 23 miles to Folkston (or take US 23 south from Laura S. Walker State Park). Suwannee Canal is 11 miles south and west of Folkston on GA 121. No charge here except for canoe (with paddles or 10-horsepower motor) and bicycle rentals. Open from 7 a.m. to 7:30 p.m. daily from March 1 to September 10 and 8 a.m. to 6 p.m. September 11 through February; (912) 496-7156.

❀❀ **CSX Rice Switchyard** — Hundreds of freight cars funnel through here daily to be uncoupled, sorted and re-coupled into trains and sent on their way across the United States. It's the largest computerized "hump" switchyard in the nation — a thrill if you're fascinated by the call of the rails. To watch it all from the control tower, phone Carl Pickett, (912) 287-4533, or terminal superintendent J. R. Odam, 287-4524, in advance. You'll find the Rice Yard on the left side of US 84 just southwest of Waycross. Proceed through the gates and follow the road to Tower A. Be very careful crossing the tracks.

❀ **Southern Forest World** — Step inside a giant cypress, climb aboard an old logging locomotive, and walk up the inside of a big model of a loblolly pine at this museum of the South's timber industry. From Waycross, drive two miles northwest on US 1/23 and turn at Augusta Avenue. Open Tuesday-Saturday 10 a.m. to 5 p.m., Sundays 2 p.m. to 4 p.m., free. Right next door, check out the 19th century print shop, 1912 steam train and depot, and regional fine art at **Okefenokee Heritage Center**; adults $2, children $1.

❀ **All-American Rose Test Gardens** — Hybrid roses developed around the country are tested here under standard conditions for Southeastern gardens. Some 2,000 named plants are in bloom from April to November. It's next to Hjort's Thomasville Nurseries as you come into town on US 84/Smith Avenue. Open daily 8 a.m. to 5 p.m., Sundays after 2 p.m., free.

❀❀ **Thomasville's Homes** — In the Victorian era, word got around snowy, smoky Chicago and Cleveland that the pine-scented air around Thomasville was a balm to health. By 1880, the town boomed with resort hotels and the "shooting plantations" of midwestern moguls. Also known for its roses, peaches and strawberries, Thomasville today remains prosperous and well-kept. See its Victorian gems on this 30-minute drive through the **Dawson Street**, **Tockwotten** and **Paradise Park** neighborhoods:

From Smith Avenue turn right onto Broad Street, then right at Monroe Street. You pass Big Oak (it's branches spread 162 feet) and turn left at Dawson Street. The **Lapham-Patterson House** at 626 Dawson Street is a wildly inventive three-story Victorian with many odd-shaped rooms (open 9 a.m. to 5 p.m. Tuesday through Saturday, Sundays after 2 p.m.; adults $1.50, kids 75 cents). **Thomas County Historical Society Museum** at 725 Dawson Street holds relics of the great hotel era in three restored homes (2 p.m. to 5 p.m. except Fridays, 226-7664). Turn around at Walcott Street and drive back on Dawson all the way to Remington Avenue. Turn left, then right onto Hansell Street and into the Tockwotten district's collection of restorations. Here you'll see the **Balfour House** with it's magnificent two-story circular veranda. Cross Smith Street, go under the railroad bridge, and emerge at forested Paradise Park, bordered by more graceful big houses. Turn right on Broad Street and end your drive at the **Neel House**, once the social center of Thomasville. (If you have extra time, Destination Thomasville, (912) 228-7673, knows everything.)

❀ **Pebble Hill Plantation** — Set in a green protected by pines and magnolias, this lavish, rambling, money-is-no-object retreat "cottage" holds paintings and relics that blend yankee and Southern ideas of genteel country living. Five

miles south of Thomasville on US 319, open daily except Mondays from
10 a.m. to 4 p.m.; $2 to enter the grounds, $5 to explore the house; 226-2344.

Places to Dine

Have a hearty, inexpensive Southern breakfast this morning in Brunswick
at the **Bluebird Cafe** on Reynolds Street (two eggs, grits or hashbrowns,
coffee, $2.50). Lunch in Waycross at the **Duck Pond Restaurant**, or picnic in
the pines at Laura S. Walker State Park.

Mom & Dad's Italian on US 84/Smith Avenue, near the Rose Test Gardens
as you come into Thomasville, gets my vote as the South's best Italian family
restaurant. Request the special house salad that's not on the menu. Early
arrival on weekend evenings will shorten your wait, (912) 226-6265. Also in
Thomasville try **Somewhere for Dinner**, 116 North Broad Street, 228-1815, for
imaginative magic from Robin Finks' kitchen (sample the heavenly walnut,
dates and sour cream appetizer!); **Melissa's** in Madison Square, 228-9844; or
for down home cookin', **Betty's Place** in Plantation Plaza on US 319 just
south of town.

Places to Stay

Choose a room in one of ten fine Thomasville homes or at **Greenridge
Plantation** ($30 to $60) through **Quail Country B&B Ltd.**, (912) 226-7218.
There's room to relax and a fishing pond at **Willow Lake Farms** on Magnolia
Road (about $40 including breakfast); call Ann Cone at 226-6372. Casual
Wright House, a restored saltbox, offers bed, breakfast and a bedtime snack,
$40, 226-2853. **Susina Plantation Inn**, 12 miles south of Thomasville, is your
last chance on this trip to stay at a fabulous country plantation. Breakfast,
dinner and room, $150, 377-7644.

Places to Camp

City of Roses RV Park, (912) 228-7275, is a very convenient campground
right in Thomasville. As you come into town on US 84, turn left at the light
on Pine Tree Boulevard, then left immediately to 2120 Old Boston Road; full
hookups $13.50. Towering pines and a lovely lake in a quiet forest setting
near Okefenokee Swamp Park make **Laura S. Walker State Park** a wonderful overnight, even though it's 100 miles from Thomasville. Waterskiing,
fishing, laundromat, $6 and $8 sites, (912) 287-4900.

Linger Longer: Heart of the Okefenokee

If the ultimate swamp experience is your goal, drive out the narrow peninsula of high ground that ends deep in the Okefenokee at **Stephen C. Foster
State Park**. Paddle (or motor) a rented canoe out past awesome 500-year-old
bald cypress trees to the headwaters of the **Suwannee River** near Billy's Island,

then cruise the river course through tupelo forests and canopies of smilax vines. Look for alligator eyes amid the thousands of water lilies. Camp overnight at the park in a cabin; call (912) 637-5274 for details.

At Homerville, take US 441 south 28 miles to Fargo, cross the Suwannee, then drive 18 miles northeast through the swamp on GA 177. From this point, its easiest to re-connect with the travel route by taking I-10 west to Tallahassee (see *Discovery Day 20*).

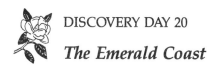

DISCOVERY DAY 20

The Emerald Coast

A GLISTENING WHITE BEACH on the Gulf Coast awaits you toward the end of today's road. But first enjoy a stop in Tallahassee and a country drive through Florida's Panhandle, a distinctly Southern region of forests, springs and gentle hills. Florida is culturally upside down: farther south it's yankee paradise, but northern Florida from Jacksonville and Tallahassee along the Gulf Coast to Pensacola is very much a part of Dixie's realm.

Does your picture of the perfect beach include gently sloping dunes at your back, tufts of golden sea oats for color, soft sand underfoot that's as white as sugar, seagulls, sandpipers, and translucent warm water stretching to the horizon? If so, the seacoast from Panama City to Pensacola should delight you. One look at the crystalline, almost etherial waters and you'll see why it's called the Emerald Coast.

Timetable Suggestion

8:15 a.m.	Depart Thomasville, head into Florida.
9:00 a.m.	See Florida's capitols in Tallahassee.
11:00 a.m.	Gaze into the depths of Wakulla Springs.
12:30 p.m.	Drive west across the Florida Panhandle.
2:00 p.m.	Arrive on the Emerald Coast, pick your beach, play in the sand and surf the rest of the day.
6:00 or so	Dine and sleep in Seaside or Destin.

Magnolia Trail: Thomasville to Fort Walton Beach (175 miles)

Depart Thomasville on US 319 and cross into Florida 15 miles down the road. Over the line, US 319 is also FL 61/Thomasville Road. Stick with FL 61 as it runs under I-10 and merges with Monroe Street, which takes you straight into the heart of **Tallahassee** (population 120,000), a bright, upbeat, yet traditional Southern city with a campus-like atmosphere (it's the home of Florida State University). The Florida State Capitol and History Museum of Florida will be to your right.

Continue south out of Tallahassee on Monroe Street (or Adams Street) and stay on FL 61 about 13 miles to the turnoff on FL 267 for **Wakulla Springs State Park**. After your visit there, turn left (west) on FL 267 and stay on it for about 25 miles to **Bloxham**. At Bloxham, FL 267 meets FL 20 which you'll follow through Bristol and across the Apalachicola River. *Move your watch back one hour here as you cross into the Central Time Zone.* Beyond Blountstown, enjoy an uninterrupted hour's ride west on FL 20 through the quiet piney countryside to **Ebro**. Don't exceed the speed limit here — the one other car you see on this often lonely stretch will likely be a cop. Turn left (south) at the stop sign in Ebro and take FL 79 through Pine Log State Forest 17 miles to the stunning white sands of the **Gulf of Mexico**. Turn right on Alt US 98 and start looking for your dream beach along the Emerald Coast.

When you've gone about seven miles, take **FL 30-A** to your left to follow the increasingly lovely beach landscape through **Seaside**, **Seagrove Beach** and **Grayton Beach State Park**. It's another 16 miles or so east on FL 30-A and US 98 through **Destin** into **Fort Walton Beach**. Feel free to continue on to Santa Rosa Island in Gulf Islands National Seashore (see *Discovery Day 21*).

In Tallahassee and Wakulla Springs you can connect with the route of Richard Harris's *2 to 22 Days in Florida* (a fine guide similar in format to this one) for an exploration of the Sunshine State all the way to Miami and Key West.

Getting to know Florida's Emerald Coast

Unlike Atlantic Florida, many miles along the Emerald Coast are still relatively open and natural. It's beaches, among the whitest in the world, are wonderful and warm most of the time, but since weather can turn chilly after November the area has developed slower than Florida's better-known coasts. You'll find long stretches where man and nature seem in balance, high-rise condos only in the distance, and the gulls and sea oats-crowned dunes in command. For these last three days, your route on the Magnolia Trail parallels the Intracoastal Waterway, a protected highway for marine traffic that courses through the estuaries and marshes behind the barrier dune islands.

Florida's history is rich with stories of seafaring conquest, pirate escapades, and international intrigue dating back to Ponce de Leon's landfall on Easter Morning 1513 — barely two decades after Columbus first arrived in the New World. Tallahassee became Florida's capital two years after the Spanish finally threw in the towel and relinquished both East and West Florida to the United States in 1821. Andrew Jackson was the first territorial governor and spent most of his time fighting Seminole Indian resistance. Tallahassee is distinguished as the only Confederate capital east of the Mississippi River that Union forces never captured.

The Best to See and Do

All of Tallahassee's recommended highlights can be seen without going more than three blocks off the travel route, but give yourself enough time

THE EMERALD COAST

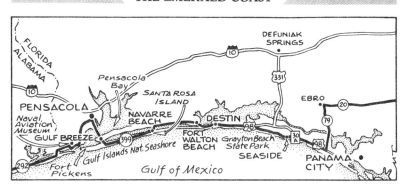

today for the best delights — those along the Emerald Coast.

❀ **Florida State Capitol Complex** — The 1902 **Old Capitol** and towering modern **Florida State Capitol** next to it offer very different free experiences. Exhibits of Florida's history from the Bourbon kings through territorial and Confederate days are found on second floor of the Old Capitol, open weekdays from 9 a.m. to 4:30 p.m., Saturdays from 10 a.m., and Sunday afternoons. The real treat at the new capitol, which has served Florida since 1978, is the view from the 22nd story observation deck, but you have to take the 30-minute guided tour of the building to get a look. Tours are conducted Monday through Friday from 9 a.m. to 4 p.m. and on weekends and holidays from 11 a.m. to 3 p.m., free.

Parking during working hours is at a premium in downtown Tallahassee. Find a space at the public garage on St. Augustine Street across from the museum. Once you're parked, the capitols, museum, and restaurants along Monroe and College Streets are easy to reach on foot.

❀❀ **Museum of Florida History** — Florida was checked out by Ponce de Leon in 1513, colonized by both France in 1564 and Spain in 1565, grabbed by the British in 1763, then relinquished back to Spain by the Treaty of Paris. Sophisticated pre-columbian Native American cultures thrived here for centuries before Ponce de Leon. Learn more about this rich heritage, and see a mastodon, Spanish doubloons, and exhibits about the citrus industry at the state museum in the R.A. Gray Building at Bronough and Pensacola streets, just west of the Capitol complex. Open weekdays from 8 a.m. to 4:30 p.m., Saturdays from 10 a.m., and Sunday afternoons, free.

❀ **Maclay State Gardens** — As you approach Tallahassee on US 319 from the north, these beautifully maintained botanical gardens in a lakeside setting will be on your right, just before you pass under Interstate 10. Noted especially for a great array of camellias, the gardens are open daily 9 a.m. to 5 p.m.; adults $3, children $1.50, cars $1.

❀ ❀ **Wakulla Springs State Park** — Glass-bottomed boats let you peer down through the crystal-clear water to see mastodon bones and artifacts lying in the maw of a largely unexplored underwater cavern that begins 120 feet below the surface. The vast spring gives forth some 200 million gallons a day, supporting a forest oasis habitat of giant cypresses quickened by swamp critters, deer, wild turkey, and lots of egrets and herons. Though I can't imagine a more lovely place for a picnic, the graceful Spanish-style Wakulla Springs Lodge, built in 1937, will entice you with excellent lunches — and an invitation to stay overnight. Once owned by a wealthy financier whose hobby was conservation, the springs were opened to the public in 1986. Wakulla Springs is open daily from 8 a.m. to sunset, admission $2 per vehicle and driver, plus $1 for each passenger (half price if you're a Floridian). The 25-minute glass-bottom boat Spring Cruise and slightly longer River Trip each cost $4 for adults, $2.25 for children, (904) 222-7279.

❀ ❀ ❀ **Seaside Community** — First you notice the soft pastel colors and crimped-tin roofs of the houses, then the rambling porches, fanciful cupolas, white picket fences, and the sandy paths that wind between the houses. Seaside looks like a restored Southern coastal village of the 1930s, but it isn't. It is a twelve year old real estate project based on the wonderfully reactionary dream of Robert Davis, whose grandfather left him 80 acres of beach. Sickened by the mindless, slapdash condo and townhouse developments he saw infecting Florida's coastlines, Davis decided to bring the best of a gentler, more sociable past back to life.

Seaside is a human-scale town that promotes neighborliness and going places on foot. Its building code is a wonder: you pick your own architect, but he can't use any material (vinyl, for instance) that was invented since 1940. You must have a porch and a picket fence, but they can't be the same as the ones next door. Lawns are forbidden, but you can plant flowers among the native shrubs. Shopping is focused in an open-air market of small stalls, and the post office is less than a ten-minute walk from every house. No security gates here — you're welcome to drop in and wander around, even stay (see *Places to Stay*). Seaside is on FL 30A just before you reach Grayton Beach.

❀ ❀ ❀ **Grayton Beach State Recreation Area** — Splendid high barrier dunes, a mile-long unspoiled beach, facilities that blend with the surroundings, and a natural lake encircled by a coastal marsh make Grayton Beach a very pleasant place to stop and take in the best of the Emerald Coast's environment. Walk the Barrier Dunes Nature Trail, which includes a loop through the sand-pruned pine woods. The 356-acre park is off FL 30A, just past Seaside. Entrance fee is $1 per car; the park closes at 7 p.m. unless you're camping here.

Places to Dine

Lunch at **Wakulla Springs Lodge** is served from noon to 2 p.m. Few of their fine choices cost much more than $5. In Tallahassee, go to **Rally's Drive In** (south on Monroe Street) for a great hamburger. Around the Capitol area you'll find several good restaurants favored by state workers, such as **Mike's Cafe** at 113 South Monroe Street and **Andrew's Deli** at 228 South Adams Street. If you have extra time in Tallahassee, drive west on Tennessee Street past Florida State University to **Crystal River Seafood**, (904) 575-4418, for a great catch at a very low price. Just west of Ebro on FL 20 you can hide out at the **Hideawhile Restaurant**.

Along the Emerald Coast in the Grayton Beach area you'll find **Creolla's**, serving West Indies creole dishes, and **Randall's**, where you might try the reasonably priced kabobs and rice or marinated beef and chicken dishes. **Bud and Alley's Restaurant** in Seaside, (904) 231-5900, gets high marks from people who live there. The **Wheelhouse** on FL 30A makes a good breakfast. A short drive north on FL 393 will take you to these interesting restaurants on US 98 in Santa Rosa Beach: **Frank LeBleau's Cajun Kitchen** (especially fun at breakfast), **Bayou Bill's**, and **Goatfeathers** for oysters. *Note:* Many restaurants in smaller communities along the Emerald Coast may be closed in winter.

The Lighthouse, (904) 654-2828, in Destin's Shoreline Village Plaza is famous for its half-priced seafood dinners from 5:30 to 6:30 p.m., but you can expect a wait. The **Marina Cafe** at the Destin Yacht Club, 837-7960, serves red snapper with scallops and a fine grouper plate (about $17), or try **Flamingo Cafe** in Destin Harbor, 837-0961. In Fort Walton Beach, there's **Seagull Restaurant**, 243-3413, on the Intracoastal Waterway and the **Bay Cafe**, 244-3550, a French-cuisine sidewalk restaurant along the water.

Key Lime pie is a super-sweet dessert treat in Florida — but you're not getting the real thing unless it's *yellow*.

Places to Stay

Lay down your head tonight anywhere along the Emerald Coast from Sunnyside to Pensacola. **Gulf View Inn**, (904) 234-6051, is a pleasant bed and breakfast (homemade breads and jellies) overlooking the Gulf along Alternate 98 in Sunnyside, just west of where you first hit the beach; rooms with bath $60, suite $75, open all year. Stay in a dreamy '20s-style cottage at **Seaside** for $100 to $250 depending on the season, or at Seaside's Motor Court for about $70 (Seaside reservations: 904/231-4224). Recently renovated **Villa Mansard**, with kitchenette suites, is on the very edge of a long stretch of open beach (Henderson Beach State Park). You can see Destin's high-rises only in the distance; call **Abbott Realty** (800) 336-4853. Typical Emerald Coast motel rooms range from about $45 in winter to $75 and up from May 1 to September 15.

Destin and Fort Walton Beach are loaded with resort, condo and motel accommodations of every kind. **Sandestin**, 267-8000, is a very complete beach resort, with tennis (on Wimbledon-style grass courts!), golf, pools, from about $90 for two. **Hotelier**, (800) 223-1561 or (904) 837-6100, lists a wide selection of Destin beachfront lodgings. Call (800) 336-3630 to find out about the variety of accommodations at **Blue Horizon** and **Driftwood** beach hotels in Fort Walton Beach.

Places to Camp

One of the nicest commercial beach camps I've come across is **Seagrove Camping Ground** on FL 30-A near Seaside. Encircled by dunes and natural coast habitat, it has a pool, laundromat, showers, and 75 pleasant sites set among native trees. Walk across the road and through the dunes to a perfect beach. Rates from $13 in winter to $15 in summer, (904) 231-5544. Camping at lovely **Grayton Beach State Recreation Area** on FL 30-A ($18 and $20 sites) is popular, so call 231-4210 well ahead of time to reserve a place. Drive through Fort Walton Beach and Gulf Breeze to get to **Ft. Pickens Campground** on Santa Rosa Island in Gulf Islands National Seashore (see *Discovery Day 21*). There's usually room, but call 932-5018 to be sure. It's $3 to get into the fort area, $10 for a site.

Useful Tips

Area code for Tallahassee and the whole Florida panhandle is 904. Check the *Limelight* section in Friday's *Tallahassee Democrat* for events in Florida's capital city. Destin is a popular port for big-game fishing (marlin, swordfish, tuna). *Shamrock II*, 267-2315, and other Destin charter boats will help you reel in the big one. Don't pick the sea oats along the Emerald Coast — their massive root systems are the secret of dunes ecology, and you can be fined.

Linger Longer

Trip #1: Redneck Riviera — I've deliberately routed you around Panama City so that you might enjoy pretty views of the Gulf relatively free of Florida beachfront blight, but some may prefer a more intense beach scene. There's none more intense than **Panama City Beach**. PCB (the beach, not the chemical) is the heart and soul of the Redneck Riviera, so named because it's a traditional playground for inland families from Georgia and Alabama, as well as Canadian snowbirds and spring break revelers. If your idea of a great time encompasses towering look-alike beachfront hotels, miles of airbrush T-shirt shops and miniature golf parks, and six-pack-and-pizza nightlife, you'll love it. Call PCB's info center, (800) 722-3224, about places to stay. Scuba dive the manmade reefs beneath the clear waters of St. Andrews Bay by contacting the Diver's Den at Panama City Harbor, (904) 234-8717, or Hydrospace Dive Shop, (800) 874-3483.

Trip #2: Apalachicola Route — If you have extra time, this drive through the coastal marshes and fishing ports south of Tallahassee makes for a very leisurely change of pace into an unseen Florida. **Apalachicola** is a rustic old fishing town far from the madding crowd, sure to relax a hurried spirit. They'll feed you and put you up at **Gibson Inn** (904) 653-2191, or the **Pink Camellia**, 653-2107. A small state museum in Apalachicola honors Dr. John Gorrie, inventor of refrigeration, man-made ice, and air conditioning.

Take US 319 south from Tallahassee, then follow US 98 through Panacea, Apalachicola and Port St. Joe to Panama City, a distance of about 130 miles. Just before you reach the bridge into Apalachicola, a turn onto FL G1A at Eastpoint will take you out to the endless, open beaches of **St. George Island**. Camp at St. George Island State Park, (904) 670-2111. Eight miles west of Apalachicola, detour onto FL 30A along the beach, and stop at **Jim McNeill's Indian Pass Store and Oyster Bar**. Order Jim's renowned dark roux gumbo. Just beyond Indian Pass you can take FL 30E to reach the beaches and dunes of Cape San Blas and the **St. Joseph Peninsula**. Stay over at St. Joseph Peninsula State Park (904) 227-1327. If the weather's nice, you may never want to leave this Gulf paradise.

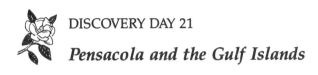

Pensacola and the Gulf Islands

LONG BARRIER ISLANDS formed by wind and tides string along the Gulf Coast for 150 miles west of Destin. Held in place by sea oats, their dunes protect the sounds and marsh environments behind them toward the mainland. Incredible varieties of wildlife — tiny hermit crabs, sea-trout and pompano, possums, soaring osprey, great blue herons — flourish in the barrier system's fecund yet fragile ecological niches.

Today's route along Santa Rosa Island and Perdido Key takes you through the Florida section of Gulf Islands National Seashore; in Alabama you'll ferry across Mobile Bay to friendly Dauphin Island. Don't be too concerned about a precise schedule — there should be time to see the main Magnolia Trail highlights and enjoy the soothing seaside ambience as well, perhaps even stroll the shallow surf out to a tidal sandbar.

Pensacola is the proud home of naval aviation. Lacy ironwork-galleried facades in the historic areas off Palafox Street hint you're getting closer to New Orleans.

Timetable Suggestion

8:15 a.m.	Morning drive along Santa Rosa Island.
9:30 a.m.	Breakfast at the Coffee Cup in Pensacola.
10:30 a.m.	Visit National Museum of Naval Aviation.
12:30 p.m.	Lunch in Gulf Shores, Alabama.
2:00 p.m.	Mobile Bay Ferry to Dauphin Island.
4:15 p.m.	Stroll through Eden-like Bellingrath Gardens.
7:00 or so	Seafood feast near Bayou La Batre or along the Mississippi Gulf Coast.

Magnolia Trail: Fort Walton Beach to Biloxi (175 miles)

Continue west from Fort Walton Beach on US 98 for 15 miles, then turn left onto FL 399 at **Navarre** and cross the Intracoastal Waterway to Navarre Beach and **Santa Rosa Island**, a paradise of white dunes, sea oats, gulls, and gentle emerald-green waters. At Pensacola Beach, turn north over Santa Rosa Sound to **Gulf Breeze** where you'll meet US 98 again. Just east of Gulf Breeze on US 98 is the Gulf Islands National Seashore visitor center and Naval Live Oaks area. This stand of giant oaks was a national tree farm created by John

Quincy Adams in 1829 to provide material for ship construction. A full-scale cross-section display at the visitor center (934-2600) shows how big wooden warships were built.

From Gulf Breeze, take the new US 98 causeway north across **Pensacola Bay** onto Pensacola's Gregory Street. The old causeway on your right has been recycled into a much-appreciated fishing pier. From Gregory Street, turn left onto Palafox, Pensacola's attractive main street. A right turn (west) on Garden Street will take you to Navy Boulevard and the entrance gate of Pensacola Naval Air Station, and out to the **Museum of Naval Aviation**. Continue west on FL 292 onto Perdido Key, where the highway becomes AL 182 as you cross the state line. Drive past Gulf State Park on the Alabama mainland to **Gulf Shores**, then continue west on AL 180/Dixie Graves Parkway along the narrow spit that separates Mobile Bay from the Gulf of Mexico.

Board the Mobile Bay Ferry at Fort Morgan for a five-mile ride to **Dauphin Island** (car and driver $8, each passenger $1, trailers $4); departures at 8:40, 10, and 11:20 a.m. and 12:40, 2, 3:20, 4:40, 6, and (except in winter) 7:20 p.m. The ferry takes you across the mouth of **Mobile Bay**, where in 1864 Union Admiral David Farragut declared, "Damn the torpedoes! Full speed ahead!" (*Note:* If the weather looks rough, call (205) 421-6420 to make sure the ferry's running. If it's not, you may have to detour north on AL 59 and I-10 through Mobile.) Fort Gaines will be on your left as you get off the ferry at Dauphin Island. Turn right (north) at the water tower and take the breathtaking high-rise bridge across the Intracoastal Waterway. Follow AL 163 through the coastal marshes, turn left onto AL 188, then right on AL 59 for four miles to reach **Bellingrath Gardens**.

Backtrack south on AL 59 and turn right on AL 188 to resume your journey through Coden and **Bayou La Batre** (pronounced *BAT-ry*), where the bayou itself is the town's main street. Turn west on US 90 at Grand Bay, cross the Mississippi state line, and follow four-lane US 90 through **Pascagoula** and **Ocean Springs** to **Biloxi**. (If you're running late, you can get on I-10 just north of Grand Bay and travel 36 miles west to the Biloxi exit.)

Getting to know Pensacola
Ever since the spot was first colonized by Tristan de Luna in 1559, just about everybody has appreciated Pensacola's position on the strategic bay at the far western end of Florida. Claimed and held on and off by Spain, France, England, the Confederate States, and the United States, governments here changed hands 13 times in 400 years. Pensacola was the first capital of the U.S. Florida Territory in 1821, and for most of this century has been the cradle of the Navy's aviation program. **Pensacola Naval Air Station,** southwest of the city, is the home of the Blue Angels precision aerobatics team; the carrier *Lexington* is based here and is sometimes open for tours.

PENSACOLA TO NEW ORLEANS

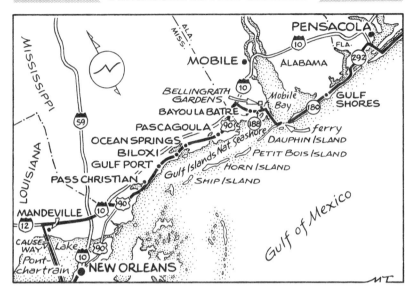

Pensacola (population 70,000) has been undergoing a nice renaissance. While you're here, take **Palafox Street** south to Government Street, turn left and drive a few blocks to Alcaniz Street for a look at **Seville Square**; folk Victorian and Creole cottages now form a pleasant district of restaurants and shops in the original heart of the city. Continue south on Palafox past the fishing fleet to Palafox Pier for a view across the bay. North on Palafox and to the west of Georgia Square is the 60-block **North Hill Preservation District** which encompasses homes in styles ranging from Queen Anne to 1930s Art Moderne.

The Best to See and Do

❀ ❀ ❀ **National Museum of Naval Aviation** — Airplanes, wonderful airplanes! The whole history of naval aviation — from the Navy's first 1911 biplane to supersonic post-Vietnam era budget busters — unfolds around you at this astonishingly complete museum. You'll see the Navy/Curtiss 4 flying boat that flew across the Atlantic eight years before Lindbergh's solo hop, an F6F Hellcat from World War II, UH-1A "Huey" helicopter, and the original prototype for the high-tech F-18 Hornet fighter — plus more than 100 other aircraft rotated out of the museum's vast collection. Buckle up in a flight simulator used to train Navy pilots. The new atrium, with four A4s of the Navy's **Blue Angels** aerobatics team hanging in formation above your head, leads to a second auditorium that doubles the number of aircraft on display and includes the carrier aircraft exhibit.

The Museum of Naval Aviation is on the grounds of Pensacola Naval Air Station, southwest of the city via Garden Street and Navy Boulevard. Free admission; open 9 a.m. to 5 p.m. every day except Christmas, New Year's Day and Thanksgiving. Call (904) 452-3604 to find out about spectacular OmniVision theater flight shows.

❀ ❀ **Coastal Forts** — Four well-preserved brick forts with colorful histories and unusual features stand at the entrances to Pensacola Bay and Mobile Bay. Pick one or two for a 30-minute visit:

Fort Pickens is out at the western tip of Santa Rosa Island. Apache chief Geronimo was held here in the 1880s. Walk out to the World War II bunkers tucked among the dunes. It costs $3 per car to enter this section of Gulf Islands National Seashore; open daily 9 a.m. to 5 p.m., 934-2635. **Fort Barrancas**, paired with Fort Pickens to guard the entrance to Pensacola Bay, is on the Naval Air Station near the aviation museum. It was occupied by Confederates in 1861, while Fort Pickens remained in the hands of Union forces. Shelling exchanges didn't hurt the forts but killed a lot of fish in the bay. Fort Barrancas has unusual design features to take full advantage of its site; open daily 9:30 a.m. to 5 p.m. (10:30 a.m. to 4 p.m. in winter), free.

Star-shaped **Fort Morgan**, veteran of the Battle of Mobile Bay, is at the end of AL 180 close to where you catch the ferry. Open 8 a.m. to sunset daily; adults $2, seniors and children 6-18 $1. When you reach land at Dauphin Island, you'll see its battle-mate, **Fort Gaines**, immediately to the left. A pentagon-shaped brick bastion complete with a moat, Confederate-built Fort Gaines has become a favorite for Civil War re-enactments. Open daily 9 a.m. to 5 p.m.; adults $2, children $1.

❀ ❀ **Dauphin Island** — Despite the storms that periodically sweep manmade structures away, Dauphin (pronounced *DOFF-in*) Island is a happy place for both visitors and residents the rest of the time. Much of Dauphin remains in a natural state, even though it isn't part of the national seashore. There's a fishing pier and a pleasant RV campground near Fort Gaines, charter boat marina, a few seafood restaurants, and that's about it. Enjoy the wildlife as you walk trails through the forested **Audubon Bird Sanctuary** to the beach. Bienville Boulevard runs out to the island's easygoing west end, where summer homes on stilts look out over some very nice public beaches.

❀ ❀ ❀ **Bellingrath Gardens** — You know by now that Dixie abounds in lovely formal gardens, but I've saved the best for last. From AL 59, turn right and drive two miles through a handsome pine forest to Walter and Bessie Morse Bellingrath's 65-acre floral fantasy, justly famed as one of the most breathtaking gardens in the world. Visitors have been welcome at this heavenly spot since 1932. In the oriental garden you walk past preening swans, yupon trees, tranquil ponds, delicate waterfalls — every prospect engenders a sense of peace. Walk the bridge over **Mirror Lake** to a floral path that leads to a view across North Bayou's wildlands. Stroll through the exotica conservatory to admire a sprawling *frangipani plumeria*. Near the Bellingrath mansion, follow the terraces, fountains and a flagstone canal leading to a grotto on the **Isle-aux-Oies River**. A maiden holds a seashell trickling water sensuously down her body. You'll feel like you've walked into a Maxfield Parish painting.

Flowers bloom year-round here: camellias and chrysanthemums through the winter months, followed by daffodils, azaleas, dogwood, spirea, and a spectacular display from 2,000 exotic rose bushes from April through December. You can even take some home with you — the gift shop offers potted plants at reasonable prices. A small cafeteria serves sandwiches and salads until 3 p.m. The gardens are open every day at 7 a.m. and the last tickets are sold one hour before dusk. Adult admission is $5, children $2.50 (under 6 free). Call (205) 973-2217 to find out what's in bloom.

❀ **Old Spanish Fort** — Originally built by the French in 1718, this fort's tabby walls of shell, mud and moss are the oldest in the whole Mississippi Valley. A hands-on museum and historic cemetery are on the site. Take Fort Drive in Pascagoula to Krebs Lake. Open daily 10 a.m. to 5 p.m.; adults $2, children $1.

Places to Eat

Earline Cleaveland's **Coffee Cup** on Cervantes Street (go north on Palafox Street, turn right on Cervantes and duck under the overpass) is Pensacola's great morning meeting place. You'll find a hearty, inexpensive Southern breakfast there and lots of chatter. Another great place for breakfast (lunch and dinner too) is the **Hopkins House**, a wonderful Old South boarding house at 900 North Spring Street, (904) 438-3979; breakfast from 6:30 to 9 a.m., closed Mondays.

Seafood lunches are excellent (but pricey) at **Perdido Pass Restaurant**, just as you cross the bridge into Alabama. Gulf Shores makes a convenient lunch stop; look for **B.J.'s Seafood** (fine homemade pies), **Hazel's Nook** (faultless biscuits), and **The Shrimpboat** (artichoke hearts). On the west end of Dauphin Island you'll find **Prissy's Restaurant** and the **Seafood Galley**. If you're hungry after your visit to Bellingrath Gardens, stop at the **Catalina Restaurant** in Coden, near Bayou La Batre.

The Mississippi coast is one of the world's great sources of food from sea and sound — you can hardly go wrong at any seafood restaurant in Ocean Springs, Biloxi or Gulfport. Ocean Springs comes first so I'll start there. **Aunt Jenny's Catfish Restaurant** serves up nicely prepared, all-you-can-eat portions (adults $7.65, kids $3.95) in a friendly atmosphere on the edge of Fort Bayou; turn right (north) at the light at Washington Avenue in Ocean Springs.

Germaine's at 1203 Bienville Boulevard (US 90) prides itself on attentive service, specialties such as crabmeat au gratin and veal angela, and famous rum cream pie, (601) 875-4426. Aunt Jenny's and Germaine's are both closed on Mondays. I like the casual atmosphere and attitude at **The Factory**, a seafood place in an old shrimp and oyster cannery just as you come into Biloxi across the bridge from Ocean Springs; have the Factory Choice — red snapper smothered in crabmeat, shallots and mushrooms ($14).

McElroy's Harbor House (435-5001) overlooks the Gulf at Biloxi's small craft harbor; friendly atmosphere, reasonable prices. Also on the water near Buena Vista Beach Club Inn are **The Pier** (374-1242), where they claim the seafood's so fresh "you'll swear you caught it yourself," and venerable **Baricev's Seafood Harbor** (435-3626). Try the soft shell crabs at **Mary Mahoney's Old French House** (374-0163), a block north of US 90 on Rue Magnolia in Biloxi. The house itself, built in 1737, is a treasure.

Places to Stay

Dozens of motels line US 90/Beach Boulevard between Biloxi and Gulfport. **Biloxi Beach Resort and Motor Inn**, (601) 388-3310, has rooms from about $70 May through August and $50 the rest of the year. **Sea Gull Motel**, 896-4211, offers both rooms and cottages ($45-$75 in summer). **Edgewater Inn**, (800) 323-9676; **Shoney's Inn**, (601) 868-8500; **Deep South Motel**, 896-7808 (quite cheap); and **Worth Motor Lodge**, 896-3641, are along this stretch. Father west in Long Beach you'll find the **Gulf View Motel**, 863-3713. **Turn of the Century** is a bed-and-breakfast cottage in Pass Christian that offers guests use of a sailboat, (601) 452-2868.

Places to Camp

Davis Bayou Campground, at the Ocean Springs headquarters of Gulf Islands National Seashore, is an ideal overnight stop just off US 90; full hookups $12, (601) 875-9057. However, they take no reservations and you must register between 3 and 5 p.m. There's a laundromat at **Biloxi Beach Campground**, 432-2755. West of Pass Christian and Bay St. Louis in Waveland, Mississippi, you'll find spacious (150 sites) and comfortable **Buccaneer State Park**, 467-3822. Kids love the wave pool there.

Care to stop earlier in the day? **Fort Gaines Campground** on Dauphin Island is close to the ferry and a short walk to the bird sanctuary, beach, and a fishing pier; sites $12, (205) 861-2742. **Gulf State Park**, (205) 968-6353, on AL 182 west of Perdido Key, has a great beach, fishing pier, and 500 sites — there's room for drop-ins even in summer.

Mobile Alternate Route

If the weather prevents enjoyment of the beach and islands, pick up I-110 at Gregory Street in Pensacola, then head west on I-10 across Mobile Bay to Mobile, Alabama. It's a one-hour drive. Mobile (population 200,000) is the Gulf's oldest French settlement (1702) and had Mardi Gras before New Orleans, but more than a short stop here may seem redundant — highlights are similar to ones you've already seen. The city's azaleas are beautiful, but I get the impression that Mobile's urban vitality is either past its prime or is yet to be realized. Climb aboard the battleship *U.S.S. Alabama* and a Navy submarine in Mobile Bay and see a huge B-52 bomber up close at **U.S.S. Alabama Battleship Park** (8 a.m. to an hour before dusk; adults $5, kids $2.50). Rejoin the main route where I-10 meets US 90 at the Mississippi state line, or take the Theodore exit if you plan to visit Bellingrath Gardens.

Today's Shortcut

If you're running late and have enough sand in your shoes, you can latch onto I-10 just north of Pensacola and blast across Mobile Bay and through the pines to New Orleans — 212 miles in four hours, non-stop.

 DISCOVERY DAY 22

Mississippi Coast Drive to New Orleans

THIS LAST DAY of your discoveries along the Magnolia Trail begins with a visit to exquisitely Southern Beauvoir in Biloxi, where Confederate President Jefferson Davis spent his final years in peace and contentment. Drive along Mississippi's Gulf Coast through Pass Christian and Bay St. Louis. The tradition of tranquil gentility along these beaches is punctuated from time to time by fierce hurricanes.

Cross the Pearl River back into Louisiana and make a dramatic re-entry into New Orleans over the waters of Lake Pontchartrain.

Timetable Suggestion

9:00 a.m.	See Beauvoir, the last home of Jefferson Davis.
10:30 a.m.	Visit Seafood Industry Museum in Biloxi.
11:00 a.m.	Drive through Gulfport, Pass Christian and Bay St. Louis, stroll the beach one more time.
Afternoon	Take the Lake Pontchartrain Causeway into New Orleans and enjoy your last day *lagniappe*.
8:00-ish	Try that restaurant you missed on Day 1 or Day 2.
9:45 p.m.	Farewell toast at the Top of the Mart, high above the Mississippi River.
Later	Sleepytime down South.

Magnolia Trail: Biloxi to New Orleans (115 miles)

Drive four-lane US 90 along the beach through **Gulfport**, **Pass Christian** and **Bay St. Louis**, then take Mississippi 43 north to join Interstate 10 West (or just stay on the four-lane, which becomes MS 607 before it joins I-10). Pass the Stennis Space Center, then cross the high bridge over the **Pearl River** into Louisiana. Near **Slidell**, switch to I-12 for a 25-mile run through the deep pine forests north of Lake Pontchartrain. Follow the signs for **Lake Pontchartrain Causeway**. After a smooth, transcendental, half-hour "voyage" on this freeway above the waters, you'll make landfall on Metairie's Causeway Boulevard; look for the ramp for I-10 East/New Orleans. Soon you'll see the Superdome and the high-rises of the CBD. You've completed your driving adventure through Dixie — you're home again in New Orleans!

Mississippi's Gulf Coast

To tell the truth, I was tempted to leave this peaceful if less spectacular stretch of beaches out of the book — and keep it for myself! After all, you've already had some wonderful beach days, and the pleasures of New Orleans beckon again just across the Louisiana line. But my conscience tells me the Magnolia Trail adventure isn't complete without it.

The shoreline of Mississippi is protected by a string of offshore barrier islands, making for shallow, life-filled waters and timid waves — usually. Along the landward side of US 90, wealthy Creoles from the Crescent City built their "cottages" for lazy, genteel summers, repairing or rebuilding them after major hurricanes. Then came *Betsy* in 1965 and 200-mile-per-hour *Camille* in 1969, a one-two punch that still makes some homeowners reluctant to build again. Through Pass Christian you'll see the foundations and grounds of gone-with-the-wind beachfront estates in the gaps between gracious old homes that survived these storms and some classy new ones, built by folks of undaunted spirit (or short memory). Very fortunately, Jefferson Davis's Beauvoir, constructed in 1853, has stood the test of the storms. Offshore, just beyond the horizon, lie the slender islands that make up the most pristine section of Gulf Islands National Seashore.

The Best to See and Do

❀❀❀ *Beauvoir:* **Jefferson Davis Shrine** — After his release from a Union prison, the Confederacy's beloved President found a final peace in the company of his family at this quiet estate facing the sea. Here he wrote *The Rise and Fall of the Confederate Government*, explaining the Southern cause. The house is filled with Davis family possessions gathered from all over the South. For over 50 years a hospital at the estate served Confederate veterans and their wives. A Confederate Museum occupies the old hospital building. Walk through quiet magnolia clearings and cross the lagoon to visit the Tomb of the Unknown Soldier of the Confederate States of America. Beauvoir is on US 90/West Beach Boulevard between Biloxi and Gulfport; open every day from 9 a.m. until 5 p.m.; adults $4, seniors $3.50, children $2, (601) 388-1313.

❀❀ **Seafood Industry Museum** — Find out how seafood from the Gulf reaches your supermarket, and trace the history of commercial fishing through old tools, photos and a display of boatbuilding techniques. Watch the film of hurricane *Camille*. The museum is at Point Cadet Plaza near the foot of the Biloxi-Ocean Springs Bridge in Biloxi; from US 90 turn north at Myrtle Street. Open Tuesday through Saturday 9 a.m. to 5 p.m., Sundays from 1 p.m., adults $2.50, students and seniors $1.50, (601) 435-6320.

❀ **J. L. Scott Marine Education Center & Aquarium** — Here you will see marine and marsh creatures native to Mississippi's coast in five distinct water-land habitats, plus a 42,000-gallon Gulf of Mexico tank with sharks, sea turtles and eels. (Worth seeing particularly if you can't get to the Aquarium of the Americas in New Orleans.) It's near the Seafood Industry Museum, just off US 90 at the Biloxi (west) end of the bridge. Open daily except Sundays from 9 a.m. to 4 p.m.; adults $2, children and seniors $1, 374-5550.

❀❀ **Mississippi Barrier Islands** — East and West Ship, Horn and Petit Bois islands lie about ten miles offshore protecting the Intracoastal Waterway and the shallow waters of Mississippi Sound. These delicate beauties of sand, sea oats, palmettos and pines form the western end of Gulf Islands National Seashore. Wilderness camping, swimming and fishing are permitted on all four islands — the trick is getting to them. **West Ship Island**, site of strategic Fort Massachusetts, is the only one accessible to by scheduled tour boats (from either Biloxi or Gulfport). The British set up here for their advance on New Orleans in the War of 1812, and Union Admiral Farragut sailed out of Fort Massachusetts to take the Crescent City in 1862. The semicircular fort has survived the brunt of several hurricanes, including *Camille* which split the island in two.

The *Pan American* sails for Ship Island from The Pier Restaurant, four blocks east of the Biloxi lighthouse on US 90, at 9 a.m. and noon daily from mid-May to Labor Day on a six-hour round-trip excursion; adults $11, children $5. Call (601) 432-2197 or 436-6010 to find out about off-season weekend schedules and departures from Gulfport Yacht Harbor on the same trip.

Horn Island is a pristine jewel of sugar-like dunes supporting rosemary and sea oats, forests of pine and live oak, and no development whatsoever. Besides a few other campers, you may have only a peregrine falcon, osprey and other coastal birds, and a few wild pigs for company. Call Davis Bayou visitor center, (601) 875-9057, or the *Shearwater,* 875-3511, to look into overnight camping on Horn and Petit Bois islands via charter boat.

❀ **Shrimp Cruise** — See first-hand what the nets haul in on a real expedition on the 70-minute Biloxi Shrimping Trip. Call (601) 374-5718 for departure times; adults $7, kids $4.

❀ **John C. Stennis Space Center** — NASA tests all its solid-fuel rocket engines here, but a lot more goes on at this multi-agency science facility. The Earth Resources Laboratory uses satellite photography of the world's oceans and land masses to predict environmental trends, and the U.S. Geological Survey runs a 30-acre flood plain simulator. You'll see the sign on I-10 as you near the Pearl River. Open every day 9 a.m. to 5 p.m., free; (601) 688-2377.

❀❀ **Lake Pontchartrain Causeway** — Broad, shallow, brackish Lake Pontchartrain is the source of tasty soft-shell crabs and the billions of shells used in roadbeds throughout the Gulf region. The 24-mile Lake Pontchartrain

Causeway, an elevated double highway that traverses the lake from north to south, is one of the world's longest bridges and a very pleasant over-the-waves drive. Toll $1.

Useful Tips

From Biloxi and nearby towns you can charter a boat for a day out on some of the best coastal fishing waters in the world. No license is required for saltwater fishing; call (601) 896-6699 to contact the captains. Angle for higher stakes aboard *Southern Elegance*, (800) 441-SHIP, and *LA Cruise*, (800) 752-1778, two casino cruise ships that go out for daily six-hour voyages into international waters (days $29, nights $39). Artist Walter Anderson's colorful and very detailed murals in the Ocean Springs Community Center are a Mississippi Gulf Coast treasure; to get inside to see them, pick up a key at the chamber of commerce, 1000 Washington Street. For more about this wonderful coast call (800) 237-9493.

Places to Eat

Annie's Restaurant on Henderson Point and **Plantation Cafe** at 115 Scenic Drive in the historic section of Pass Christian make good lunch stops, or pick up a shrimp po-boy at **Lil' Ray's** on US 90 in Waveland. **The Landmark** is a comfortable place for lunch or dinner on old Main Street in Bay St. Louis, (601) 467-3033. Mandeville's quaint main street on the north shore of Lake Pontchartrain has a pleasant restaurant or two where you can fuel up before crossing the lake into New Orleans.

If you make it back to New Orleans by lunchtime, exit at West End Boulevard to reach the cluster of seafood restaurants on the Lakefront. Turn back to *Discovery Days 1* and *2* for my New Orleans dining suggestions.

New Orleans Lagniappe

In Louisiana, *lagniappe* (pronounced *LAN-yap*) means a little something extra, most often free. Treat yourself to an afternoon in New Orleans, making up your own lagniappe to complete your odyssey in Dixie. Maybe it'll be just hanging out at the wonderful old Napoleon House in the Quarter, or taking a pedal boat out on the little bayou in City Park, or getting aboard the free Algiers Ferry at the end of Canal Street for an easy trip to the West Bank and back. Other possibilities:

❀❀ **Barataria Unit/Jean Lafitte National Historical Park** — Jean Lafitte ran his own little fiefdom and harbor in these secluded swamps, from which he raided ships, smuggled contraband and played a cool political hand in the early 1800s. He provided arms and men to help Andrew Jackson defeat the British at the Battle of New Orleans. Several wilderness environments — a forest canopy of live oaks and hickories, swamplands of cypress and tupelo, waterfowl-nurturing marshlands — have been carefully laced with trails, boardwalks and canoe routes by the National Park Service. Take the Crescent City Connection (Mississippi River Bridge) to the West Bank and get on the West Bank Expressway. Turn left at Barataria Boulevard/SR 45 and go south seven miles. The switch from mind-numbing sprawl to quiet wilderness is sudden and delightful. (Try to avoid the expressway and bridges at peak commuter hours.) Barataria is open daily 9 a.m. to 5 p.m. every day and it's free.

❀ **Battle of New Orleans/Chalmette** — In 1815 Andrew Jackson managed to rally Creoles, Kaintucks, free men of color, pirates, and a few Choctaw Indians into a spirited fighting force that soundly trounced the British at Chalmette. Jackson became a national hero and New Orleanians began to think that being part of America wasn't such a bad idea after all. Peer through the restored wood and mud ramparts and imagine the British advancing across the broad field. Take Rampart Street/St. Claude Avenue and St. Bernard Highway downriver about six miles. Open 8 a.m. to 5 p.m. daily except Mardi Gras, free. Call (504) 589-4430 to find out about later summer hours.

❀ **Algiers Point** — This quiet old neighborhood is directly across the Mississippi from the French Quarter. A ferry boat right at the end of Canal Street takes pedestrians over to Algiers Point landing for free (car round-trip $1). It's a great escape from the liveliness of the Quarter and you'll have splendid views of St. Louis Cathedral, the bridges, the skyscrapers, and river traffic on your 15-minute voyage. Enjoy a cup of gumbo and salad (about $4) with your Dixie Beer at the **Dry Dock Cafe**, which you'll see from the landing. The Algiers Ferry runs until 9 p.m.

❀ **Mardi Gras World** — Blaine Kern's talented crew (krewe?) works year-round on a fleet of Carnival floats that are works of art in their own right, and you're invited to watch it happen. Take the Algiers Ferry to the West Bank and look for the Mardi Gras World van at the dock — or walk ten minutes along the levee (toward the bridges) to 233 Newton Street in Algiers. Open daily 9:30 a.m. to 4 p.m.; admission to self-guiding tour $3, (504) 361-7821.

❀❀❀ **Your Own Heart** — Dixie, as you've discovered, is a place of exquisite emotions and enchanting stories, mostly a slow dreamy land, where the arts of human relationship are given high value and somehow there's always time for them. Today, before you go, take some moments alone to reflect on where you've been and what you've experienced that touched you as memorably amusing, amazing, fascinating, or profound. Recall also the new people you've encountered along the way. You may find that in subtle and interesting ways you've changed — for the better, of course.

Soon you'll be home and your days in Dixie will be but memories, but parts of your journey may steal into a permanent place in your heart. May they dwell there in comfort, and may they rise again on the sweet scent of magnolias!

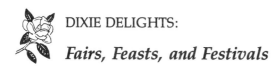

DIXIE DELIGHTS:
Fairs, Feasts, and Festivals

COME EARLY SPRING, the Deep South awakens with Mardi Gras, historic homes pilgrimages, and the blessing of fishing fleets along the Gulf Coast. Good times swell throughout the warmer months with food and music festivals, sportsmens' tournaments, and NASCAR stock car racing. Here are a few of the shindigs that occur annually which are (more or less) along the Magnolia Trail route. With each state and each event, I've listed a number you can call to get exact dates and complete information:

❀ **NEW ORLEANS** (504) 566-5031 or (504) 566-5011

Mardi Gras, February or March. Carnival officially begins on Twelfth Night (January 6) and climaxes the day before Ash Wednesday, but be there a week before Fat Tuesday for a full Mardi Gras experience. (504) 566-5068.
Louisiana Jazz and Heritage Festival ("Jazz Fest"), Late April and early May. (504) 522-4786, 568-0251.
Spring Fiesta (home and garden tours), after Easter. (504) 581-1367.
La Fete (food festival), July. (504) 525-4143.
Sugar Bowl, New Years Day. (504) 525-8603.

❀ **LOUISIANA** (800) 33-GUMBO or (800) 633-6970

Mardi Gras is celebrated in nearly every town in the state, Tuesday before Ash Wednesday. Call the Louisiana Association of Fairs and Festivals, (318) 463-9350.
Audubon Pilgrimage, St. Francisville, March. (504) 635-6330.
Festival Internationale, Lafayette, April. (318) 265-5810.
Louisiana Crawfish Festival, St. Bernard, April. (504) 271-6025.
Louisiana Praline Festival, Houma, early May. (800) 688-2732.
Breaux Bridge Crawfish Festival, May. (318) 332-6655.
Okra Festival, Kenner, June. (504) 468-7274.
Louisiana Catfish Festival, Des Allemands, July. (504) 758-7542.
Louisiana Oyster Festival, Galliano, July. (504) 632-2224.
Cajun Music Month *(Fete des Acadiens)*, Lafayette, August. (318) 981-2364.
Cajun Heritage Festival, Galliano, August. (504) 632-4391.
Delcambre Shrimp Festival, Delcambre, August. (318) 685-2653.
Tangipahoa Black Heritage Festival, Hammond, September. (504) 345-9134.
Festivals Acadiens, Lafayette, September. (318) 232-3737 or (800) 346-1958.
Gumbo Festival of Chackbay, Thibodaux, October. (504) 633-7302.
Andouille Food Festival, LaPlace, October. (504) 651-9111.
International Rice Festival, Crowley, October. (318) 783-3067.
Cajun Country Outdoor Opry (music), Houma, October. (504) 872-0297.

Bonfires on the Levee, along the River Road from Baton Rouge to New Orleans, December. (504) 566-5068.

❀ **MISSISSIPPI**   (800) 647-2290 or (601) 359-3414

Dixie National Livestock Show, Jackson, February. (601) 960-1891.

Natchez Spring Pilgrimage (antebellum home tours), Natchez, March & April. (800) 647-6742 or (601) 446-6631.

Vicksburg Pilgrimage, Vicksburg, late March and early April. (800) 221-3536 or (601) 636-9421.

Landing of d'Iberville (historic reenactment), Gulfport/Biloxi, April. (800) 237-9493.

Natchez Trace Festival, Kosciusko, April. (601) 289-2981.

Gumtree Festival, Tupelo, May. (601) 841-6521.

Jubilee Jam (arts and music), Jackson, May. (601) FEST.

Blessing of Shrimp Fleet and **Fais-Do-Do**, Biloxi, early June. (601) 435-6294.

Deep Sea Fishing Rodeo, Gulfport, early July. (601) 896-2100.

Flagship Boat Festival, Pascagoula, September. (601) 762-3391.

Grand Village of the Natchez Indians Festival, Natchez, September. (601) 335-3523.

Fall Pilgrimage, Natchez, October. (800) 647-6742.

Mississippi State Fair, Jackson, October. (601) 961-4000.

International Food Festival, Bay St. Louis, October. (601) 467-9048, 467-0630.

Scottish Highland Games, Biloxi, November. (601) 432-5836.

Gingham Tree Festival, Lucedale, November. (601) 947-7341.

Heritage Music Festival (blues, rhythm & blues), Vicksburg, November. (601) 636-9421.

❀ **ALABAMA**   (800) ALABAMA or (205) 242-4169

Mardi Gras, Mobile (older but smaller than New Orleans' Mardi Gras), February or March. (800) 666-6282.

Azalea Trail Festival, Mobile, following Mardi Gras. (205) 433-5100.

International Festival, Huntsville, early April. (205) 883-8147.

Crawfish Festival, Dauphin Island, April. (205) 861-6992.

Huntsville Depot Springfest, Huntsville, April. (205) 539-1860.

Spring Fling (water carnival), Huntsville, April. (205) 882-1057.

Bellingrath Gardens Rose Show, throughout May. (205) 973-2217.

Sea Oats Festival (jazz, arts and food), Gulf Shores, May. (205) 968-7511.

Alabama Jubilee & Hot-Air Balloon Classic, Decatur, Memorial Day weekend. (205) 350-6983.

Alabama June Jam (annual "Alabama" band concert), Fort Payne, June. (205) 845-1646.

Blessing of the Fleet, Bayou La Batre, June. (205) 824-2415.

W. C. Handy Music Festival (jazz, gospel, R&B), Florence, August. (205) 766-7642.

National Shrimp Festival, Gulf Shores, October. (205) 968-7511.

✿ **TENNESSEE** (615) 741-2158 or (615) 741-7994

Wildflower Pilgrimage, Gatlinburg/Smoky Mountains, late April. (800) 822-1998.
Summer Lights (music festival), Nashville, June. (615) 259-6374.
Country Music FanFair (meet your favorite stars), Nashville, first week in June. (615) 889-7503.
National Mountain Music Festival, Pigeon Forge (Dollywood), June. (615) 453-4616.
Riverbend Festival, Chattanooga, June. (615) 756-2212.
Italian Street Fair, Nashville, early September. (615) 329-3033.
Tennessee State Fair, Nashville, September. (615) 259-1960.
Grand Ole Opry Birthday Celebration, Nashville, October. (615) 889-7503.
Fall Color Cruise and Folk Festival, Chattanooga, October. (800) 322-3344.

✿ **NORTH CAROLINA** (800) VISIT NC or (919) 733-4171

Festival of Flowers, Asheville, April. (704) 255-1700, 252-2711.
Coca-Cola 600 NASCAR Stock Car Race, near Charlotte, May. (704) 455-2121. Call (904) 253-0611 for complete NASCAR schedule.
Unto These Hills (Indian outdoor drama), Cherokee, June through August. (704) 497-2111.
Shindig-on-the-Green, Asheville, Saturday evenings during July and August. (800) 548-1300, (704) 258-3916.
Grandfather Mountain Highland Games, Linville, July. (704) 733-2013.
Belle Cher (arts and music), Asheville, late July. (704) 259-5807.
Mountain Dance and Folk Festival, Asheville, early August. (800) 257-1300.
World Gee Haw Whimmy Diddle Competition, Asheville, early August. (704) 298-7928.
Mineral and Gem Festival, Spruce Pine, August. (704) 765-9483.
Southern Highland Handicraft Fair, Asheville, October. (704) 298-7928.
Swannanoa Sourwood Festival, Black Mountain, August. (704) 669-2300.
Music in the Mountains, Burnsville, September. (704) 682-7215.

✿ **SOUTH CAROLINA** (803) 734-0235 or (803) 734-0122

Festival of Wines, Charleston, February. (803) 571-5208.
Black Heritage Tour, Beaufort, February. (803) 525-0628.
Heritage Classic PGA Golf Tournament, Hilton Head Island, April. (803) 671-2448.
Spoleto Festival USA, Charleston, May and June. (803) 722-2764.
Freedom Weekend Aloft (hot air balloons), Greenville, around July 4. (803) 282-8501.
Beaufort County Water Festival, Beaufort, July. (803) 524-0600.
Southern 500 Stock Car Race, Darlington, Labor Day weekend. (803) 393-5931.
Taste of Charleston (food festival), Charleston, September. (803) 723-7641.
Candlelight Home and Garden Tours, Charleston, October. (803) 722-4630.
South Carolina State Fair, Columbia, late October. (803) 799-3387.

❀ **GEORGIA**   (800) VISIT GA or (404) 656-3545

St. Patrick's Day Parade, Savannah, March 17. (800) 444-2427.

First Saturday Festival, Savannah, March through November. (912) 234-0295.

Savannah Tour of Homes and Gardens, March. (912) 234-8054.

Motorcraft 500 Stock Car Race, Atlanta, March. (404) 946-4211.

Forest Frolics, Waycross, April. (912) 283-3742.

Night in Old Savannah, April. (800) 4445-2427.

Thomasville Rose Festival, April. (912) 226-9600.

Beach Festival, Jekyll Island, July. (912) 635-3400 or 265-0620.

Pogo Fest (honoring Walt Kelly's cartoon swamp critters), Waycross, October. (912) 283-3742.

Rock Shrimp Festival, St. Marys, early October. (912) 822-6200.

Atlanta Journal 500, near Atlanta, November. (404) 946-4211.

❀ **FLORIDA**   (904) 487-1462

Springtime Tallahassee, late March. (904) 224-5012.

Daytona 500 NASCAR Race, Daytona Beach. (904) 253-0611.

Fiesta of Five Flags, Pensacola, May. (904) 434-1234.

Billy Bowleges Festival, Fort Walton Beach, early June. (904) 244-8191.

Hog's Breath Challenge (catamaran races), Fort Walton Beach, late May. (904) 244-2722.

Pensacola Seafood Festival, September. (904) 433-6512.

Destin Seafood Festival, early October. (904) 837-6241.

Destin Fishing Rodeo, October. (904) 837-6734.

Florida Jazz Festival, Jacksonville, October. (904) 353-7770.

Boggy Bayou Mullet Festival, Niceville, October. (904) 678-2323.

Florida Seafood Festival, Apalachicola, November. (904) 653-9419.

Index

Order *Discovering Dixie* for yourself or as a gift!

If your bookstore doesn't yet carry **Discovering Dixie** *along the Magnolia Trail*, ask them to order it for you — or use this handy form and our clip-out envelope to order direct from the publisher. We invite you to include your suggestions to help keep *Discovering Dixie* up to date.

OCEAN TREE BOOKS
Post Office Box 1295
Santa Fe, New Mexico 87504

Sirs:
☐ Please send me _____ copies of **Discovering Dixie** @ $11.95.
☐ Please send the Ocean Tree title(s) checked on other side.

   I have enclosed a check or money order for the full amount, plus $2.00 for the first book, and 50 cents for each additional book.

Name _____

Address _____

City _____ State _____ Zip _____

☐ Please send **Discovering Dixie** *along the Magnolia Trail* as my gift to:

Name _____

Address _____

City _____ State _____ Zip _____

Please enclose a card: "Gift from _____."

Adventurous Spirits and Inspirational Ideas from Ocean Tree Books!

Check the titles you want and use the order form on the opposite side of this page to order *Discovering Dixie* and other Ocean Tree Books titles. Include $2 for postage and packing for the first book, and 50 cents for each additional book. *Canadian orders: Please remit in U.S. dollars with postal money order. Bookstores: Write for Ocean Tree's discount and terms policies.*

☐ **Santa Fe On Foot.** *Elaine Pinkerton*
The top-rated guide to the Southwest's City Different. Revised!
0-943734-05-3 $7.95

☐ **Discovering Dixie Along the Magnolia Trail.** *Richard Louis Polese*
Introduce yourself to the South with this handy travel guidebook.
0-943734-18-5 $11.95

☐ **Gandhi Through a Child's Eyes.** *Narayan Desai*
Intimate memoir by a man who spent his boyhood with the Mahatma.
0-943734-23-1 $8.00

☐ **Peace Pilgrim: Her Life and Work in Her Own Words**
The spiritual and practical classic by America's wandering saint.
0-943734-29-0 (paperbound) $10.00; 0-943734-20-7 (hardcover) $14.95

☐ **Victories Without Violence.** *Ruth A. Fry*
More than 70 true stories about overcoming personal danger.
0-943734-06-1 $6.00

☐ **A Road to the Future.** *Mikhail S. Gorbachev*
Complete text of the United Nations speech that changed the world.
0-943734-13-4 $5.95

☐ **Peace Like a River.** *Sue Guist*
Personal account of a nine month walk across America.
0-943734-17-7 $8.95

OCEAN TREE BOOKS

Post Office Box 1295 · Santa Fe, New Mexico 87504 · (505) 983-1412

- -

Fold here and fasten on front and sides with tape.

Fold along the dashed lines to make an envelope.

- -

_____

_____

_____

```
PLACE
FIRST CLASS
POSTAGE
HERE
```

OCEAN TREE BOOKS
Adventure Roads Travel
Post Office Box 1295
Santa Fe, New Mexico 87504

☐ Book Order
☐ Note for Mr. Polese re: *Discovering Dixie*

We invite you to help make *Discovering Dixie* an even better guidebook. Use this page to tell Mr. Polese about your travel experiences along the Magnolia Trail, your own restaurant and accomodations suggestions, and things that should be included, deleted or corrected.

Clip along this line.

(This page makes its own envelope. See other side.)